D1478273

The Last Ride

Murder, Money, and the Sensational Trial That Captivated Nashville

Martha Smith Tate

Green House Press

The Last Ride

Green House Press, A Division of Acme Garden Productions, Inc.
Atlanta, Georgia

Book design and cover by Mia Broder
Cover photograph/newsprint: used with permission from the Nashville Public Library, Special Collections, Banner Newspaper Collection.
"There is no such thing as justice, in or outside the courtroom:" Copyrighted 1936, Associated Press, License # 2344772
Car illustration by Mia Broder

Title: The last ride: murder, money, and the sensational trial that captivated Nashville/Martha Smith Tate

First edition

Library of Congress Cataloging-in-Publication Data has been applied for

Includes bibliographical references

ISBN: 979-8-9867406-0-7 (Hardcover)
ISBN: 979-8-9867406-1-4 (E-book)

Identifiers: BISAC:	TRUE CRIME / Murder / General / TRU002000 LAW / Criminal Procedure / LAW027000 / Nashville, Tennessee HISTORY / South (AL, AR, FL, GA, KY, LA, MS, NC, SC, TN, VA, WVA) HIS036120

Manufactured in the United States of America

For my daughters, Anne and Laura, whose love of books has been a constant inspiration

PREFACE

My two daughters grew up hearing the story of the tragic murder of Haynie Gourley which took place on May 24, 1968, on Elm Hill Pike in Nashville, Tennessee. Even when they were pre-teens, they would ask me to tell over and over what happened to my college friend's father and describe the dramatic events that followed. It was a yearly ritual on our vacation to Pawleys Island, South Carolina, to have Friday night story time, where they would gather their friends to hear local tales of the Gray Man or Alice's Grave. I would always end with the story of the death of Haynie Gourley and the search for his killer. They would hang on every word, fascinated by an event that took place years before they were born.

When I entered Vanderbilt University as a freshman in the fall of 1963, one of the heartthrobs in our class was Billy Gourley. Billy was tall and slender, had dark brown eyes, thick black hair he kept slicked down, a perennial tan, and a decidedly cool manner. He pledged Sigma Alpha Epsilon, one of the top fraternities on campus, and even though he was from the wealthy Nashville neighborhood of Belle Meade, he lived in the dorm. His father, Haynie Gourley, owned Capitol Chevrolet, one of the largest Chevrolet dealerships in the Southeast, and Billy was often seen around campus driving a brand-new Corvette or an Impala convertible.

In the fall of my sophomore year, I answered the phone in our dorm suite one day, and a voice with a thick Southern drawl asked for "Moth-a." That was my first encounter with the famous Billy Gour-

The two Nashville daily newspapers often covered Vanderbilt University social events. This photograph appeared in *The Tennessean* on May 2, 1965, after the Sigma Alpha Epsilon fraternity's annual Black and White formal dance. L-R, Billy Gourley, the author, Emily Binning, Keith Caldwell, and Sam Dewey. © *The Tennessean – USA TODAY NETWORK*

ley. I was thrilled and flattered that he asked me out. I went to a few parties with him, and he took me to the big SAE formal called Black and White (girls wore white or black dresses). Much to my disappointment, no romance developed. We remained friends, however. I hung out at his fraternity house during my years at Vanderbilt, and he started calling me "Bag" (after the popular James Brown song), and the name caught on with some of his fraternity brothers. It was not at all flattering, but I was pleased by the attention.

After we graduated in 1967, I moved to Atlanta to teach school and saw Billy from time to time. Often when I went to Nashville, I spent the night at his parents' home. His mother and father were gracious and welcoming, as was his sister, who was very beautiful and always warm and friendly. The entire family lived a charmed life.

In the early part of May 1968, I was in Nashville for a weekend and went out with Billy and some friends. Soon afterwards, I received an invitation to join several sorority sisters from the class below mine for a house party at Sea Island, Georgia. On Friday, May 24, 1968, a fellow teacher from Atlanta and I left after class and drove the five hours to the coast, arriving in time for a late supper.

As we sat around the table, I could tell something was wrong. I worried that I shouldn't have brought my friend along. It was not that my sorority sisters were unfriendly, but I could sense an awkward reserve of some kind.

It was only at bedtime that Charlotte Callis, who was from Nashville, came into the room and told me that Billy's father had gone for a ride with another man that morning, and when they returned to the dealership, Mr. Gourley was dead. By then, Billy was working full time at Capitol Chevrolet, so I knew he must have been right there when the car came back with his father.

That next morning, my friend and I drove back to Atlanta, and I flew to Nashville on Saturday afternoon. I had just seen Mr. Gourley two weeks before, and he was his usual jovial self. I couldn't believe he had been killed, much less in such a horrific manner. He had been shot three times—just below his ear, in his neck, and in his chest. The murder was all over the front pages of both Nashville newspapers and was the lead story on the three broadcast networks. The funeral was the next day, and the church was packed. Billy was grief-stricken and in shock. A lot of his friends came from out of town to the service.

Before I left that June to spend the summer in Paris, I went to Nashville, and Billy and I drove to Memphis just to get away. He talked about his father, how much he loved and admired him, that he had lost his best friend. He wondered aloud why one of the Capitol Chevrolet employees who had been a close friend of the family and a protégé of his father had not been to see his mother or talked to him. He thought that was strange and maybe held a clue. I remember his saying over and over, "If they could only find the gun." I sensed that he had an idea who the killer was, but he never said.

Throughout the fall and winter of 1968 and into the spring of 1969, Billy and I kept in touch. In March 1969, the grand jury handed down an indictment for the murder. A trial was set to begin on July 14. I arrived on July 21, the first day of testimony.

All anyone in the city could talk about was the trial. The two daily newspapers and the three broadcast networks covered every aspect of every day. The entire transcript, word for word, was published in both the *Nashville Banner* and *The Tennessean*. Nashville was a divided city regarding the guilt of the defendant. Nowhere were the events discussed as much as around the dining room tables of Belle Meade. Everyone I knew thought the accused man had killed Billy's father, although the accused man's friends were adamant that he was not capable of committing such a heinous crime.

The atmosphere was tense in the courtroom. The voices of the opposing attorneys thundered through the room. I was awestruck. I had spent the previous year flopped on the sofa after teaching all day, watching Perry Mason at five o'clock. The drama in that Nashville courtroom far eclipsed anything I had ever seen on television. Every day was a circus, with crowds jostling to get in the doors to get a seat. Photographers camped out like paparazzi, stalking the Gourleys, the defendant's family, and the famous lawyers trying the case. Each day was suspenseful, with a parade of witnesses being built up and then just as quickly torn down by the opposing side.

The end came just before nine o'clock on the evening of Saturday, August 2. I was with Billy and his family in the district attorney's office next door to the courtroom when it was announced the jury had reached a verdict.

I came back to Atlanta, and on September 1, 1969, I headed west to San Francisco with my Nashville pal and sorority sister Kathi Woods. We ended up that winter working in Taos Ski Valley, New Mexico, and the next September I moved to Paris. I lost touch with Billy, only to see him again at our Vanderbilt class reunions. By then, we were both married.

After writing for the *Atlanta Journal & Constitution* for twenty-two years and producing 240 episodes of the HGTV series *A Gardener's Diary*, I was approached to write a book about the murder of a beautiful young law student in Birmingham, Alabama. The project was taking a lot of research and work. In my heart, I knew the story I wanted to write was the life and death of Haynie Gourley. For nearly fifty years, I had been haunted by the outcome of the trial. I wanted to set out the facts of the case to see where they led. Both my daughters were excellent writers and voracious readers and kept pressing me to write a book. My answer was always the same: Neither Billy nor his sister had ever given an interview to the press since the day of the verdict, despite persistent requests from newspapers, magazines, and countless authors. I felt sure he would not want to revisit the trauma that broke his heart and turned his life upside down.

I saw Billy at our 50th Vanderbilt reunion in October 2017 but said nothing about what I wanted to do. We still had that special friendship bond, so I was heartened to think he might change his mind and talk to me about a book.

The next year, as the fiftieth anniversary of Haynie Gourley's death approached, I knew I could not let this story remain untold. I had to take a chance. There had never been an in-depth examination of the case. I found magazine articles that were dramatically written, but they were full of errors. Also, having been right there in that courtroom, I could tell that the writers had not used primary source material and did not have a sense of the drama that gripped Nashville for an entire year and culminated in the moment the verdict came down. I felt I could do the story justice, having told long and short versions of what happened for so many years.

One of my New Year's resolutions for 2018 was to ask Billy if he would allow me to interview him for a book. I set a deadline for late April. I worked on an email for weeks and finally got up the nerve to press "send" on the appointed day.

Billy called me almost immediately. He said he had talked it over with his wife and his son. Both thought it was a good idea. "I'm all in," he said. "I'm ready to talk."

I promised him it would only take me a year to write the book. I didn't factor in the travel I had already planned, another book I promised to edit, and I won't go into how I didn't quit everything else and write every day. I made several trips to Nashville. Billy and I rode up and down Elm Hill Pike where the murder occurred. He arranged interviews with Hal Hardin, who was the assistant district attorney at the trial, and with John Lentz, who was the lawyer for Bob Frensley, a major player in the story. Billy also put me in touch with Jimbo Cook, a fraternity brother and close friend who attended every day of the trial and knew it by heart. Jimbo's father had been one of Haynie's best friends. Jane Hindman Kyburz, my little sister in our sorority who grew up in Nashville, was able to locate both Sherman Nickens, the Metro police's chief detective on the case, and Larry Brinton, the head crime reporter for the *Nashville Banner* who covered the murder and trial. She set up interviews and drove me to Nashville. Another sorority sister and Billy's friend from childhood, Joanne Fleming Hayes, shared stories of what it was like growing up in Belle Meade in the decades of the fifties and sixties.

I am not the only one still captivated by Nashville's most notorious murder and trial. A 2014 book, *Disastrous Deaths: From the Dueling Grounds on Red River to Murder on Elm Hill Pike* by Ridley Wills II, contained a long chapter on Haynie Gourley's murder. In 2016, the Nashville School of Law produced an hour-long video re-enactment of the news coverage of the murder and trial. Assistant district attorney on the case, Hal Hardin, was featured on a podcast in 2018 called "Who Shot Haynie?" part of the "Back in the Day" history series produced by Ken Fieth at the Nashville archives. When I walked into the library in downtown Nashville in June 2018 to begin my research, there was a long glass display case filled with photographs and newspaper clippings about the murder of Haynie Gourley and the 1969 trial. Larry Brinton, who, after his stint as a crime reporter for the *Nashville Banner*, had a second career in television news as a commentator and investigative reporter, also did a podcast about the murder; a third podcast featured two young women discussing the crime. In 2020, a lawyer in Nashville published a novel loosely based on the case. As I write this, the historical committee of the Nashville Bar Association is planning a retrospective of the most famous and controversial criminal trial in Nashville history.

My original idea was to start with the week before the murder and go to the end of the trial. But that all changed when Billy answered questions I had sent to him about his father. After what Billy told me about Haynie's childhood, I changed course. With subscriptions to Ancestry.com and Newspapers.com, I was able to trace Haynie's own fascinating story and the social history of the Gourleys, as well as access articles about the murder and police investigation. With the entire 2,400-page transcript available through *The Tennessean,* I was able to use source material with exact quotes from witnesses and attorneys. I also had my own vivid recollections of sitting in that tense courtroom, hearing the gasps of onlookers as witnesses revealed one shocking detail after another, my heart beating wildly at every twist and turn as the trial headed to its conclusion.

Because most of the people I interviewed participated in the prosecution's case, there is a definite bias to the book. Their opinions are only used as thoughts each person had about the murder and trial at the time and are identified as such by insets. All other accounts come directly from quotes in the newspapers or from the transcript of the trial or from interviews I conducted.

On the 50th anniversary of his father's death, Billy spoke publicly about his father for the first time since May 24, 1968. He appeared on camera and told a reporter from WSM-TV: "I want my dad to be remembered. I want his legacy to continue. He was a great father and a great person. He was a prominent face in a very different Nashville. I don't want this city to forget."

Like Billy, I want the generations below us to know about Haynie Gourley's extraordinary life and to give readers the opportunity to study the facts of the case and draw their own conclusions. Most of all, I do not want the story to be lost to memory or given over to myths surrounding the case.

Nashville has changed drastically since I was in college, especially in recent years. Cranes hover over downtown, and I hardly recognize the greatly expanded Vanderbilt campus. Many of the big farms in Brentwood and on the road to Franklin have been carved into subdivisions. Towns that were isolated back then are now part of the metropolitan area. Also, Nashville is a tourist destination and home to many world-famous performers. It's not unusual to spot a celebrity having lunch downtown or walking along the leafy streets of Belle Meade. Open-air tour buses offer rides through the city.

But even with all the growth, Nashville is still a special place with a character that's hard to define, one that draws people in, but which has its roots in the struggles and triumphs of the past. I hope this book will go a long way in painting a picture of what Nashville was like at another time, in a decade that was both turbulent and gentle. Above all, I am hoping to bring to light what happened on May 24, 1968, when Haynie Gourley took the last ride of his life.

— Martha Tate, Atlanta, Georgia, August 2022

PROLOGUE

On Friday morning, May 24, 1968, Nashville, Tennessee, woke to a humid, summer-like day. A chance of thunderstorms was predicted for the afternoon. Already at eight in the morning it was sticky outside.

It had been a mild spring. The oaks and maples and lindens lining the streets of Belle Meade, the city's wealthiest enclave, were in full leaf. In backyard gardens, roses and peonies were at peak bloom in this part of the Iris City, so named by the Tennessee State Legislature in 1933 to honor the many iris hybridizers who had planted thousands of the flowers all around town.

In the bedroom of his elegant home on Belle Meade Boulevard, Haynie Gourley pushed the knot of his blue-striped tie into place and pulled on the gray coat of his favorite suit.

Walking over to the dresser, the portly, bespectacled seventy-two-year-old founder and president of one of the South's most lucrative automobile dealerships and a widely known name in Nashville, opened the top drawer and pulled out a square linen handkerchief. He carefully folded it into his breast pocket, adjusting the points to show exactly two inches. He was a fastidious dresser, and everything from his highly polished black wing-tip shoes to the cap of snow-white hair, which he kept combed neatly away from his forehead, had to be just so. He liked his suits tailored with exactly the right amount of shirt sleeve visible at the wrists. Haynie favored cuff links, and this morning picked out a square-shaped gold pair engraved with his monogram.

Satisfied that everything was in order, he took a yellow pack of Juicy

Fruit gum from a plate on the dresser top and slipped it into his coat pocket. He only chewed a half-stick at a time, usually in secret, but it was a habit he'd had for decades. He had once been a heavy smoker, but his physician and friend Tommy Frist had succeeded in getting Haynie to cut down to five cigarettes a day. Haynie picked up a half-empty pack of Dorals and slid it into his pocket with the gum. Finally, he took his brown leather wallet off the dresser and tucked it into the back-left pocket of his suit pants.

As he walked into the breakfast room, Henrietta Green, the family's live-in housekeeper, greeted him with a cup of coffee and a piece of toast and handed him the morning paper.

Haynie glanced at the front page. A photograph at the top showed a smiling Allen R. Cornelius Jr., who had just won the Democratic nomination for Division III criminal court judge for Davidson County. Cornelius was shaking hands with attorney Joe Binkley, a friend of Haynie's.

For the past ten years, Cornelius had been a general sessions judge, hearing traffic and city ordinance violations and civil cases. He was not widely known, but the events of this day would change all that. In a little more than a year, the thin, graying 48-year-old would preside over the most famous murder trial in Nashville history.

In a photograph down page, youths were burning a French flag. Strikes and riots had paralyzed France all during the month of May. Haynie, a self-made millionaire, had proudly taken his family to Europe on the luxury liner SS France three summers ago, staying at the Savoy in London and the Ritz on the Place Vendôme in Paris. Another article said the peace talks to end the Vietnam War seemed to be stalling once again. Former U.S. Ambassador Averell Harriman and special envoy Cyrus Vance were making no progress in negotiations with the North Vietnamese.

The world might be coming apart, but Haynie's own life couldn't be better. Just two nights before, something happened to ensure that his longtime dream for his twenty-three-year-old son would come true.

Thanking Henrietta for his breakfast, Haynie called to his wife to say he was leaving for work. Every morning, Josephine Gourley saw her husband off at the front door. Today, though, she walked down the steps with him.

Already, the buzz of riding mowers could be heard crisscrossing the vast lawns of nearby mansions. The scent of fresh-cut grass hung in the air.

Haynie asked Josephine about her plans for the day.

"I'm getting my hair done later on this morning." At fifty-six, his wife was still a beauty and a fashion plate. Haynie took out his wallet and handed her a hundred-dollar bill, then climbed into his black '68 Chevrolet Caprice sedan, let the electric window down, and kissed Josephine good-bye.

"I've finally got my boy where I want him," he said, smiling and pausing a moment before he put the car into reverse. "This is the happiest day of my life."

In a matter of hours, the afternoon paper, the *Nashville Banner*, was frantically rolling its presses, turning out two extra editions for the second time in its ninety-two-year history. Judge Cornelius was still on the front page, but he now appeared in a small headshot below the fold. At the top was a photograph of Haynie at the opening of his new headquarters a month earlier, standing proudly next to his friend Buford Ellington, the governor of Tennessee.

Giant bold headlines exploded across the page:

W. HAYNIE GOURLEY, OWNER OF CAPITOL CHEVROLET, SLAIN

PART [I]

The Child is Father of the Man
— William Wordsworth, from the poem "My Heart Leaps Up," 1802

CHAPTER [1]

In the darkened cave, Thomas Kilgore dared not move. One sound would mean instant death. Only inches away from his head were several men from a local Cherokee tribe. They had followed him to his hiding place in this cave-rich region just south of the Kentucky border in what would become the state of Tennessee.

Kilgore thought his hideout was safe. He had lived here all during the summer of 1778 without incident. The only way into the cave was through the knee-deep waters of a tributary of the Red River, so he was confident he could not be traced. But on this day some warriors spotted him and gave chase. Kilgore outran his pursuers and reached the cave with only moments to spare. He crawled into a small hole high in the inner chamber, pulled up his rope and rolled a large stone over the opening just as the men entered the cave.

He waited. Kilgore could tell the men were baffled by finding no trace of the man who had disappeared into the mouth of the one-room cave.

At last, they gave up and left.

Having heard rumors of the region's natural resources from hunters and traders, Kilgore, already in his sixties, traveled on foot from North Carolina and reached the area in 1778. He found old growth forests that sheltered walnut trees with trunks measuring eleven feet across. The rich, black soil around the Red River was endlessly deep. It seemed ideal for a settlement.

Kilgore planted corn when he arrived. In late summer, he harvested some of his crop and left for home. He returned the next year with his family and built a fort for protection. More settlers followed, and the town of Cross Plains, named for its location along a trail followed by hunters and traders, sprang up only three-fourths of a mile from Kilgore's fort.

As it grew, the town attracted newcomers. Among those who came to Cross Plains in the 19th century was William Longfellow Haynie, a native of Alabama who settled in the area in the early 1870s. On June 8, 1875, at the age of twenty-five, he married a local girl, Annis Gideon Payne, who was only fourteen at the time and a descendant of early settlers of the region.

William Haynie became a schoolteacher, having obtained his education at Neophogen College, a short-lived institution founded in 1873 in Cross Plains by Professor J. M. Walton. In 1877, William and Annis had a daughter, Annece. Another girl, Paulette "Hattie," was born in 1881. Sadly, Annis Haynie died at age twenty-two when Annece was five and Hattie not even two years old.

The motherless Annece grew into a teenager known for her beauty. She was a gifted pianist and an excellent student. Her father, who became superintendent of the Robertson County Schools, was considered one of the prominent citizens of Cross Plains. He was proud of his accomplished older daughter and had high hopes for her continuing her education.

But Annece had other ideas. She had fallen head over heels in love with a local farm laborer named William Peter Gourley. William Haynie was alarmed at his daughter's choice of beaux and discouraged the relationship. Peter Gourley did not fit in with Haynie's hopes for Annece. Peter had little education and seemingly few prospects for betterment, though he was undeniably handsome.

One night when Annece was seventeen, Peter, who was nineteen, dragged a ladder through the muddy streets of Cross Plains to the Haynie home. Under the cover of darkness, Annece crawled out of a window to meet Peter waiting below.

William Haynie learned of his daughter's elopement the next morning when Annece failed to come downstairs. His discovery came too late. Peter and Annece had run away and married.

In February 1896, when she was eighteen, Annece gave birth to a boy and named him William Haynie Gourley, after her father. Two years later, in 1898, another son, Everett, was born, followed by a third son, James Pasco in 1900. In 1902, the couple had a fourth child, a daughter they named Margaret. A fifth child, a boy, Raymond Miller Gourley, came along in 1903.

Annece was now the mother of five children under the age of seven. She found herself overwhelmed and unhappy. There was little time for piano or reading or social gatherings. Annece had lost her own mother at such a young age, and now, with no one to help her, she grew despondent. With Peter in the fields all day, she had the sole responsibility of looking after five children. Her state of melancholia deepened with each day that passed.

By the next February, when Haynie turned eight, Peter was desperate for a solution to his wife's distress. Night after night, Peter came home to find Annece increasingly in despair. Her life in Cross Plains, she told him, had become unbearable. She felt hopeless.

When Annece finally reached a breaking point, saying she could no longer cope with her situation, the husband and wife came up with a scheme. They announced that the family would be traveling to the St. Louis World's Fair when school let out. Annece's spirits suddenly lifted. People heard about their plan and thought a vacation would be good for the harried couple.

But Annece and Peter were harboring a dark secret. The couple left on the trip, but no one in the town knew or even suspected that in just a few short weeks the lives of the seven members of the Peter Gourley family would be forever changed.

***

John Offut's wagon bounced over the dirt road, sending his seven passengers swaying back and forth. The two mules clopped along, straining under their load. Even though the riders were wedged between carpetbags filled with clothes, the going was rough. The wagon wheels threw up dust, stinging eyes and settling on anything not covered. The twelve miles between Cross Plains and the town of Springfield, Tennessee, seemed to take forever, given that the mules stopped at intervals, refusing to budge, then stubbornly bumped forward again.

The discomfort of the wagon ride hardly bothered the three older Gourley boys. They were too excited about taking their first train trip. Offut, a distant cousin of their mother, pulled up to the depot at Springfield and helped the family down from the wagon. Peter Gourley held two-year-old Margaret while Annece put one-year-old Ray down and dusted him off.

The black locomotive came chugging in. The family climbed aboard, deposited their bags, and the train steamed off. Everett and Haynie waved happily from a window as Offut stood on the platform. He had promised Annece he would meet the return train in two weeks.

In April 1904, the Louisiana Purchase Exposition opened to great fanfare. Covering 1,200 acres, the monumental project was a year late in its completion. But from the moment it debuted to John Philip Sousa leading his famous band in rousing marches and President Teddy Roosevelt in faraway Washington, D.C., pulling a switch to electrify millions of lights and send dozens of fountains jetting into the air, it was an instant success.

Popularly known as The St. Louis World's Fair, the exposition drew twenty million visitors from all over the United States and from around the world. Fairgoers were dazzled by the sheer extravagance of the colossal buildings that rivaled the magnificent palaces and museums of Europe. Created in painstaking detail, the giant exhibition halls were adorned with friezes and statues of marble and bronze, many of them ornate replicas of the world's architectural gems.

At night, millions of electric lights lit up the pavilions and glimmered on the surface of the Grand Basin, which covered several acres. Fountains shot high into the air with giant plumes of spray, and water cascaded down statue-lined steps into the huge pool.

Canopied tour boats glided through canals and lagoons and under bridges, passing by the exhibition halls, vast columned structures with colonnades and glittering domes, each more elaborate than the next.

For visitors like Annece and Peter Gourley who had never traveled abroad, the fair provided an opportunity to experience the grandeur of Europe. Tourists could stroll along broad avenues lined with trees and gardens and walk under monumental arches, modeled after structures in Paris and Rome built to commemorate famous victories in history. Haynie liked seeing all the people, and he was especially proud of his beautiful mother, dressed like the other ladies in her crisp high-necked white blouse with tucks in the front bodice. She wore lace-up boots and a long black skirt. Her dark hair was loosely pinned up beneath her straw boater hat with its black band. She looked elegant as she pushed the wicker baby pram among the crowds.

Forty-three of the forty-five states had exhibits. Pennsylvania brought the Liberty Bell for display; California shipped in hundreds of thousands of almonds to cover a giant elephant form and fill over-sized baskets and see-through containers. An ornate building representing Missouri was studded with corn cobs; Illinois crafted a larger-than-life statue of Abraham Lincoln for its impressive building.

There was plenty to delight children. For the Gourley boys, the fair was a magical extravaganza at every turn. In one of the cavernous halls, life-size replicas of dinosaur skeletons were on display along with a giant blue whale suspended from the ceiling. In the international area, there were live camels from Egypt and huge wrinkled elephants from Asia, decorated with elaborate gem-encrusted collars. On a raised platform, Pygmies brought from Africa performed tribal dances.

What the boys delighted in most was the child-size railroad that circled the fair, offering rides that gave an overview of the exhibits and passed by a live enactment of a battle from the Second Boer War. Every time the boys finished a tour, they begged to go again. They were also mesmerized by miniature battleships that motored along the canals with adult captains aboard, creating an oddly out-of-scale sight.

Along the midway, also known as The Pike, there were daily parades and booths selling ice cream cones, the latest rage from New

York. The entire family rode the elaborate carousel and ventured into the Creation concession, where boats passed through a labyrinthine cave leading to a giant cavern with scenes from the book of Genesis. A Tyrolean village, backed by towering, three-dimensional snow-covered mountain peaks, featured an outdoor restaurant that served German food.

In one area along the Pike, Geronimo, the famous Apache leader and medicine man, sold pictures of himself for ten cents. Children surrounded him, begging their parents for dimes.

Towering above the midway was the 264-foot-high Ferris wheel, which had been disassembled from the 1893 Chicago fair where it was first introduced and brought to St. Louis and rebuilt for the Louisiana Purchase Exposition.

One of the biggest thrills for the Gourley boys was seeing the private automobiles that rumbled over the fair's wide avenues. Great crowds gathered around these recent inventions and clamored for a ride on one of several motorized open-air buses.

Standing there wide-eyed, eight-year-old Haynie could not have imagined that these new-fangled contraptions would one day determine his future, and ultimately his fate.

After the family spent two weeks touring the exposition, Peter Gourley accompanied his wife and children to Union Station in St. Louis to see them off. He told the older boys he would be staying on in the city for a while and that he would see them soon.

The family walked through the massive hall under the soaring sixty-five-foot-high, gold leaf ceiling with its 800-light chandelier suspended above the crowds. On the platform, Peter stood and waved as Annece and the children boarded an overnight train to return to Tennessee.

Settling down in the railroad car, Annece put her five children to bed. They were all fast asleep when, sometime in the middle of the night, Annece got off the train at one of the stops along the route and disappeared into the darkness.

***

The next morning, the train, its engine belching steam, rumbled to a stop in Springfield. John Offut waited for the family to step down onto the platform.

A handful of passengers detrained and went on their way.

But no one else got off, and there was no sign of Annece and the children.

Puzzled, Offut jumped onto the train as it was about to leave the station and was met by a porter who led him to the five children, the two youngest sobbing loudly.

When questioned, Haynie spoke up and said he could not find his mother when he had awakened earlier in the morning. He had called out to her, but she had not answered. With the little ones hungry and needing their diapers changed, he and six-year-old Everett had run frantically through the cars. People shook their heads when asked if anyone had seen their mother.

The train was halted and all the cars searched, but there was no sign of Annece. Haynie was panic stricken, thinking his mother had somehow fallen off the train. What he did not know at that moment, standing on the platform of the depot in Springfield, was that he would never see his mother again. She was gone forever, and so was his father. Annece and Peter had abandoned their five children, and, without a word to anyone, vanished without a trace.

***

The four Gourley boys and their sister Margaret were now alone in the world, left to depend on the charity of others. This devastating loss marked the beginning of a nightmarish childhood for Haynie, growing up without ever knowing why his parents had left him and his brothers and sister on that train. Neither Annece nor Peter contacted anyone in Cross Plains. The children, shocked and bewildered, were separated from one another, and with no relatives able to care for them, were taken in by different townspeople, many of whom did not have the means or the desire to support them.

Weeks and months and years passed with no word from Annece or Peter. With no money of their own, the children were bounced from pillar to post. In the 1910 census, Haynie's younger brother, James Pasco Gourley, called "J.P.," then ten years old, was listed as a "boarder" in the home of a Cross Plains family named Jernigan.

When Haynie should have been starting fifth grade, he had to go to work in the surrounding tobacco fields and take odd jobs to earn his keep. From time to time, he was handed over to a different family in Cross Plains. He never had a permanent home and never knew when he would find himself at someone's back door, wondering where to go. The census of 1910 listed Haynie, then fourteen years old, as a ward of John Freeland, a farm laborer, and his wife Mary Freeland of Cross Plains. Haynie's sister and brothers lived under similar circumstances. Only Margaret would go past the sixth grade in school.

***

Haynie grew to be a nice-looking young man, with a broad face and dark hair which he kept combed neatly to the side. Despite the hardships of his childhood, he developed a jaunty, almost mischievous personality. He had a winsome smile and was outgoing and friendly and had a reputation as a light-hearted jokester.

But for a young man in his teens, there were no opportunities in Cross Plains outside of farm work. He was determined to find a way to earn money to support his younger brothers and sister. When Haynie was nineteen, he set off for Nashville, thirty miles to the south of

Cross Plains and the capital of Tennessee. The city was growing, with a population now pushing 100,000.

Like Cross Plains, Nashville and its environs had been occupied by Native American tribes including the Cherokees, Chickasaws, and Shawnees. This part of middle Tennessee was known as the "bloody ground" due to the battles fought over its rich hunting grounds.

About the time Cross Plains was founded, a North Carolina man named James Robertson, a friend of Thomas Kilgore's who lent his name to the northern Tennessee county Kilgore had settled, led a group of some 250 men and boys overland to establish a permanent settlement near a site known as the French Lick, arriving on Christmas Day 1779. Robertson's fellow North Carolinian, Colonel John Donelson, set out by boat with a flotilla of families and provisions, and, after a thousand-mile journey wracked by hardship and several fatal encounters with hostile tribes along the Ohio and Tennessee Rivers, arrived via the Cumberland River on April 24, 1780.

The men from the two expeditions signed the Cumberland Compact, setting up a civil government and naming the settlement Nashborough after the North Carolina Revolutionary War general Francis Nash. In 1784, the name was changed to Nashville. In 1796, Tennessee became the sixteenth state but did not yet have a permanent capital.

With the arrival of the first steamboat in 1819, Nashville grew to become a distribution center for the mid-South, trading in tobacco, corn, and lumber. Prosperous merchant enterprises expanded. Large farms and plantations, including Andrew Jackson's Hermitage, John Harding's Belle Meade Plantation, and the Overton family's Travellers Rest, covered thousands of acres. All depended on slave labor, and in downtown Nashville there was a busy slave market.

In 1843, Nashville became the permanent capital of Tennessee. Newly-built railroads linked Louisville, Chattanooga, and Atlanta, and by 1860, Nashville was a thriving town with close to 14,000 inhabitants.

The Civil War brought vast changes. Because of its location, Nashville became an important center for the distribution of supplies for the Confederate army. Much of the South's arsenal was produced in the city and then shipped to battle sites.

In February 1862, Union troops seized the city and commandeered the ironworks for their own production of artillery. An attempt by Confederate forces to free Nashville in 1864 failed, and the city remained occupied by Union troops until the end of the war in 1865. As such, many freed and runaway slaves found refuge here and would make Nashville their permanent home.

After the war, the influx of wealth from the North added yet another building block to the city's character, especially in the area of higher education. Fisk University, founded in 1866, became one of the first private colleges for African Americans in the nation. On the west side of downtown, Vanderbilt University was established in 1873 with a million-dollar gift from New York railroad and shipping magnate Commodore Cornelius Vanderbilt. Across 21st Avenue from the university, the George Peabody College for Teachers was founded in 1875, also with money from the North. The next year, Meharry Medical College became the first medical school for Black students in the South. In 1890, Belmont Women's College was formed and occupied the Acklen mansion and estate not far from the Vanderbilt campus.

Around 1892, city leaders began to plan a celebration for the 100th anniversary of Tennessee's statehood. Because there were so many institutions of higher learning, Nashville was becoming known as "The Athens of the South." Building on that theme, the planners of the centennial celebration commissioned an exact replica of the Parthenon in Athens, Greece, to be built on a site near Vanderbilt University. The immense structure, which was originally constructed of brick, wood, and plaster, became a tourist attraction.

But during the early years of the twentieth century, the replica began to deteriorate due to Nashville's often-humid climate in summer followed by cold, damp winters. Construction of a permanent building began in 1920 and was completed in 1925, this time fashioned from reinforced concrete. Rising on a gentle knoll above Centennial Park, a popular gathering place for Nashville residents on Sunday afternoons, the massive Parthenon would soon become the most recognizable symbol of the growing city.

When Haynie arrived in Nashville in the summer of 1915, he rented a room in a boarding house and began looking for work. He took odd jobs at first, but one day he saw a "Help Wanted" sign in the window of a tailor's shop on Fourth Avenue and applied for a job as a salesman of men's made-to-order suits. The tailor was skeptical since the young man from the country had no experience, but something about his confident manner and enthusiasm prompted the man to give him a try.

Armed with a brochure, measuring tape, and fabric samples, Haynie set out to call on downtown offices and soon returned with his first order. He owned no nice clothes of his own, so when the suit was ready to be delivered, he donned the clothes himself for a few days in order to look nice to sell another suit. When the second suit was finished, he turned the first suit over to its owner. He kept up this system until he could afford to buy his own suit of clothes. To make himself look presentable, he would place his suit pants under the hard mattress in his boarding house room every night to keep them pressed.

Despite his limited resources and the tricks he had to resort to, Haynie found he liked being a salesman. He was good at it, and the owner of the shop was pleased with his results. Haynie was soon making enough to send money back home to his two youngest siblings in Cross Plains.

***

Haynie had just turned twenty-one when the United States entered World War I in April 1917. He immediately enlisted in the Army and was sent to Camp Sevier in Greenville, South Carolina. When he and the members of his regiment arrived at the camp, Haynie was dismayed to find there were only a few tents and no buildings. Haynie and the other men had to put in long hours felling trees to build barracks which would eventually house 30,000 soldiers.

After almost a year of training, Haynie was eager to see action. Finally, on May 26, 1918, as part of the U.S. Army's 114th Field Artillery, Battery E, Haynie boarded the transport ship *Karoa*, which left from the port of New York bound for Europe.

The volunteer regiment from Nashville was immediately thrust into the intense heat of battle along the Western Front, landing in the horrific trenches of the Argonne Forest and the Woevre plains near Verdun in northern France. The Argonne Forest was especially treacherous, given the hilly terrain and the relentless assaults by the Germans. The attacks which would start around 2:30 a.m. made it impossible to get much sleep. Rations were scarce, and some days Haynie was grateful to find raw cabbages to eat, left in the fields by farmers who had been driven out of their homes by the fighting.

To add to the misery, it rained nearly every day from May until November, and Haynie slogged through the endless mud, his rifle and gas mask at the ready and a pack slung over his back. His battalion was under constant German attack. Haynie never knew if he would see the next day, but "we were too busy fighting to allow for feelings." Men were dying all around him, and the sharp smell of exploding shells penetrated the air he breathed, sometimes landing so close he was peppered with shrapnel. With the incessant fire raining down on him, Haynie made a promise to himself, one that would become the credo of his life: "This is no time to worry about my own fears. I have a job to do."

On November 11, 1918, when the announcement came that an armistice had been signed and the fighting was over, Haynie and the men of Battery E were stunned by the silence that descended over the ravaged land.

Haynie had survived abandonment by his parents, a crippling childhood, and now he had escaped death in the trenches.

His luck was changing.

***

Having "served with distinction," Corporal William Haynie Gourley returned to Nashville at the end of 1918. He took lodging in a fifty-room boarding house located on Sixth Avenue downtown where his younger brother Everett, also home from the war, rented a room. But Haynie did not return to the tailor's shop. He was now confident that he had a knack for selling, and he set his sights on something much bigger.

At the end of World War I, the automobile business was growing like wildfire in Nashville. By 1919, there were just under 12,000 cars registered in the city. The two newspapers, the afternoon *Nashville Banner* and the morning *The Tennessean*, were running full pages of news articles about the burgeoning industry. Numerous dealerships were cropping up downtown, some taking out quarter-page ads offering new and used cars for sale.

In early 1919, Haynie landed a job at the Southern Automobile Sales Company, the largest dealer of used cars in Nashville. His skills as a suit salesman easily transferred to an industry with many more opportunities. By June 1921, he had become assistant manager of the company.

News of Haynie's talent as a salesman spread quickly, and in September of that same year, he was recruited by the newly opened Ford dealer, George Cole Motor Company, where he was named manager of used car sales.

Haynie's star had begun to rise.

Haynie Gourley (in back seat wearing a bow tie) in a Reo, one of the first cars in Cross Plains, Tennessee, 1925. *Courtesy of Rita A. Read, Cross Plains Heritage Commission*

All through the 1920s Nashville continued to grow, fueled in part by the automobile business. Other industries arrived to make the city their headquarters, including DuPont and the General Shoe Company, which would become Genesco, and which brought in more employees and purchasers of automobiles. More cars also led to more roads and the creation of suburbs. Lawns grew larger, and sidewalks disappeared.

By 1924, automobiles were clogging traffic and challenging trolleys for space on downtown streets. Broadway west to Sixteenth Avenue became known as Auto Row, with showrooms, auto parts stores, and tire dealers opening up along the strip, displacing former mansions.

In 1928, a traffic count taken at Eighth Avenue and Broadway found that twenty-eight thousand cars passed through the intersection every day.

Haynie was a familiar figure on Auto Row throughout the 1920s. His name appeared almost daily in ads in the *Nashville Banner* and *The Tennessean*. His photograph headed many articles published about the rapidly expanding industry and his meteoric rise in the business.

In 1929, he was promoted to general manager of the George Cole Motor Company. Word among the dealers was that Haynie Gourley had "unusual abilities" as a salesman and as an innovator in promoting new models. In 1930, he was recruited as manager of the Graham-Paige Company, which distributed the Graham car, a make that would last only a little more than a decade, but which sold well under Haynie's leadership. To introduce the Graham to the public, Haynie had the showroom decorated to match the colors of the new models. People flocked to his grand opening. Other firms took notice.

***

From its founding, Nashville was a place of contrasts. The circumscribed world of automobiles Haynie Gourley came to know in the 1920s in downtown Nashville couldn't have been more different from one occupied by a recently formed group on the west side of the city.

Around 1920, some teachers of literature at Vanderbilt University, along with several students, began meeting on alternate Saturday nights in a private home. They were primarily poets and essayists who shared their work with each other and carried on scholarly discussions into the night.

The group became known as The Fugitives. The best-known members were John Crowe Ransom, Allen Tate, Donald Davidson, William Ridley Wills, and Robert Penn Warren. From 1922 until 1925, they published their works in a small literary magazine, *The Fugitive*. Their movement made Vanderbilt University a leader in what would come to be known as the "New Criticism," which would influence college English classes across the country during the first half of the twentieth century.

Some members of this erudite society formed a second group known as the Southern Agrarians, who championed a return to Southern culture based on the region's agricultural roots, a reaction to the nation's fast-moving industrialization. Promoters of this school of thought included the poet, novelist, and essayist Andrew Lytle; the poet Allen Tate; Donald Davidson, poet, essayist, and historian; John Crowe Ransom, poet, professor, and essayist; and Robert Penn Warren, who would gain fame for his novel *All the King's Men*. Warren later became the first poet laureate of the United States.

While Haynie Gourley's world would never intersect with these lofty academics, the automobile would end up catapulting him into a very different Nashville, one he could never have dreamed of when he walked through the door of a tailor's shop in 1915.

In the 1930 census, Haynie Gourley was listed as a "lodger" in the column designating home ownership in Nashville. He now had more than ten years' experience in automobile sales and management. The population of Nashville had grown to 153,860, and there were more than 40,000 registered automobiles in the city.

Unbeknownst to Haynie, back in 1921 something had occurred across the state in Memphis that would forever change the trajectory of his life. A twenty-seven-year-old man named James Dobbs borrowed $25,000 to open a car dealership. Dobbs, along with his thirty-seven-year-old friend and business partner, Horace Hull, began selling Fords out of a modest brick building at 600 Madison Avenue in downtown Memphis.

Dobbs was a brilliant salesman, and Hull was the mastermind behind the financial end of the business. In just three years, their Memphis dealership was generating annual gross sales of $1.25 million. In 1928, Dobbs and Hull received an offer of $250,000 for the business. They decided to sell. But the stock market crash of October 1929 and the onset of the Great Depression wiped out the new owner. Dobbs and Hull purchased the business back when the dealership was repossessed.

To expand on their success in Memphis, the two automobile men opened a Ford dealership in Nashville with a third partner, W. B. Maclin. Horace Hull and James Dobbs soon heard about Haynie Gourley's talent and recruited him to come work for them. Haynie left the Graham-Paige Company to take a position as sales manager for Hull-Dobbs-Maclin Ford, joining the firm in January 1931. An article in *The Tennessean* appeared on March 1, 1931, touting Haynie's credentials: "One of Nashville's best-known young automobile men, W. Haynie Gourley, recently joined the Hull-Dobbs-Maclin Company as general sales manager. W. B. Maclin, general manager, says the firm is indeed fortunate in obtaining the services of Mr. Gourley."

Haynie's photograph began appearing in ads for the dealership, along with another salesman named L.D. Crick. The two were dubbed "just a couple of hometown boys." The folksy moniker caught on, and by May of 1931 Haynie and Crick, now household names, bought Maclin's interest in the company. The *Nashville Banner* proclaimed Haynie Gourley "one of the best-known men on Auto Row" with a "splendid background of accomplishment."

In 1932, major changes occurred at the Hull-Dobbs Company. First, the headquarters moved to 510 Broadway between Fifth and Sixth Avenues. Second, the firm switched from its franchise as a Ford dealership and began selling Chevrolets. Haynie was put in charge of the business as vice-president and general manager and ran its day-to-day operations while Horace Hull and James Dobbs remained primarily in Memphis. With the promise of loans from Hull and Dobbs, who had come to depend on Haynie's leadership, Haynie was able to make a deal to purchase the dealership.

That year, Haynie began his acquisition of Hull-Dobbs, which he renamed Capitol Chevrolet Company. Haynie now had his own automobile franchise. He was adept at organizing big events to introduce the new models that came out each year. People were instinctively drawn to him, and he had a gift of making every person who walked through the doors of Capitol Chevrolet feel special. His skills were beginning to translate into sales. Dreams way beyond his expectations were beginning to come true.

CHAPTER [2]

In the 1930s, Nashville, like cities all over the country, suffered bread lines and joblessness. At the same time, however, the town's social scene was thriving.

Dance clubs had become a popular form of entertainment in Nashville at the end of the 1920s, and the trend continued throughout the 1930s. Unlike in some other cities or frontier towns where these sorts of establishments attracted a roughcast clientele and oftentimes became scenes of rowdy confrontations, the Nashville dance clubs drew crowds of college students and respectable young professionals in addition to well-heeled, newly married couples from the more affluent southwest side of the city. Teenagers from "good" families worked the concessions, watching couples dance to the music of live, mostly African American orchestras.

In 1934, it was at one of these dance clubs that Haynie, now thirty-eight, met a twenty-two-year-old beauty with dazzling, iridescent-blue eyes named Josephine Saunders who was in Nashville visiting her married sister. From the moment Haynie saw her across the room, he was smitten.

Josephine Saunders had graduated with a dramatic arts degree from Martin College in Pulaski, Tennessee. Slender with lustrous dark hair, Josephine had enjoyed a privileged upbringing. Her father owned a successful Buick dealership and served as mayor of Waverly, Tennessee, county seat of Humphreys County, located seventy-five miles west of Nashville.

At twenty-two, the high-spirited Josephine, who had attracted many beaux during her high school and college years, was fascinated by this older man who, despite his age, possessed boyish looks and a playful, good-natured temperament.

Haynie had not come from a background Josephine's parents considered even remotely in keeping with the status of their popular, lively daughter. In addition, Gertrude and Andrew Saunders harbored doubts about the sixteen-year age difference between their daughter and her persistent thirty-eight-year-old suitor. They were also disturbed by the fact that the romance seemed to be progressing too quickly.

After courting for only six weeks, Haynie asked Josephine to marry him. Her reply was, "But I don't love you." He answered with a devilish smile, "That's okay. You will." Further, he impressed her with his claim that he was taking in $4,000 a month in his business, a fortune considering the Depression was in full swing. Without her parents' knowledge, the two slipped away to Franklin, Kentucky, and married on November 25, 1934. They honeymooned for almost a month in the U.S. Northwest and Canada.

Haynie and Josephine settled in Nashville, moving into the popular Gainesborough, a handsome stone apartment building on Harding Road. Haynie's business was doing well, but it was only after he and Josephine had wed that Haynie confessed he was not earning $4,000 a month. In fact, he admitted, the amount was what he *owed* on his loan each month. Josephine took the deception in good stride and was soon impressed by his keen business acumen and his easy self-confidence. It didn't take long for her to fall in love with her much older husband. She would from then on refer to him as "My Haynie."

***

"Record crowd thronged the display rooms of Capitol Chevrolet to get a glimpse of the new Chevrolets for 1935," read the caption under a photograph in the *Nashville Banner* on January 13, 1935, showing crowds packed into the downtown dealership. "Congratulations to

Haynie Gourley as Chevrolet Showing Sets First Day Record."

Haynie was good at marketing. To entice customers to his business, Haynie ran an ad that appeared in the *Nashville Banner* on May 20, 1935, offering oil changes for eighty-nine cents that included five quarts of oil. He also advertised a "paint all over" job for $17.99.

In November of that year, the new 1936 Master and Standard Chevrolets went on display. Large crowds again packed the showroom of Capitol Chevrolet Company, and over 2,000 visitors passed through the building over the weekend, again setting a record.

Haynie Gourley, standing, at Capitol Chevrolet's downtown offices at 510 Broadway. Seated is Charlie Rolfe, Haynie's business partner from 1937 until Rolfe's death in 1953. *Courtesy of Billy Gourley*

At the beginning of 1936, Haynie was elected president of the Nashville Automobile Trade Association. The business continued to grow, and in 1937, Haynie brought in an investment partner, Nashville native Charles Rolfe Jr., who was twenty-nine. Haynie knew Rolfe from their days at Hull-Dobbs-Maclin. While there was night-and-day difference in their upbringing and education—Rolfe had attended the prestigious boys' preparatory school, Montgomery Bell Academy, graduated from Vanderbilt University, and was a member of the elite Belle Meade Country Club—the abandoned boy from Cross Plains and the privileged city boy became fast friends.

The Gourley-Rolfe partnership was a successful one, and Haynie was doing well enough to buy a one-story, white-columned brick home on Estes Road, six houses down from the Rolfe residence and not far from the boundary of the city of Belle Meade, Nashville's wealthiest neighborhood.

It did not take long for the society pages of the *Nashville Banner* and *The Tennessean* to recognize the star quality of the Gourleys, who were pictured at galas, and mentioned when they attended social functions or hosted a Valentine's Day party. One of the *Nashville Banner*'s columnists described them as members of Nashville's "smart set."

Gregarious with a ready smile, Haynie loved a good time and made friends easily. He joined the Richland Country Club, founded in 1901 and located just off Harding Road. At Richland, he learned to play golf and developed a love of the game. From the outset, Haynie's scores and performance in tournaments were frequently listed in the sports pages of both Nashville newspapers.

Meanwhile, Josephine Gourley was making a splash of her own. She was glamorous and possessed an exuberant personality. She also loved to entertain. By the late thirties, she was hosting bridge luncheons and afternoon teas and threw herself into charity work, mainly as a member of the Fannie Battle Social Workers and the Traveller's Aid Society.

On October 5, 1939, Haynie and Josephine had a daughter, Josephine Ann "JoAnn" Gourley. As a toddler, she appeared in numerous newspaper photographs with her "attractive mother."

From 1940 on, the couple together or Josephine on her own made the papers practically every week. The society editors were especially taken with Jo's sartorial elegance. She was noted for her outfit for the 1940 Kentucky Derby, a "gray and white polka dot dress, matching gray wool coat, topped by a silver fox scarf." At a tea in 1942, a columnist wrote that Mrs. Haynie Gourley's "unusual beauty was set off by the delicate pink shade of her dress and hat."

On March 29, 1945, Jo and Haynie had a son, born at St. Thomas Hospital. They named him William Haynie Gourley Jr. and called him

Billy. He, too, along with his pretty sister, would capture the attention of newspaper photographers and society editors for years to come.

He would also one day play an outsized and unwitting role in his father's destiny.

***

All throughout the Depression years, Haynie maintained close ties with the Memphis car dealers, James Dobbs and Horace Hull. The three men had become close friends. When the United States entered World War II in December 1941, much of the production of steel and other materials used in cars was given over to the war effort. Dobbs and Hull bought up new and used car inventories from dealers and stockpiled them in warehouses across the South. This meant Haynie continued to have access to cars to sell as automobile production ground to a halt, keeping his business alive.

When World War II ended in 1945, the return of soldiers from abroad created a huge demand for automobiles. Capitol Chevrolet's sales skyrocketed, and within a year, Haynie Gourley was a wealthy man. Haynie and Josephine were beginning to be mentioned as attending the same parties as members of the vaunted Old Nashville society. While the couple's social life was centered around the Richland Club, more and more, their names were listed as guests of members of the exclusive Belle Meade Country Club.

Josephine's keen sense of style and beautiful clothes constantly drew the attention of society columnists, and Haynie was becoming a well-known golfer. One sportswriter with the *Nashville Banner* wrote about Haynie's antics on the golf course, referring to him as "the Chevrolet dealer who drives a Cadillac."

In the fall of 1948 when Billy was three years old, the family moved into a house on Belle Meade Boulevard, the main thoroughfare of the most exclusive section of Nashville, populated mostly by long-established, wealthy families. All along cross streets like Jackson Boulevard, Iroquois Avenue, Tyne Boulevard, and Chickering Road stood elegant mansions with acres of lawn stretching to the street. Within the walls of these great houses, Nashville's wealthy elite employed butlers and live-in servants to tend to their families.

Belle Meade Boulevard was divided by a wide, grassy median and ran from Harding Road past the Belle Meade Country Club and up to the stone gates at the entrance to Percy Warner Park. The forested hills and rolling meadows of the park added to the expansiveness and beauty of Belle Meade.

The Gourleys completely renovated the one-story, four-bedroom house, adding four tall columns on the front portico and painting the red-brick exterior white. A fifth bedroom was added for Henrietta Green, the family's live-in housekeeper and cook.

The *Nashville Banner* described the interior décor as having "all shades of green, and chartreuse rugs and dark green walls." The living room opened onto a back terrace swathed in pink rambling Dorothy Perkins roses, which bloomed in late May and would soon provide a striking floral backdrop for dinner parties in mild weather.

By the late 1940s, Haynie had become well-established in Nashville's civic and business life and was earning a reputation for his generosity. He had joined the Lions Club back in the 1920s and supported several charitable organizations, notably the Community Chest and the United Givers. He and Josephine were active members of Vine Street Christian Church, located on Seventh Avenue North in downtown Nashville. In June 1948, Haynie and Charlie Rolfe made a gift of a new Chevrolet to the church's longtime pastor, the Reverend Dr. Roger T. Nooe. Haynie would keep this tradition up, changing out models for the church's senior minister every year.

Haynie was also a devoted fan of Vanderbilt football, and he and Josephine attended all the home games, often hosting pre-game parties. A headline splashed across the society page of *The Tennessean* on Sunday, October 30, 1949, proclaimed, "The Haynie Gourleys Are Hosts at Breakfast Preceding Football Game: Vanderbilt vs. Auburn." Two large photographs showed the women wearing corsages of football chrysanthemums, and the men in suits and ties, all gathered around tables topped with Vanderbilt-themed arrangements.

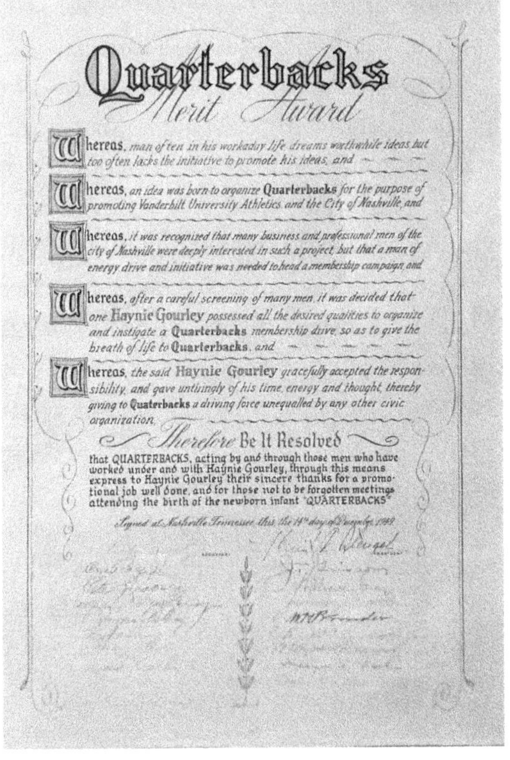

Quarterbacks
Merit Award

Whereas, man often in his workaday life dreams worthwhile ideas but too often lacks the initiative to promote his ideas, and

Whereas, an idea was born to organize **Quarterbacks** for the purpose of promoting Vanderbilt University Athletics and the City of Nashville, and

Whereas, it was recognized that many business and professional men of the city of Nashville were deeply interested in such a project, but that a man of energy drive and initiative was needed to head a membership campaign, and

Whereas, after a careful screening of many men, it was decided that one Haynie Gourley possessed all the desired qualities to organize and instigate a **Quarterbacks** membership drive, so as to give the breath of life to **Quarterbacks**, and

Whereas, the said Haynie Gourley gracefully accepted the responsibility, and gave untiringly of his time, energy and thought, thereby giving to **Quaterbacks** a driving force unequalled by any other civic organization,

Therefore Be It Resolved

that QUARTERBACKS, acting by and through those men who have worked under and with Haynie Gourley, through this means express to Haynie Gourley their sincere thanks for a promotional job well done, and for those not to be forgotten meetings attending the birth of the newborn infant "QUARTERBACKS"

Signed at Nashville Tennessee this the 14th day of [illegible] 1949

Merit award presented to Haynie Gourley, 1949. *Courtesy of Bill Gourley III*

As a crackerjack salesman, Haynie had a natural gift of persuasion. For a year, he had been working on a pet project called Quarterbacks—an organization formed to promote athletics at Vanderbilt University and in the City of Nashville. For his work in heading up a successful membership drive, he received a citation which spelled out his growing influence in the community: "Haynie Gourley gracefully accepted the responsibility and gave of his time, energy and thought, thereby giving to Quarterbacks a driving force unequalled by any other civic organization."

On December 1, 1949, *The Tennessean* recognized Haynie's contribution, describing the new athletic booster club's makeup.

"The 'Quarterbacks' were organized at the start of the new era in Vanderbilt football last summer. Its membership has climbed toward the 1,000 mark, including many non-Vanderbilt men, many non-college men, and many from nearby towns—all interested in the advancement of Vanderbilt's football fortunes."

Haynie was one of the non-college, non-Vanderbilt men. He never talked about his upbringing or revealed that he had only made it through fourth grade. When frequently asked where he had attended college, he would answer, "I received my degree from H. and K. University," then laughing heartily, adding, "The school of Hard Knocks."

Further down in that same December 1st column, written by Joe Hatcher, a former sports editor for *The Tennessean*, was a story about Bill Powell, one of Vanderbilt's current football stars. Powell had been accused, "perhaps unfairly," noted the columnist, for the penalty of holding against a bitter rival, the University of Tennessee, causing Vanderbilt to lose in the last minutes of the game.

Neither Bill Powell nor Haynie Gourley could have imagined that in twenty years' time, their names would be splashed across the front page of this very newspaper for weeks on end, or that they would be inextricably bound by a single act that would define both their fates.

CHAPTER [3]

In the early 1950s, something amazing was taking shape in an imposing building at the corner of Broadway and Fifth Avenue, directly across the street from Capitol Chevrolet's showroom. It was a phenomenon that would help define the city's character and make Nashville famous the world over.

On Monday, March 21, 1949, Haynie and Josephine attended the opening night of Irving Berlin's *Annie Get Your Gun* at the Ryman Auditorium. Completed in 1892, the Ryman had its beginnings as the Union Gospel Tabernacle, built by riverboat captain Thomas Ryman, who had attended a downtown tent revival and was moved by the preaching of noted evangelist Rev. Sam Jones. To provide a permanent setting for Jones's preaching, Ryman had the tabernacle built at 116 Fifth Avenue North in downtown Nashville. From the beginning, the building was used for more than preaching, becoming a venue for lectures, operas, ballets, circuses, concerts, plays, and even an ice-skating show.

In addition to Rev. Jones's revivals, the tabernacle attracted world-famous celebrities. Susan B. Anthony and Booker T. Washington both lectured on the original platform, which was replaced by a stage built in 1901 to accommodate the opera *Carmen*. In 1904, on the occasion of Thomas Ryman's funeral, Rev. Jones announced the name of the tabernacle would be changed to Ryman Auditorium. In 1906, the world-famous French actress Sarah Bernhardt starred in her signature role in *Camille*, and in 1907 President Theodore Roosevelt took the stage for a ten-minute lecture that turned into a half-hour talk.

The first ticket event to sell out was the 1913 appearance of Helen

Keller and Anne Sullivan. Anna Pavlova, the celebrated Russian ballerina, danced there in 1918. In that same year, to raise money for war bonds, Charlie Chaplin performed his antics, including his famous waddle, to a standing-room-only crowd. It was Chaplin who was the inspiration for adding a balcony to provide another layer of seating.

Other performances were given by the Italian tenor Enrico Caruso, the magician Harry Houdini, the humorist Will Rogers, the famous opera singer Marian Anderson, and actresses Ethel Barrymore, Helen Hayes, Tallulah Bankhead, and Katherine Hepburn, the latter reprising her role in *The Philadelphia Story*. First Lady Eleanor Roosevelt also made an appearance as she traveled around the country on a lecture circuit.

However, for all the famous people who appeared there, it was the Grand Ole Opry that put the Ryman Auditorium on the map and would make Nashville the country music capital of the world.

The Opry began as a radio show in November 1925, broadcasting from the fifth story studio of the National Life & Accident Insurance Company at the corner of Seventh Avenue and Union Street in downtown Nashville. The insurance company's motto was "We Shield Millions," thus the station's call letters WSM. The one-hour show was called the WSM Barn Dance and aired on Saturday nights, featuring what was then called hillbilly music.

George Hay, the founder of the Grand Ole Opry, was hired from Chicago's WLS radio station where he had made a success with his National Barn Dance show. In 1927, he renamed WSM's show the "Grand Ole Opry."

By the 1930s, the Opry had expanded to four hours on Saturday evenings and was broadcast at 50,000 watts, enough power to send a clear signal to some thirty states. The hugely popular show outgrew the National Life & Accident studio and three other locales before it was moved to the Ryman Auditorium in 1943. Crowds lined up for blocks to enter the 3,000-seat auditorium to see the country music greats perform on its stage, among them Roy Acuff, Eddy Arnold, Hank Williams Sr., and Ernest Tubb in the 1940s, to Chet Atkins, Kitty Wells, Hank Snow, the Carter Family, Lester Flatt and Earl Scruggs, and Johnny Cash in the 1950s, and Patsy Cline, Loretta Lynn, Willie Nelson, and Tex Ritter in the early '60s.

On a radio show in 1950, the WSM disc jockey David Cobb called Nashville "Music City." The name took hold, and Nashville was well on its way to becoming a major center of the music and recording industry, gaining worldwide recognition that would continue to attract performing artists from around the globe.

When country music hit Nashville's airwaves on WSM radio, Haynie did not take to the genre with its Tennessee twang and songs of love and loss and growing up poor. He'd had enough of those sentiments in his early days. On his travels with Josephine, he had developed a taste for the soft string music that often wafted through the lobbies of grand hotels and the strains of orchestras playing romantic ballads he could dance to. On the few occasions Billy asked his father what it was like for him growing up, Haynie would answer that he had made it his practice to enjoy the here and now and think only of good things.

"I left my past behind long ago," he told his son. Billy knew by his father's tone of voice that the subject was closed and not to ask again.

There would be only one other occasion when Haynie would bring up the struggles of his early years, and that would be on a night that would prove to be a defining moment for both him and his family.

***

The decade of the 1950s brought more and more attention to the Gourleys, especially Josephine, who ramped up entertaining in her new home. On Thursday, January 19, 1950, a columnist at *The Tennessean* waxed effusively about a "get together" hosted by Mrs. Haynie Gourley at her home on Belle Meade Boulevard, describing the decorations as "a veritable bower of yellow tulips, buttercups and purple iris, stunning with the green and chartreuse decor of the home." In another entry in the society pages of *The Tennessean*, a writer gushed over Josephine Gourley's most outstanding feature: "Quick now, name me a gal with prettier azure eyes than Mrs. Haynie Gourley."

Josephine was also proving herself to be a leader, now heading up various committees and fund-raisers at Belle Meade's neighborhood Parmer School, where her children were elementary students. She, too, was persuasive. She had a bigger than life personality. She would corner a donor, grabbing her hands and calling her "honey" or "darling" and showering her with compliments. This gesture became Josephine's signature greeting. She would treat both close friends and new acquaintances this way, holding them spellbound with her iridescent blue eyes and her brand of intense warmth and charm.

The Gourley family in Sea Island, Georgia, 1955, as pictured in the society pages of the *Nashville Banner. Nashville Public Library, Special Collections, Banner Newspaper Collection*

Haynie could now afford the best for his family, and he took great pleasure in spoiling his wife and children. He loved taking them on trips, staying in the best hotels wherever they went—the Broadmoor in Colorado Springs, the Plaza in New York, the Drake in Chicago, and the Mayflower in Washington, D.C. In September 1950, Haynie and Josephine were staying at the Plaza in New York when they took in a World Series game and attended the Army-Colgate football match-up. In April 1954, the family spent the Easter holidays at the Plaza and dressed in their Sunday best to attend the big parade on Fifth Avenue.

As they had done since the early days of their marriage, Haynie and Jo kept up their yearly trip to the Kentucky Derby with friends from New Albany, Indiana. Fort Lauderdale, Miami, and Delray Beach in south Florida became destinations every winter, and the family spent summer vacations at the ritzy Cloister on Sea Island, Georgia, mingling with the other wealthy guests, playing golf and tennis, horseback riding, bicycling, and shooting skeet. They dined each evening in the Cloister's opulent rooms, while at noon the more casual Beach Club with its large swimming pool next to the ocean was a gathering place for youngsters and teenagers and for ladies to enjoy a Southern-style lunch of frozen fruit salad and cheese straws.

***

Sales at Capitol Chevrolet were booming, but on September 24, 1953, tragedy struck. Haynie's partner Charles Rolfe Jr., died unexpectedly of heart failure after spending two weeks in the hospital. Rolfe was only forty-five years old, eleven years younger than Haynie. This was a huge blow to Haynie, who was fond of his business partner and depended on their partnership to keep the company running smoothly and to have the freedom to travel. The Rolfes and Gourleys had become good friends and frequently took trips together. Charlie Rolfe was a favorite of young Billy Gourley, slipping the boy a silver dollar each time he came down to Capitol Chevrolet with his father.

Shortly after Rolfe's death, Haynie ran an ad in the newspaper, saying that all trucks and used cars must be sold immediately to satisfy the Charles Rolfe estate. In 1954, Haynie bought Rolfe's stock from his widow.

Once again, Haynie Gourley was sole owner of Capitol Chevrolet Company.

By the mid-1950s, Haynie's social status in Nashville reached a new high when he was invited to join the ultra-exclusive Belle Meade Country Club. The club was founded in 1901 by descendants of John Harding, who, in 1807, acquired property along the Natchez Trace and developed Belle Meade Plantation. Harding's son, William Giles Harding, inherited the original house and land and greatly expanded both. In the early 20th century, most of the acreage of the plantation was sold and developed and taken into the city of Belle Meade.

Originally known as Nashville Golf Country Club, Belle Meade Country Club moved in 1915 to its permanent location at 815 Belle Meade Boulevard, a half mile from the Gourley home. From the club's beginning, candidates were chosen from men of prominence, most all of whom had family ties dating back to the captains of industry and the governing class in the early days of Nashville and the state of Tennessee.

The process of election to membership in the club was highly secretive and restrictive. Legacy and family connections were of utmost importance, and membership was passed down through generations. Sons were first in line for consideration. Since only men could join Belle Meade Country Club, some lucky sons-in-law who had married well were accepted. Other men who were partners in elite law firms or top executives in major companies were the next to be proposed but were favored only if they possessed the right pedigree. Many members had graduated from Harvard, Yale, and Princeton or from prestigious Southern schools, namely Vanderbilt, the University of Virginia, the University of the South, and Washington and Lee. Most could trace their heritage back generations.

The chances of someone with a fourth-grade education and no family connections being asked to join one of the snobbiest clubs in the country would normally be zero. But Haynie and Josephine had long been friends with important members who had included them in large parties in the ballroom or in the more intimate settings of the club's quiet rooms.

With his invitation to membership, Haynie joined in foursomes on the club's golf course, although he remained active in the Richland Club and made it a habit of having lunch with his friends there on a weekly basis.

Josephine now signed her own ticket at the Belle Meade Country Club when she met friends for lunch, ordering one of the club's signature dishes, the frozen tomato, which, oddly, was not a tomato at all, but an odd concoction of tomato soup, canned pineapple, mayonnaise, cream cheese with a dollop of ketchup. The Gourley children became regulars at the club's swimming pool and snack bar and joined in hosting parties with their classmates.

Also in the mid-fifties, Haynie acquired one of the much sought-after boxes at the prestigious Iroquois Steeplechase. The event, a type of horse race with hurdles and jumps, was first held in Nashville in 1941 and became an annual event, taking place on the second Saturday in May in Percy Warner Park. The race was always a grand occasion in Belle Meade society, with pre- and post-Steeplechase parties held in the homes of Nashville's elite horsey set, a rarefied world of wealth and fox-hunting and thoroughbreds and historic farms with miles of fencing and hundreds of acres of rolling fields. Mason Houghland, master of Hillsboro Hounds, and his son Calvin Houghland Sr., owner of Bright Hour Farm, Guilford Dudley of Northumberland, and John Sloan of Maple Grove Farm, were among the founders of the Steeplechase.

On the eve of the race, Belle Meade members placed their bets at a Calcutta party, held at the club. Then, Saturday evening after the race, the Hunt Ball, with the signature scarlet and black colors of the Hillsboro Hounds festooning the ballroom of the Belle Meade Country Club, was one of the highlights of the social season. Mr. and Mrs. W. Haynie Gourley, as they were most often listed in the newspapers, were now regulars at this black-tie affair and involved in the entire weekend's activities centered around the Steeplechase.

With all this new-found prestige, Haynie had not forgotten where he came from. He never pretended to be well-bred, and in fact, some of the society types considered him to be "rough around the edges."

But his outlook was always positive and optimistic, and people liked him. He was not about to let any bad memories or his lack of proper background overshadow his enjoyment of life in this elite world that had taken him into its fold.

***

Thanks to their father's success, the Gourley children, JoAnn and Billy, lived an existence that would have been the envy of any pre-teen or teenager coming of age in the 1950s. Life in Belle Meade was one big social whirl, with skating parties at the Hippodrome rink on West End Avenue; square dances at Mrs. Brown's Coffee Shop with live music provided by The Dew Drops and their famous fiddler; hayrides at historic farms on Franklin Road; and high school sorority and fraternity formal dances, all with orchestras and "combos" like the popular Beach Nutz. Even small teen parties in Belle Meade often included dancing to a live band.

In the summer there was camp. On August 21, 1953, the society editor of the *Nashville Banner* wrote that JoAnn Gourley was seen "hopping off the train after two months at Camp Green Cove in Tuxedo, North Carolina." Along with some buddies from Belle Meade, Billy spent a month each summer at Camp Greenbrier in the mountains of West Virginia, where his parents would come to pick him up, always staying at the nearby Greenbrier Hotel with its garden-inspired interior décor and upscale clientele.

JoAnn Gourley attended the all-girls private Harpeth Hall School and during her freshman year was invited to join SAP, one of the most prestigious local high school sororities and one with many Belle Meade daughters as members. The SAPs, whose acronym was a highly guarded secret, held their formal dances at the Belle Meade Country Club. More casual events took place at several venues around the city or in private homes. At a Hawaiian themed party, SAP members transformed a popular spot, Gossett's Barn, into a giant ship. Another SAP party at a member's house was described as a "barbeque and house hunt," followed by dancing to the Kings of Rhythm.

An auburn-haired beauty with a sparkling personality, JoAnn was a regular at dances hosted by Alpha Chi, a top high school fraternity. Her dates often had prominent Nashville family names like Cheek or Sloan. The *Nashville Banner* placed JoAnn at one such formal party at the downtown Maxwell House Hotel on Friday, May 7, 1954, where teenagers were dancing "under a balmy spring sky studded with stars, with the girls floating in ballerina-length dresses to the music of the Owen Bradley Orchestra."

During her high school years, JoAnn was a prolific hostess herself, holding "Coca-Cola parties" in summer, "chocolates" in winter, and luncheons to entertain out-of-town camp friends. Hardly a week went by without a reference to the teen's comings and goings.

***

During the 1950s, Tennessee native and Vanderbilt graduate Dinah Shore had become nationally famous with her own television variety show on NBC, sponsored by the Chevrolet Motor Company. There was hardly a television viewer in America who was not familiar with the famous jingle, "See the U.S.A. in your Chevrolet," sung with gusto in Shore's slightly raspy voice on every episode of *The Dinah Shore Show*.

It was a proud moment for Haynie when the blonde, personable entertainer made an appearance at his showroom. Crowds gathered outside to peer in at the celebrity, who waved and blew kisses to her admirers. Haynie couldn't have asked for a better advertisement for Capitol Chevrolet. He would talk about the event for years.

Chevrolet's new models for the upcoming year were now introduced in the fall, usually in late September, instead of in January. Haynie had always had a knack for marketing. The roll-out of new models was no small occasion in the 1950s. People looked forward to seeing the changes from year to year. The unveiling was always a big to-do. Even young children knew which cars were which year, and parents would bring them downtown to the dealerships for the event. Haynie liked keeping the public in suspense, so he covered his showroom windows with brown paper for a few days while he changed out the previous year's models. No one was allowed to see the new Chevrolets until the manufacturer gave the go ahead. Then, with great fanfare, the brown paper was ripped away to reveal the latest models.

Haynie was asked to be a member of Chevrolet's National Dealer Planning Commission and often flew to Detroit and Cincinnati for meetings. Back in Nashville, he made plans to acquire more space for the dealership, which already covered an entire block in downtown Nashville. Sales were booming, and some of the service areas had to be located across the street from 510 Broadway as well as on nearby lots. He even installed his own gas station opposite the main building. Chevrolets were now the best-selling cars in America, lagging behind Ford for only two years out of the decade.

That moment in 1932 when Hull-Dobbs switched from a Ford dealership to a Chevrolet franchise had been Haynie's lucky day.

Meanwhile, the lively Josephine Gourley continued to be a force to be reckoned with. Long known for her exquisite taste in clothes, she kept up with the latest fashions from New York and Paris. Risley Lawrence, a direct descendant of one of the founders of Nashville and a well-known tennis player and employee of the Third National Bank, along with his wife Elizabeth, attended the same church and knew the Gourleys from afar. The handsome younger couple had a standing joke that at the beginning of every season, the women of the church would anxiously wait to see what Josephine Gourley was wearing so they would know what to go out and buy for themselves.

Further acclamation of Josephine's wardrobe chic came on September 9, 1959, when a bold headline in *The Tennessean* announced the newspaper's First Annual List of Best-dressed Women. Mrs. W. Haynie Gourley along with Mrs. Sam Fleming and ten other society matrons were selected by a "secret committee."

"Black is Mrs. Gourley's preferred fashion color," noted the writer. "Her favorite dinner dress is a black peau-de-soie sheath. She likes basic tailored suits that can be worn with a variety of accessories, particularly different small cloche hats."

***

The year 1957 held changes for the family. In the fall, Billy entered the private boys' preparatory school, Montgomery Bell Academy, as a seventh grader, and JoAnn headed to Washington, D.C., enrolling as a freshman at the all-female Holton Arms Junior College.

Haynie and Josephine were busy helping plan a new sanctuary for the Vine Street Christian Church, which, after sixty-eight years in downtown Nashville, was to be relocated to Harding Road, adjacent to MBA and not far from Belle Meade. Haynie was instrumental in raising $900,000 for the construction, and Josephine sat on the building committee. The new sanctuary was designed by the noted Nashville architect Edwin Keeble. Keeble also designed the Life & Casualty Tower downtown, Memorial Gymnasium at Vanderbilt University, and the Veterans Administration hospital in Washington, D.C. He was also the architect for many important homes in Nashville, including Northumberland for Guilford Dudley Jr. and Maple Grove for the John Sloans.

Vine Street Christian Church's soaring steeple reached a height of 187 feet, with a six-foot-tall cross at the top. The distinctive narrow proportions of the church only served to make the steeple all the more dramatic. Keeble's steeple designs amusingly became known as "Keeble's needles."

The dedication for the new sanctuary was held on Sunday, October 12, 1958. In two more years, the church would be the scene of a very happy event for the Gourley family. In less than ten years, however, the pews would be packed for a very different occasion, due to a circumstance no one could ever have anticipated.

***

These were halcyon days for Jo and Haynie. In 1958, Haynie's good friend Buford Ellington had been elected to his first term as governor of Tennessee. Haynie was made a "colonel" on the governor's staff, which gave him certain privileges, including a special number on his license plate to indicate his status as a good-will ambassador for the state. The lower numbers were reserved for government officials and rose in importance to include private citizens. Sam Fleming, president of one of the largest banks in Nashville, was assigned the number 33. The number on the Gourley family's license plates was 58, prestigious enough to let the Tennessee Highway Patrol know that someone important was behind the wheel.

In late 1959, Haynie had completed the expansion of his downtown dealership, renovating a former ice plant he owned at Fifth Avenue and Demonbreun Street for exclusive use in truck sales and service, and making a total investment of $100,000 in improvements. In the previous five years, Capitol Chevrolet's total sales for new and used vehicles had exceeded $3,500,000.

Josephine kept up a busy schedule of entertaining and charity work. She was now a member of the exclusive Centennial Club, an invitation-only meeting place for upper class women to host luncheons and teas and bridge parties.

Haynie's circle of friends and golfing buddies had grown to include Nashville's mayor and the governor of Tennessee, along with some of the wealthiest and most influential business owners, executives, and professionals in the city. As a member of the private Cumberland Club located in the Life & Casualty Tower, Haynie often lunched with city leaders in an atmosphere that was decidedly old-line men's club, with leather chairs and framed prints of hunt scenes.

CHAPTER [4]

Celebrating the beginning of a new decade, Haynie and Josephine Gourley rang in the 1960 New Year at the Belle Meade Country Club, dancing to Owen Bradley's orchestra playing "Auld Lang Syne."

Starting in the early 1940s, Bradley's orchestra became the most sought-after dance band among Nashville's well-heeled society. Early on, Bradley's vocalists included the future pop stars Snooky Lanson and Kitty Kallen of the television show *Your Hit Parade* fame. Later, Dottie Dillard and Bob Johnstone became popular lead singers, known all around Nashville. For over two decades, Bradley was a mainstay at the Belle Meade Country Club, playing for most of the important balls and large private bashes. He was also in demand at Vanderbilt University's social events and at Nashville's private prep schools and high school fraternities and sororities. JoAnn and Billy Gourley and their friends, having attended so many functions where Bradley played, knew well the orchestral strains of "Goodnight Sweetheart," always the last song, signaling the end of the evening.

Belle Meade society felt a sort of proprietorship when it came to Bradley. And Haynie, who loved to dance and was often the last to leave the floor, had twirled Josephine around to the orchestra's familiar tunes into the wee hours at the club.

What few in the smart set and the Gourley family knew or could even imagine was that Owen Bradley, so familiar to them as the band leader playing their favorite tunes, had forged a career that far overshadowed his performances at their parties. In fact, his other work would inspire a movement that would have a profound and lasting influence on Nashville's place in the American music industry.

Born in Westmoreland, Tennessee, in 1915, Owen Bradley moved to Nashville as a small boy. Early on, he learned the piano, and by the time he was a teenager could play several instruments, including the harmonica, steel guitar, trombone, and the organ. By age fifteen, he had formed his own band and was playing roadhouses and local night clubs.

When he was twenty, Bradley joined WSM-AM radio where he worked as a musician and arranger. In 1942, at the same time he was becoming *the* band for society parties, he was named WSM's musical director.

In 1947, Paul Cohen, an executive at Decca Records, hired Bradley to open a Nashville office and work as a music arranger for the label's recordings. Bradley produced and recorded some of Decca's biggest talents, including Ernest Tubb and Kitty Wells. In 1950, he produced Red Foley's million-seller "Chattanooga Shoe Shine Boy." He led the recording session for Kitty Wells's 1952 blockbuster hit "It Wasn't God Who Made Honky Tonk Angels," which helped revolutionize the place of women in country music.

In 1950, Capitol Records opened a Nashville branch, followed by the Mercury label's arrival in 1952, RCA in 1957, and Columbia in 1962.

When Cohen left Decca in 1958, Bradley was named head of its Nashville division, where he, along with famous guitarist, country music icon, and record producer Chet Atkins of RCA, ushered in a new era in the genre. It was this innovation that would brand Bradley and Atkins as star makers and expand the popularity of country music.

In 1950, the team of Roy Acuff and Fred Rose, whose publishing company had discovered Hank Williams, presaged a new sensation with their recording of Patti Page's "Tennessee Waltz."

The world-famous song of losing a love at a dance was originally on Side B of the long-forgotten "Boogie Woogie Santa Claus." Using backup singers and adding instruments like strings and piano to the plaintive sounds of the steel guitar, the record became one of the greatest hits of all time. It was still "country" music, but the extra instrumentals and vocal harmony helped it make the leap to the top of the pop charts. By the end of the year, the recording had sold over two million copies.

Bradley was soon embracing this technique, enhancing the voices of country singers by adding guitar, bass, drums, piano, strings, and background harmony, which gave their songs a wider appeal. His arrangements, along with those of Chet Atkins, became known as the "Nashville Sound." Some of the singers Bradley produced became mega-stars. Patsy Cline and Loretta Lynn were among the first, and soon Brenda Lee had twelve hits on the Top Ten Billboard chart. Many other famous artists benefited from Bradley's musical arrangements and the cross-over opportunities made possible by the "Nashville Sound."

In 1954, Bradley and his brother Harold repurposed a World War II surplus Quonset hut to use as a recording studio. The lightweight structure was attached to a house the brothers owned at 804 16th Avenue South, not far from the Belmont College and Vanderbilt University campuses. RCA's Chet Atkins built Studio B two blocks away on 17th Avenue South.

Bradley's studio, which other producers frequently used to record many famous country and pop stars, was one of the building blocks of Nashville's world-famous Music Row. The district, comprised of several interlocking streets, would become a major center of the music industry, attracting other recording labels, artists, songwriters, and producers from all over the country and abroad.

***

Davidson County was a "dry" county, meaning alcohol could not be served in any public eating establishments in Nashville. As a result, Saturday nights in Belle Meade in the 1950s and '60s revolved around private dinner parties, where waiters in white coats handed out highballs and served the likes of shrimp remoulade, roast partridge, and a

Southern staple, beaten biscuits, which were hard round, labor-intensive delicacies traditionally served with country ham.

On numerous occasions, the Gourleys dined at Boxwood, the imposing mansion belonging to Josephine and Sam Fleming, located on the corner of Harding Place and Belle Meade Boulevard, across from the Belle Meade Country Club. Fleming, a gracious, distinguished-looking man whose great-great grandfather had been governor of Tennessee, was president of the Third National Bank, and besides being a good friend of Haynie's, was the executor of his will and the banker for Capitol Chevrolet Company.

There were special parties on holidays held in the homes of some of Nashville's wealthiest and oldest families. Haynie and Josephine were often on the guest lists of these exclusive affairs. At Maple Grove Farm, John and Margaret Sloan's hunt teas were legendary. Although the Gourleys were not part of the fox-hunting set, John Sloan was a friend of Haynie's, and he and Josephine were often included at dinner parties at the Sloans' English manor-style home in Brentwood.

Haynie also enjoyed some perks of his new-found status. For twenty years, the couple had stayed at the Plaza Hotel on frequent trips to New York. Haynie was on a first-name basis with Ralph Rugierro, the storied manager of the hotel. On short notice Haynie could call Rugierro and request tickets for the latest Broadway hit. The reservations would be waiting for the Gourleys when they arrived at the Plaza.

In the early winter of 1960 Haynie and Josephine took their annual trip to south Florida. Horace Hull, of Hull-Dobbs, had remained close friends with Haynie, often staying overnight at the Gourley home when he came to Nashville from Memphis. Every year, Hull invited Haynie and Josephine to stay at a condominium he owned in Fort Lauderdale, Florida.

In February 1960, Haynie was having lunch at the Coral Ridge Country Club in Fort Lauderdale with a group of Nashville men. Haynie loved a good joke, so when Robert Doggett said to him, "I'll bet that member behind you can whip you with one arm tied to his side," Haynie looked around at the man in question.

"He doesn't look so tough. Who is he?"

"Rocky Marciano," replied Doggett.

Haynie jumped up, shook Marciano's hand and exclaimed, "I can't wait to tell my son back in Nashville that I almost put on the gloves with the former heavyweight boxing champion of the world."

For once, the Nashville men had gotten the best of Haynie, who was usually the prankster in the crowd.

***

In the early 1960s, Belle Meade was a very insular community. Everybody knew each other. Children knew their friends' parents and vice versa. Adults and children alike rarely ventured outside their comfort zone, with grown-ups participating in charity work and holding dinner parties or playing bridge or golf. The younger set attended pool parties or dances. Sidewalks were rare in Belle Meade, but young teens could obtain a limited driver's license at age fourteen. They were supposed to drive only to school, to the grocery store, or to church. But in Belle Meade, visits to friends' houses were routine, and the teens were rarely stopped by police.

Unless they were directly affected, few in this rarefied society were involved in the simmering civil unrest that was beginning to brew in downtown Nashville at the end of 1959. The events that occurred a few short months later in the city would trigger a movement that would reverberate throughout the South and foment lasting change in Nashville and the rest of the United States.

One leader of this nascent movement in downtown Nashville was James Lawson. The son and grandson of African American Methodist ministers, Lawson attended Oberlin College in Ohio where he grew up. He became a missionary to India in 1954 when he was twenty-six. While in Nagpur, India, he studied the passive resistance teachings of Mahatma Gandhi. After returning to the United States, Lawson became further inspired by Dr. Martin Luther King Jr.'s advocacy of non-violent methods to achieve social change. In 1958, Lawson enrolled in Vanderbilt University's Divinity School to study for the ministry.

In the evenings, Lawson began holding workshops in local church basements for a handful of students from Fisk University, Tennessee State A&I, and the American Baptist Theological Seminary. He taught non-violent strategies he had learned from Gandhi and from Dr. King. Out of these meetings came plans to desegregate lunch counters in downtown Nashville stores.

In 1960, Black people could purchase merchandise in Nashville department stores but could not sit down at any of their lunch counters or restaurants. In late 1959, Lawson met with two downtown department store owners, one a friend of Haynie's, to ask them to voluntarily allow a few Black students to be served in their establishments. The executives refused, claiming the action would cost them business.

On December 5, 1959, Lawson sent Diane Nash, an English major at Fisk University, along with John Lewis, a student at the American Baptist Theological Seminary, to make a trial run at a lunch counter downtown by taking a seat and attempting to order food. They were immediately asked to leave, which they did.

Undeterred, Lawson came up with a plan to desegregate lunch counters at Woolworth's, S. H. Kress, McLellan's, and Walgreen's Drugs. Lawson was working with the backing of the Nashville Christian Leadership Conference, an extension of Dr. King's Southern Christian Leadership Conference.

In Lawson's training sessions, which were now attended by dozens of volunteers, he used role playing techniques to practice for the sit-ins, directing some students to act as vicious hecklers while others had to resist any sort of fighting or talking back. Lawson's strict rules consisted of practicing stillness and silence and showing no animosity toward anyone committing a hostile act against them.

The sit-ins officially began in mid-February 1960. The students were refused service but continued their efforts day after day. By the end of the month tensions had escalated, and young whites began to spit on the Black students, kicking them in the back, pulling them off stools, and even burning them with cigarettes. Still, the students sat passively and did not move. At the sit-in on February 27, a particularly brutal day, white youths pushed one demonstrator down a flight of stairs and fled when the police arrived. Eighty-one Black students, but no whites, were arrested. The students were fined but refused to pay and were sentenced to thirty-three days in the county workhouse.

At Vanderbilt University, two members of the school's Board of Trustees, both from Belle Meade, took note of the fact that Lawson had been the instigator of the protests and called for his resignation from Vanderbilt Divinity School. Lawson refused. On March 4, 1960, he was expelled from the school by Chancellor Harvey Branscomb. The next day Lawson was arrested. The dean of Vanderbilt's Divinity School, Robert Nelson, resigned in protest and personally paid Lawson's bail. On the frigid day of Lawson's expulsion, dozens of divinity students, almost exclusively white, protested in front of the divinity school building on the Vanderbilt campus, holding up signs and walking about in the snow and ice left over from a winter storm the day before.

A prominent Nashville African American lawyer Z. Alexander Looby defended the students arrested in the sit-ins. On the morning of April 19, 1960, Looby's home in Nashville was all but destroyed by a dynamite blast. Miraculously, Looby and his wife were not injured, but the explosion knocked out over 140 windows at nearby Meharry Medical College.

That afternoon, some 3,000 protestors—mostly students—marched in silence to City Hall where their leaders, Diane Nash and C. T. Vivian, another Civil Rights leader studying for the ministry at the American Baptist Theological Seminary, confronted Nashville mayor Ben West.

"Do you believe it is morally wrong to discriminate against a person solely based on his race or color?" Nash asked the mayor. West answered yes, agreeing with Nash and Vivian that segregation was morally wrong and that it was reprehensible to sell people merchandise, but refuse them dining service. The reaction of the mayor's constituents was immediate and harsh. But West stood his ground. His acknowledgement was a turning point in the students' cause. By May 1960, the downtown lunch counters were desegregated.

The success of the sit-in struggle in Nashville paved the way for other similar movements, which spread quickly across cities throughout the South. This was hardly the end of racial trouble in Nashville, but the accomplishments of 1960 became an important steppingstone for future Civil Rights icons who would go on to make their marks in history.

CHAPTER [5]

At the beginning of her sophomore year, JoAnn Gourley transferred to Southern Methodist University in Dallas, Texas. While on Christmas break back in Nashville, her name began to appear in the society pages as the date of another Belle Meade resident, William "Billy" Bainbridge III. In early June 1959, JoAnn was on a tour of Europe for two months with other Nashville friends, a sort of rite of passage for society college girls. In the August 10 issue of the *Nashville Banner*, a columnist wrote, "Welcome home to the summer continentals," mentioning JoAnn's name and ending the bit with, "There's no place like home—except Europe, of course."

A few days later, on August 14, the *Nashville Banner*'s Talk of the Town society column took note of JoAnn Gourley's attendance at a dance at the Belle Meade Country Club. Her date was William Bainbridge III.

That fall, JoAnn enrolled in Vanderbilt University for her junior year and continued dating Billy Bainbridge. The following February on Valentine's Day 1960, *The Tennessean* ran a large photograph showing Bainbridge giving roses to his "sweetheart." Later in the spring, he popped the question. By June, JoAnn Gourley was wearing a pear-shaped diamond engagement ring.

On June 3, 1960, the lead article on the society page of the *Nashville Banner* read, "Of outstanding social interest is the announcement made today by Mr. and Mrs. William Haynie Gourley of the engagement of their daughter, Josephine Ann to William Lafayette Bainbridge III."

During the week leading up to their September 10 wedding, JoAnn and Billy were honored at a dizzying array of "glamorous" parties. Luncheons and showers and breakfasts and dinner parties filled the calendar all week.

On Saturday night, September 10, 1960, Josephine Ann Gourley married William Lafayette Bainbridge III in a formal ceremony at the Vine Street Christian Church. Following thirteen bridesmaids down the aisle, Haynie Gourley gave his daughter away and took his seat by Josephine. The church was decorated with clipped boxwoods and lit by cathedral candles forming an aisle from the chancel steps to the altar, behind which was a massive arrangement of white Ascension lilies.

At the Belle Meade Country Club reception, Haynie Gourley danced with his daughter to Owen Bradley's orchestra. The tiered wedding cake was surrounded by smilax vine and flanked by "epergnette arrangements of white Butterfly roses."

Billy Gourley looked up to his big sister and was proud of her beauty and warm, engaging personality, and he immediately took to his new brother-in-law. JoAnn was now married to the scion of a prominent Belle Meade society family. She would go on to be the youngest chairman of the Bal d'Hiver, the mid-winter ball sponsored by Kappa Alpha Theta sorority alumnae to raise funds for their charities. The black-tie affair was held each year at the Belle Meade Country Club. JoAnn was also invited to join the Junior League of Nashville, an honor reserved for only the top young society women.

In early 1963, an article in the business section of *The Tennessean* quoted Haynie Gourley as saying that 1962 was one of the best years in Capitol Chevrolet's history, and "the outlook for 1963 is very bright."

The dealership enjoyed an exemplary reputation, and Haynie, with his distinctive black-rimmed glasses and jovial manner, was well known throughout Nashville. Many residents of the well-to-do Black neighborhoods had traded with Capitol Chevrolet since the 1940s. Haynie was also known for helping out when someone couldn't afford a needed repair. Haynie knew all too well what it was like to be destitute and have nowhere to turn. Billy would often hear his father say to a customer, "You can catch up with me when you can." Billy knew full well that his father never expected to see any money.

Haynie's family would only later learn the extent of how many people he had helped.

***

In May 1963, good news came. Just after the Iroquois Steeplechase and Hunt Ball, Haynie and Josephine received an invitation that would leave no doubt as to the couple's place in Belle Meade society.

In the latter part of the nineteenth century and the first few decades of the twentieth century, the Maxwell House Hotel, built by John Overton in the 1860s and located in downtown on the northwest corner of Fourth Avenue North and Church Street, was Nashville's most prestigious hotel where celebrities and well-heeled visitors stayed when visiting the city. In its heyday, the five-story, 240-room hotel played host to seven U.S. Presidents, along with Thomas Edison, William Jennings Bryan, Annie Oakley, and William Sydney Porter, better known as the short story writer O. Henry.

In 1884, a traveling wholesale grocer from Kentucky named Joel Cheek moved to Nashville, and along with a British business partner began experimenting with different coffee blends. In 1892, Cheek gave the kitchen at the Maxwell House Hotel a twenty-pound bag of one of his coffee blends. When the bag ran out and regular coffee was substituted, hotel patrons demanded that Cheek's coffee blend be reinstated.

Cheek and his partner named their coffee after the hotel, and by the 1920s, Maxwell House Coffee became the nation's best-selling coffee. Whether it was true or not, the story was widely circulated that Teddy Roosevelt had a cup of the coffee while staying at the hotel and declared that it was "good to the last drop." However it came about, the phrase became the well-known slogan of Maxwell House Coffee.

Leslie Cheek Sr., the son of Joel Cheek's cousin, was an early investor in the Maxwell House brand, and when it was sold to General Foods in 1928, he became immensely wealthy.

The story goes that Leslie Cheek's wife, Mabel Wood Cheek, had purchased a gilt mirror that was too tall to fit into their present home. Cheek was alleged to have said to his wife, "I suppose we will have to either sell the mirror or build a house to fit it." Mabel chose the house.

Leslie Cheek Sr.'s Maxwell House Coffee fortune was used to build a grand English country estate next to Percy Warner and Edwin Warner parks in Nashville. The Cheeks engaged architect Bryan Fleming of Ithaca, New York, who had created estates for Andrew Carnegie and William Scripps, to design the house and landscape.

Fleming traveled to England to gather antique furnishings and architectural elements for the house and grounds, the treasures arriving in Nashville in five railroad cars. Fleming laid out the extensive gardens and designed several handsome outbuildings.

The 36-room Georgian mansion was finished in 1932 and christened "Cheekwood," a blend of the husband and wife's last names. The grand house contained eleven bedrooms, twelve bathrooms, two elevators, a hidden staircase, and a library that held 2,000 volumes collected by Mabel Cheek.

The couple had a son and daughter, Leslie Jr. and Huldah, who traveled with their parents all over the world. When the Cheeks were in Nashville, they frequently hosted family and friends and threw lavish parties.

Leslie Cheek Sr. died suddenly in 1935 at the age of sixty-one. Mabel Cheek continued to live in the house until her death in 1946 at age seventy-two. She deeded the estate to her daughter Huldah, who married one of the founders of the Nashville Symphony, Walter Sharp. The couple continued to reside at Cheekwood and in 1957 offered the estate and surrounding fifty-five acres to the city of Nashville. Funds were raised by several civic organizations to create a fine arts museum and botanical garden. The estate was opened to the public on May 31, 1960.

Jane Dudley, the glamorous blonde wife of the wealthy and dashing Guilford Dudley Jr., president of Life and Casualty Insurance Company and future ambassador to Denmark, was playing tennis at the Belle Meade Country Club when she pitched her idea for a fundraiser to benefit Cheekwood to the president of the new horticultural and arts center.

One of Nashville's leading hostesses and an international socialite, Jane Dudley envisioned a grand, white-tie gala in Cheekwood's Swan Garden overlooking the rolling hills of Nashville. Enlisting the support of men and women from the top rungs of Nashville society, she planned the first annual Swan Ball, to be held on the second Saturday in June 1963.

The men's committee read like a who's who of important Nashvillians: John Bransford, Sam Fleming, J. C. Bradford, Robert S. Cheek, Gov. Frank Clement, Guilford Dudley Jr., Walter Sharp, John Sloan, James Stahlman, Albert Werthan, and Vanderbilt Chancellor Alexander Heard.

From the beginning, it was understood that only the elite of Nashville society would receive invitations, along with Hollywood celebrities, socialites from Palm Beach and New York, and even royalty from Europe.

An invitation to the Swan Ball would soon become a coveted prize for members of Nashville society. People checked their mailboxes daily for the envelopes containing invitations and would immediately send in their acceptances, lest they miss the cut-off of only a few hundred guests from around the world.

"Everybody who was anybody received an invitation to the first ball," a society editor wrote a few years later.

Lester Lanin's world-famous orchestra played at the first ball, and fabulous jewels were on display, a custom that would continue to be a highlight of the annual ball.

Among the chosen ones were Haynie and Josephine Gourley. Dressed in white tie and tails and guiding the elegant Josephine into the glittering party, a smiling Haynie savored the moment, his hard-scrabble youth far behind him.

***

Life may have been refined in Belle Meade, but Nashville in 1963 was not a clean or a particularly safe city.

Portions of downtown were crime-infested and could be dangerous after dark. Printers Alley was not yet the popular destination it would become. While the southwestern neighborhoods were mostly prosperous, other areas to the north and east were not so lucky. Poverty was widespread in both white and Black sections, and pollution invaded every part of the city, including the Cumberland River. Female students entering Vanderbilt University in the fall of 1963 were advised not to bring white blouses because the amount of soot in the air would soon turn the clothing gray.

But these were not big concerns for the Gourley family. The second half of 1963 for Josephine and Haynie was jam-packed with social functions. In June, Billy had graduated from MBA, and in September he enrolled in the Class of '67 at Vanderbilt.

On the Wednesday before Christmas 1963, Haynie and Josephine hosted their first big bash at the Belle Meade club with a Christmas buffet and dance. Haynie had wanted to do this for ages. Afterwards, he was proud to read the *Nashville Banner*'s description of the party: "Jo and Haynie Gourley were hosts par excellence at the loveliest and gayest Christmas buffet supper Wednesday at the Belle Meade Country Club." *The Tennessean* similarly described the occasion as featuring a "bountiful buffet laden with shrimp, fried oysters, beef tenderloin, tasty asparagus casserole around a huge green Christmas tree trimmed with hundreds of red satin bows." The writer continued, "Josephine Gourley was radiant in a white brocade cocktail dress fashioned along empire lines. The Sam Hollingsworth combo had guests dancing around the buffet table in the ballroom." Decorations also included wine coolers filled with Yuletide roses and silver candelabra with avocado-colored tapers.

All this pleased Haynie to no end. He had missed out on so many Christmases in his early life, but he had made sure that his own family experienced the magic of the season. He had a ball at his own party. Josephine had done a bang-up job with the decorations, and he had loved every minute of it.

***

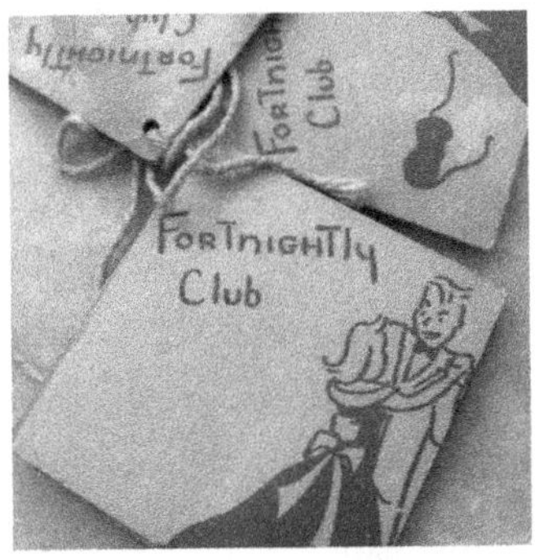

Fortnightly dance cards, 1958.
Courtesy of Jane Hindman Kyburz

William Haynie "Billy" Gourley Jr.'s childhood could not have been more different from his father's. He was adored by parents who doted on him and his sister.

From an early age, Billy had an appeal about him that won him friends. He was a handsome little boy, and when he was nine years old, he made the papers frequently, attending skating parties at the Hippodrome roller rink and "house parties" given by Belle Meade parents for their sons. Twenty of his fifth-grade classmates at Parmer School attended a party for his eleventh birthday where his parents served hot dogs, hamburgers, and Cokes at their Belle Meade Boulevard home and then proceeded to Percy Warner Park for a game of baseball, the event chronicled in the society pages of both dailies.

As was the fashion in many cities across the South, pre-teens attended dance classes where basic ballroom steps and party etiquette were taught. In Nashville, this tradition was called the "Fortnightly," so named because the classes met every other week and were hosted by a Miss Hank Fort, a well-known singer and entertainer. The dances took place in a grand old house on West End Avenue. On October 5,

1956, Billy was pictured in an outsized photograph in *The Tennessean*, wearing a sports jacket and shirt and tie and casually leaning against a stereo holding a 33 1/3 rpm record. The article was entitled "Young Ivy Leaguers," and the photo caption read: "Proper attire for the eleven-year-olds is the red and black plaid informal coat shown by Billy Gourley, son of Mr. and Mrs. Haynie Gourley, who will wear this snappy coat with charcoal slacks tonight when he attends his first Fortnightly dance class."

In the fall of 1957, when Billy entered the seventh grade at Montgomery Bell Academy, he joined several of his friends from Belle Meade who, like Billy, were regulars at Camp Greenbrier in West Virginia.

That Christmas, he and a close group of buddies from school threw a dance party in the Andrew Jackson room at the Belle Meade Country Club for some of their friends. One of two photographs in *The Tennessean* showed Billy's pal Ben Gambill pouring punch for three of the lucky seventh graders. The second pictured Billy and two of his co-hosts picking out 45 records with some of the invited girls.

The social whirl of his elementary school days picked up speed in high school. During the summer of 1959, before Billy entered the ninth grade, the local high school fraternities and sororities held rush parties. Billy, along with some of his closest friends from Belle Meade, was invited to join Alpha Chi fraternity.

Throughout his freshman year, there were hayrides and square dances and theme parties. Billy was invited to the SAP sorority's formal Christmas dance where Owen Bradley's orchestra played at the Belle Meade Country Club. Billy's fraternity held a winter ball, where the freshman class pledges were introduced. He was also invited to formal dances sponsored by another top sorority, Kappa Delta Theta.

During his sophomore year, Billy's name continued to pop up in both daily newspapers, listing his dates to various high school fraternity—or sorority—sponsored parties, basketball games, or dances at two all-girl preparatory schools, Harpeth Hall and St. Cecelia Academy.

In the summers, Billy worked at Capitol Chevrolet, filling up cars at the Capitol-owned gas station across the street from the main entrance or cleaning out bins in the parts department. When he was old enough to drive, he shuttled cars from the service department check-in to the repair shop. Summer nights, he was back on the social circuit, attending parties almost every evening.

Billy enjoyed an especially warm, close relationship with his father. There was never an ill word spoken between the two of them. Billy was touched by what little he knew of his father's past and how hard Haynie had worked to overcome the pain of his childhood. He knew well that it was his father's dream for him to take over the dealership. Haynie had said over and over to his children, "This is what I've worked all my life for, for you and your sister to have what I never had." Billy wanted to enjoy college and have fun, but he was always aware of his father's ambitions for him, and he meant to make him proud.

One day during the summer before his senior year at MBA, Billy was working at Capitol Chevrolet when he walked into Haynie's office holding several envelopes with college applications.

Billy had his heart set on attending either the University of North Carolina at Chapel Hill or Tulane University in New Orleans. Haynie had never asked a favor of his son and had always been happy to go along with Billy's choices. Haynie was delighted when Billy chose golf as a varsity sport at MBA, but he never pressured him about taking up any particular sport or about his grades. In turn, Billy had great respect for his father and never gave him any trouble.

But this time, Haynie spoke up.

"I think the best thing for you to do is to go to Vanderbilt," Haynie said. "Someday you are going to take over Capitol Chevrolet. If you stay here, you can build up relationships and grow friendships with the people you'll be doing business with."

Billy didn't hesitate and dropped his idea for going to college anywhere else. It was an easy decision. He would apply to Vanderbilt and stay in Nashville.

In the fall of 1963, Billy entered Vanderbilt University, and even though his parents lived only twenty minutes from the school, he elected to live in the dorm with the other freshmen.

While he was rushed by several of the top fraternities, in the end he pledged Sigma Alpha Epsilon. Having reached six feet two inches in height, he had olive skin, black hair, brown eyes, and long eyelashes. Because of his good looks and his laid-back, "cool" manner, he was immediately popular with the Vanderbilt sorority girls. An invitation from Billy Gourley to a fraternity party was considered a coup. Billy wasn't keen on dancing, but he liked to stand on the sidelines, his arm around his date, and sway to the live bands playing the latest Motown hits.

Well-liked in the fraternity, his pledge brothers knew him as "always happy and a lot of fun, the kind of guy you wanted to hang out with," and as "a very kind, generous guy with a big heart, always lending his car, just handing over the keys anytime without hesitation, no questions asked."

Between classes, he was a fixture, along with his fraternity brothers, at the Commodore Room on the Vanderbilt campus, a cafeteria-snack bar combination where he swigged Dr. Peppers and made comments to the sorority girls who passed by, dressed in their McMullen blouses, cable-knit cardigans, and Pappagallo shoes.

Billy wore a sort of "uniform" which consisted of a blue, long-sleeved, button-down oxford cloth shirt, which he wore with the sleeves rolled up exactly twice on his forearms, khaki pants, a brown alligator belt and Weejuns, a type of penny loafer wildly popular in the '60s, which he wore without pennies and without socks. When his father, who was an immaculate dresser, noticed Billy sitting sockless in church, he issued a rare order to his son.

"From now on, I don't want to look down in church and see your ankles. You put on some socks." Billy obeyed his father, but around campus, he, like most of his fraternity brothers, continued to go sockless.

By his sophomore year, Billy was zipping around campus in a silver

Corvette. In back of the Kappa Alpha Theta sorority house, a sign read, "Parking for members only," but for three years, Billy parked in the lot anyway. No one ever said a word.

During holidays and summers, Billy was a popular escort for Nashville's debutantes. His pal since kindergarten years, Joanne Fleming, daughter of the Gourley family's banker Sam Fleming and in the class below Billy at Vanderbilt, often tapped Billy as a date for deb parties given in her honor. During the summer of 1965, he was her escort at the Cotton Ball in Chattanooga and took her to several parties at Christmastime.

Both Josephine and Haynie had always been supportive of their children's schools, heading up fund-raisers and events and attending their activities. At the beginning of Billy's sophomore year at Vanderbilt, Josephine Gourley was elected president of the Minerva Club

Haynie and Josephine Gourley (right), arrive at the Belle Meade Country Club for the Iroquois dinner and Hunt Ball after the Steeplechase, May 9, 1964. Also pictured, Mr. and Mrs. Morris Moughan. © *The Tennessean-USA TODAY NETWORK*

composed of mothers of Vanderbilt SAEs. The group entertained new members and served as a welcome committee for SAE pledges.

In addition, Josephine and Haynie welcomed Billy's college friends into their home. One pledge brother described Josephine Gourley as "warm and just wonderful," and Haynie as "so nice and friendly."

***

With daughter JoAnn happily married, son Billy enjoying Vanderbilt, and the business doing well, 1964 was a good year for Haynie and Josephine. They continued to entertain at a breathless pace and worked in trips to New York and Fort Lauderdale. They attended the Iroquois Steeplechase and Hunt Ball in May and the second annual Swan Ball in June. This time, the Swan Garden at Cheekwood was transformed into a copy of the Doge's Palace in Venice. To reach the party, one crossed the Rialto Bridge, with *papier maché* swans floating in the canal below.

"I just can't believe I'm in Nashville," swooned one party goer.

Once again, Josephine and Haynie hobnobbed with ambassadors, European royalty, and visitors who listed their domiciles as "New York and Palm Beach."

Josephine also made some changes to their home. She hired Dan Burton, whose interior design firm was all the rage in Belle Meade, to update her interiors. While nothing as imposing as the mansions along Belle Meade Boulevard, the Gourleys' home was spacious with large rooms. Using a softer palette, Burton's makeover was stylish and elegant, but comfortable and not overdone. Josephine made sure she included all the elements to create just the right atmosphere for a wealthy household in 1960s Nashville. Walking into the Gourley home, you were met with the faint scent of eucalyptus, a popular touch in upper class homes at the time.

Like other members of the Belle Meade set, Josephine employed a live-in housekeeper. Henrietta Green had worked for the Gourleys since Billy was two years old, taking Sundays off to spend at her brother's house. She was a slight woman who wore her hair in a neat bun at the back of her neck. She was never without a smile or a kind word. She adored Haynie, and the feeling was mutual. When Billy was living at home, Henrietta spoiled him by rising at 6:00 a.m. on Saturdays to make her special homemade cinnamon rolls for his breakfast. She was also known among Billy's friends for her fried chicken, "the best anywhere." If Billy didn't always mind his mother, he never disobeyed Henrietta. She was the one who would make sure he had an umbrella if rain was predicted or check to see if he and JoAnn had everything they needed before they left for school. She was loved and treated as part of the family and had a grace about her that endeared her to everyone.

The Gourleys often welcomed overnight guests to their home. Horace Hull from Memphis was a frequent visitor, as was Thomas Jackson, Chevrolet's zone manager from Louisville, and E. M. "Pete" Estes, a General Motors big wig in Detroit. Billy's fraternity brothers were always welcome. Most were from out of state and welcomed the chance for a homemade meal and a night away from campus. An occasional girlfriend of Billy's came to visit as well.

When guests turned in for the night, they found their bedspreads had been pulled back to reveal silky monogrammed blanket covers. Visitors in the Gourley home were awakened in their room in the morning by Henrietta Green, carrying a white wooden breakfast tray with fresh-squeezed orange juice and a bouquet of flowers.

***

Haynie had not been out of the country since his stint in World War I in France. His parents had not bothered to obtain a birth certificate for him, and now that he wanted to take his family on a trip to Europe, he was unable to obtain a passport.

In 1963, he applied for a birth certificate, which was granted in June 1964. On his application were affidavits from a Mattie E. Offut, whom Haynie listed as an aunt from Cross Plains, Tennessee, and J.D.

Freeland from one of the households that took him in after he was abandoned in 1904. His brother Everett, who lived in Nashville and who was two years younger than Haynie, had obtained a birth certificate in the 1940s, so he also signed the application.

In July 1965, Haynie, Josephine, Billy, and JoAnn and Billy Bainbridge set sail on the luxury liner the SS France out of New York. Billy had a shipboard romance, and the whole family reveled in the five days spent crossing the Atlantic on the elegant and graceful liner. The Gourleys stayed at the best hotels in London and Paris. The plans were to continue to Lucerne, Switzerland, and then on to Florence and Rome, where they would take a flight back home.

Their trip was cut short in Paris when Billy Bainbridge injured his back, and the whole family flew home. After surgery, Billy Bainbridge made a full recovery. Haynie promised he would treat the family to another trip to Europe in the summer of 1968 to complete their tour.

As it turned out, that trip would never take place.

The family in Paris, summer 1965: L-R, Haynie and Josephine Gourley, William Bainbridge III, JoAnn Bainbridge, Billy Gourley. *Courtesy of Billy Gourley*

CHAPTER [6]

By 1965, Capitol Chevrolet was still growing and now occupied an even greater hodge-podge of buildings and parking lots downtown. The sprawling complex included a paint and body shop at Fifth Avenue and Demonbreun Streets, car and truck rental services in another building, commercial truck sales elsewhere, and a gas station across the street from the main entrance. The check-in for the service department was one place, and the cars had to be driven up the street to another building to be worked on.

Haynie was now sixty-nine years old. He was in good health, but was putting in long, hard hours at the dealership. He was anxious to find a way to have more time off to spend in Fort Lauderdale so he could get his fill of golf, and Josephine could escape Nashville's unpredictable winters and enjoy seeing friends they'd made on their visits over the years. In order to have this freedom, Haynie needed someone to help with the day-to-day operation at the dealership.

In the spring of 1965, when Billy was a sophomore in college, Haynie found exactly the person he was looking for. Thirty-seven-year-old William E. "Bill" Powell was a former college football star and had entered the automobile business after graduating from Vanderbilt in 1950. He was general manager of Hippodrome Oldsmobile in Nashville where he had worked for eleven years. Powell was known for his management skills and since his days at Vanderbilt had built a wide circle of friends and acquaintances around town. He had a reputation for being easy-going and affable. Haynie recognized that Powell was just the person to build on Capitol Chevrolet's success.

In May 1965, Bill Powell accepted Haynie's offer and became general manager of the dealership. He was welcomed in an ad in the sports pages in the Friday, May 14, 1965, edition of *The Tennessean*:

> W. Haynie Gourley, Owner of
> Capitol Chevrolet Company
> is pleased to announce the appointment of
> William E. (Bill) Powell
> As General Manager
> Mr. Powell has been associated with the local sales and service of automobiles in an executive capacity for the past 15 years. He is married to the former Helen Suddoth and they have two children. A graduate of Vanderbilt University where he starred in football, he serves as a deacon at the First Presbyterian Church. He is a member of the Exchange Club and Hillwood Country Club.
> Bill issues a cordial invitation to his friends and former customers to visit him at Capitol Chevrolet.

Powell, who was adopted, grew up in Arkansas where he had been a star athlete in high school, excelling in football and track. For years after he graduated, he held the state record in the sixty-yard dash. Although offered twelve college football scholarships, the six-foot-four, 240-pound Powell chose Vanderbilt, where he ran track and played center on the football team. He was named Southeastern Conference player of the week on three occasions and four times was player of the week at Vanderbilt. The 1948 Commodores under Coach Red Sanders had a stellar season, winning eight games in a row.

At Vanderbilt, Powell was known as "Big Bill" and was popular and well-liked by his teammates. Like Billy, he pledged Sigma Alpha Epsilon. He was also elected to the Vanderbilt Honor Council, made up of respected student leaders charged with investigating any rare instances of cheating that might occur at the school.

Before his senior year, Powell married his college sweetheart, Helen Suddoth, a pretty Vanderbilt co-ed from Nashville, who was a member of a top sorority, Delta Delta Delta. Right out of college, Powell was offered a position by Sam Fleming at Third National Bank, one of the two largest and most prestigious banks in the city. Powell turned down the offer in favor of a sales position at Palmer-Hooper Motor Company, a Lincoln-Mercury dealer in Nashville.

Tall, with a longish face, receding hairline, and easy smile, Powell was sturdily built but fit, if not trim. Haynie liked the fact that Powell's family closely resembled his own—two children—an older girl, Mary Helen, thirteen, and a younger boy, Bill Jr., eleven. Both attended Parmer school, just as JoAnn and Billy Gourley had. The Powells were great sports enthusiasts, and Mary Helen was captain of the school's cheerleaders and young Bill a star player on the Parmer football team. In the summers, the family enjoyed water skiing and spending weekends at their cottage on Little Creek.

"We entertain all summer because we love people, and informal entertaining is what we like best," Helen Powell said in an article in the November 28, 1965, edition of *The Tennessean*.

Helen Powell, like Josephine Gourley, was dedicated to volunteer causes. She was president of the Delta Delta Delta sorority's Nashville alumnae chapter and of the Junior Board of the Florence Crittenton Home, which tended to the concerns of the unwed girls living there until their babies were born.

In 1963, the "likeable twosome," as the Powells were described in the article, built a spacious Georgian brick house in Belle Meade on a hill at the corner of East Brookfield and Chickering Road, less than five minutes from the Gourley home. Helen Powell's sister Roberta Witherspoon and her husband John lived next door.

Haynie was delighted with Powell's ideas to grow the business by adding more services. Because of their age difference, the two quickly developed what they both called a "father-son" relationship.

At the start of 1966, with a first-class general manager to run the dealership, Haynie felt a new freedom to pursue his golf game and travel with Josephine. In February, the couple spent four weeks instead of the usual two in Miami and Fort Lauderdale.

In May, Haynie and Josephine fell back into what had become their regular social schedule in Nashville. In June, they were present at the fourth annual Swan Ball where Josephine Gourley and her daughter made fashion news. "Mrs. W. Haynie Gourley was on hand in Malcolm Starr's hot pink crepe with empire waist and heavily beaded bodice." At the time Starr was the number one designer whose gowns were seen at elite country clubs across the nation. A photograph in *The Tennessean* pictured Mrs. W. L. Bainbridge III "performing her duties as a Swan Ball beauty," dressed in "Harvey Berlin's white crepe gown cut along Grecian lines," and "wearing a simple strand of pearls with her strapless dress with a vertical bow at the shoulder."

***

That summer, a big change was made at Capitol Chevrolet.

Bill Powell had been at the dealership for a year, and in the late spring of 1966, Haynie asked Billy, now a junior at Vanderbilt, to sit down and talk.

"Bill Powell wants to buy into the business," Haynie told his son. "I'm thinking about doing this."

Haynie explained that Powell would purchase 25% of the stock and have the title of executive vice-president and general manager.

"Our family would still own the majority, seventy-five percent of the business."

Haynie continued. "Before I do this, though, I want your approval. You'll be coming into the business after you graduate. The main reason I'm doing it this way is so that I can count on him to teach you how to run Capitol Chevrolet. I'm going to ask him to set up a program to train you to take my place as soon as you're ready."

Billy was finishing his junior year at Vanderbilt, and the future seemed far away, but he was quick to give his approval.

"Seems like the pie is plenty big enough to give up twenty-five percent," he told Haynie. "You've worked hard all your life. You deserve some time off. I think it's a great idea."

In June 1966, Haynie asked his long-time friend John Glenn, a certified public accountant with Peat, Marwick and Mitchell and the secretary-treasurer of Capitol Chevrolet, to draw up the paperwork for Bill Powell to become a stockholder in the company. It was written into the contract and understood by both the Gourley family and by Bill Powell that a key part of the deal would be to put Powell in charge of developing a program to train Billy Gourley to become the dealer and eventual owner of Capitol Chevrolet. Powell readily agreed to this requirement.

On July 20, 1966, Powell borrowed $200,000 from Sam Fleming at Third National Bank and became a shareholder in Capitol Chevrolet. His title was changed to executive vice-president and general manager, with Haynie remaining as president. Powell began to spread the news that he was a part owner of Capitol Chevrolet and set about making his mark on the business.

Pleased with Powell's performance and happy with the warm relationship they had forged, Haynie eagerly signed the agreement, confident that his son would have a trusted mentor to guide him into the family business.

But Haynie overlooked a basic provision in the contract that seemed unimportant at the time. Paragraph Three named Powell as a co-franchisee, meaning that in the event of either man's death the other would become the sole owner of the franchise, with the exclusive right to sell new Chevrolet automobiles. The contract made it clear that Bill Powell, owning one-fourth of the company and having years of experience in the industry, met the requirements to become the dealer in the event of Haynie Gourley's death. Billy was only twenty-one and still a college student. He would not be eligible to enroll in the highly regarded Dealers' Sons School in Detroit for three more years. To become a General Motors franchisee, Billy would need both experience and the satisfactory completion of the training course in Detroit. For the time being, then, Bill Powell was written into the contract as Haynie's successor.

Haynie never gave a thought to the possibility that his signature on a document drawn up by his own accountant could spell the end of his hard-fought dream and the beginning of a lasting nightmare for his family.

***

In the late spring of 1966, Andy Rittenberry, a recent Vanderbilt graduate from Cowan, Tennessee, asked his friend Billy Gourley, about to finish his junior year at Vanderbilt, if Billy's father might consider hiring him for the summer while he waited to enter medical school in the fall. Andy's mother had been a classmate of Josephine Gourley's in college. Billy set up a meeting with Haynie, who gave Andy a job in the service department.

Andy's main duty was to drive cars dropped off at the service check-in over to the building where the actual work was done. An unofficial job Andy held was to drive to Belle Meade in a new 1966 four-door Impala and bring Josephine Gourley to downtown stores to shop, then deliver her back home with her packages.

But during that summer Andy began to sense that there was some sort of friction at the dealership. Although Andy found himself at the absolute bottom of the rung at Capitol, he soon learned about an undercurrent of competitiveness among the employees. Bill Powell had only been at Capitol for a year, but one of the service department workers explained to Andy that in this organization, you were either a Gourley man or a Powell man. In other words, each worker was assumed to be loyal either to Haynie Gourley or Bill Powell.

Andy had never spoken to or been introduced to Bill Powell, whom he described as "a big, strong man, physically imposing and very fit-looking." Andy saw Powell only in passing, but by the end of the summer he had developed a negative feeling about him. He found

Powell to be somewhat imperious compared to Haynie Gourley, who was friendly and always giving Andy a pat on the back. Andy also perceived that there was discontent among the Capitol employees.

However, if there was any sort of discord between Haynie and Bill Powell, Haynie seemed not to be aware of it. In fact, Haynie continued to refer to his partnership with Powell as a father-son relationship. The business was growing rapidly under Powell's supervision, and Haynie never missed an opportunity to let everyone know how pleased he was with his executive vice-president and general manager.

Andy Rittenberry did not tell Billy about the loyalty divide or the uneasy feeling he had about the highly charged atmosphere at Capitol Chevrolet. He knew that everyone considered Billy Gourley as the "crown prince" who would someday inherit Capitol Chevrolet. It was hard for Andy to picture Bill Powell letting this happen. To Andy, it seemed that Powell was already acting like he owned the place.

Only later would Andy realize there might have been something to the troubling perceptions he formed that summer.

CHAPTER [7]

On October 15, 1966, a grand ball was held to celebrate the 65th anniversary of the Belle Meade Country Club. The white tie affair was an extravaganza that included music from different eras. Owen Bradley, whose orchestra had been a mainstay at the club during the 1940s and '50s and who had retired to concentrate on his rapidly growing recording business, made an appearance with his combo during the informal dinner hour.

A special treat was the appearance of Francis Craig, whose orchestra had played for sorority and fraternity dances and debut balls held at the club during the 1930s. In 1947, Craig's hit "Near You," was the number one song in the United States for twelve weeks in a row and became familiar to every Nashvillian, regardless of era. Craig had attended Vanderbilt University and as a student there in 1922, wrote the school's enduring fight song, "Dynamite," played at every football game and sporting event at the university. For this special anniversary celebration, Craig played "Near You" on the piano while Belle Meade members gathered around and sang along. Francis Craig died unexpectedly a month later at the age of sixty-five.

The Tennessean ran an article about the evening and mentioned only thirteen of the hundreds of couples who attended. Josephine and Haynie Gourley made the cut, along with a dozen other well-known members.

Haynie, feeling at home at the club, wanted his protégé to enjoy the perks of his new status as part owner of Capitol Chevrolet, so he sponsored Bill Powell for membership. The process could take as long as two years before Powell might become a full-fledged member. Powell's brother-in-law John Witherspoon, the husband of Helen Powell's sister Roberta, was already a member, and Powell, even though he, too, lacked the social credentials of most members, was still remembered as a Vanderbilt football star. Haynie thought his chances of getting in were good. Powell belonged to the Hillwood Country Club, a newer upscale club, but Haynie knew it would be an advantage for the business to have his executive vice-president in the Belle Meade Country Club, and he was eager for the Powell family to enjoy the privileges of membership.

It would not be long before Haynie would be sponsoring Billy Gourley for a junior membership, so Haynie would have both his "sons" in the club with him.

The best news of 1966 came late in the year. On Wednesday, November 30, Haynie and Josephine became grandparents. JoAnn Bainbridge gave birth to a son, William Gourley "Bill" Bainbridge, at St. Thomas Hospital. Haynie and Josephine were beside themselves with excitement, as was Billy Gourley, and little Bill was immediately taken into the fold of the blissful, loving Gourley-Bainbridge family.

***

On January 11, 1967, a headline appeared on the front page of *The Tennessean*: "Capitol Chevrolet to Move."

"Officials of Capitol Chevrolet Co. are planning a new Murfreesboro Road headquarters that will be the largest automobile agency plant in Nashville." The article went on to say that construction was about to begin on the new facility just east of downtown.

The dealership had long been bursting at the seams in its location at 510 Broadway and the surrounding streets. The business was essentially land-locked with nowhere else in the immediate vicinity to expand.

It was increasingly inefficient to operate in such a confined space. In addition, the new-car showroom was outdated and could only hold a handful of vehicles.

For years, Haynie had been harboring a dream about a new building, one that would be both accessible to customers and offer ample parking, a particular problem downtown. Commercial truck sales were booming, and the used car division was doing a brisk business but sorely needed more parking spaces as did the recently added rental car department. Powell was planning a new leasing department, and room was needed to accommodate other new divisions in the works. It was clear that it was time to make a move.

Haynie had looked at a dealership in Houston that was exactly the state-of-the-art facility he had in mind. He envisioned an ultra-modern building with a glass-encased showroom with the capacity to park all the newest models, and an expanded parts department where enough stock could be kept on hand, avoiding the necessity of having to order parts for repairs. The present quarters for the parts and service departments were especially cramped, resulting in too much wait time for customers. He and Bill Powell began to look for a building site.

An area just east of downtown was experiencing a building boom, and several automobile dealerships were moving away from the city in search of more space. Haynie and Bill Powell found the perfect eight-acre parcel at 600 Murfreesboro Road. The site offered easy access to nearby Interstate 40 and other main thoroughfares connecting to downtown and both the eastern and the southern suburbs.

The location would allow enough space to construct an impressive, multi-level building that could accommodate all of Capitol's departments, with room for future expansion. Ample space for visitor parking and a large used car lot made the site ideal for new headquarters. Haynie worked diligently with the architects on the design of the complex, making sure all his specifications were met.

An arrangement was made with a local physician who owned the land. Instead of Capitol Chevrolet making the million-dollar-plus investment, an agreement was worked out with Dr. Bruce P'Pool, specifying that he would finance and own the building, then lease it back for twenty years to Capitol Chevrolet.

Haynie's accountant advised him not to assume responsibility for the long-term lease due to his age. John J. Hooker Sr., the Gourley family's attorney, agreed. Both men wanted to avoid any complications with Haynie's estate in the event of his death.

On August 29, 1966, a month after thirty-eight-year-old Bill Powell had bought into the business, he and his wife Helen became co-signers and personal guarantors of the twenty-year lease with Dr. P'Pool. The obligation was $85,000 a year.

***

While the year 1967 saw construction of the new building begin, elsewhere in Nashville racial tensions were flaring. The 1966-67 Vanderbilt basketball team had one of its best seasons ever. In the fall of 1966, Perry Wallace entered Vanderbilt from Nashville's all-Black Pearl High School, where he had been a straight-A student and class valedictorian. He became the first African American scholarship recipient to play basketball in the Southeastern Conference.

The team itself welcomed Wallace, but when Vanderbilt traveled to other colleges around the South, Wallace faced verbal taunts and rough treatment from players and fans while on the court. In Nashville, he was banned from attending services at the University Church of Christ across from the campus because of his race, although the church was not affiliated with the school. But there were also overtly racist Vanderbilt professors and students who resented his presence at the school and openly shunned him.

In early April 1967, Vanderbilt sponsored its fourth annual Impact Symposium, where national figures were invited to speak on current topics.

Billy Gourley was a senior when 5,000 students and faculty members packed Memorial Gymnasium to hear Dr. Martin Luther King Jr., Senator Strom Thurmond of South Carolina, the Beat Generation poet Allen Ginsburg, and Stokely Carmichael, head of the Student Non-violent Coordinating Committee (SNCC).

On the first night of the two-night symposium, Dr. King gave a sermon-like speech advocating non-violence and challenged the audience to answer a question: "How can a man pull himself up by the bootstraps if he has no boots?" He received a standing ovation. The next day, Stokely Carmichael followed with a rousing speech, calling younger Blacks to action. Mayor Beverly Briley blamed Carmichael for racial unrest during his visit to Nashville, claiming his firebrand talk at Vanderbilt set off demonstrations and several incidents of violence in the city.

The confrontations with police hit the papers. Haynie had never participated in any of the politics concerning racial issues. At this moment, he was occupied with overseeing the construction of the new building, oblivious to the trouble simmering across town.

After graduating from Vanderbilt in May 1967, Billy Gourley joined the Tennessee Air National Guard. He was assigned to Lackland Air Force Base in San Antonio, Texas, for six weeks of basic training.

Billy left Nashville for Texas in July 1967. The father and son had never been apart for so long. Even when Haynie was in Florida for a few weeks, he had Billy fly down to play golf with him. Haynie wrote to his son every day. Billy treasured the letters from his "best friend," and one night received a harsh reprimand from his drill sergeant after he was caught with a flashlight reading one of his father's letters under the covers.

After Billy finished basic training in November 1967, he returned to Nashville and joined Capitol Chevrolet full-time, expecting Bill Powell to have his training program ready. The new building was under construction, and the dealership was still downtown. Haynie wanted Billy to come in as an officer or as an assistant manager with an executive office in the new building, but Bill Powell flatly rejected the idea. Instead, Billy was assigned to the new car sales department, and when he approached Powell for guidance, he was brushed off. Powell made no assignments and left Billy on his own, feeling like he was just "winging it."

Billy was careful not to be pushy or to insist on becoming an officer, although he did ask Powell if it were possible. Powell said no. Billy hoped to transition into management in order to get some experience under his belt before attending the Dealers' Sons School in Detroit the next year.

But he could sense that Powell did not want him around. There was little to no communication between the two. Billy was reluctant to go to his father, fearing it would only upset him. He figured that Powell would soon come through for him. But Powell made no assignments and ignored Billy.

When Powell joined Capitol Chevrolet, he hired his adoptive father Roy Powell as manager of the body shop. One day when the new building was nearing completion, Billy was in the showroom when Roy Powell came through with several visitors, pointing out all the new building's features.

"My son built all this," Roy said, waving his hands around.

Billy could hardly contain himself. Haynie had talked about building a new facility for years, long before Bill Powell was even hired. Haynie had started with nothing thirty-five years earlier, built a reputation for Capitol Chevrolet, made it through the Great Depression and World War II, and now Roy Powell was giving credit to his son who had only been with the company for a little over two years.

Another thing nagged at Billy. Powell appeared to fawn over Haynie, calling him "Boss," or "Mr. G." Billy thought there was something phony about the way Powell addressed his father. But Haynie seemed pleased with Powell, and to Billy's knowledge the two had never had an unpleasant word pass between them.

Billy continued to observe Powell, but something just didn't seem right. He didn't dislike the man, but he couldn't put his finger on exactly what bothered him, so he kept quiet.

CHAPTER [8]

Capitol Chevrolet executives in front of the new showroom, completed in spring 1968. L-R, Jimmy Allen, new car sales manager; Charlie McCaffrey, service manager; Haynie Gourley, founder and president; Bill Powell, executive vice president and general manager. *Nashville Public Library, Special Collections, Banner Newspaper Collection*

The new year of 1968 held great promise for the Gourley family. Son Billy was working at Capitol Chevrolet. Haynie was making money hand over fist and had friends in high places. His name and face were recognized almost everywhere in the city. He especially reveled in what he'd never known as a child—a loving, close-knit family. He liked being able to provide them with financial security and privileges he could only have dreamed of during his wretched youth.

Haynie was anxious for news about Bill Powell and the Belle Meade Country Club. By late 1967, an invitation had not yet come through, but Haynie felt confident about Powell's chances. Billy had already joined as a junior member.

In the spring of 1968, Haynie received the good news. Bill Powell had been invited to join the Belle Meade Country Club. Haynie was ecstatic that both his "boys" would be members of Nashville's most prestigious and venerable social institution.

With Bill Powell in charge of day-to-day operations at Capitol Chevrolet, Haynie was able to plan more golf outings and was looking forward to a three-week stay in south Florida in March.

Meanwhile, Haynie and Josephine continued to entertain. In January 1968, they hosted a breakfast at the Centennial Club for a special bride-to-be, the daughter of their good friends Dr. Tom Frist and his wife Dot. The Frists' daughter, a senior in college, was engaged to one of Billy's SAE fraternity brothers. Dr. Frist had been Haynie's physician for years. Already prominent at several area hospitals, Dr. Frist was making plans for the launch of the Hospital Corporation of America, a company he anticipated would bring about a revolutionary change in America's healthcare system.

But Haynie's biggest thrill of 1968 was the completion of Capitol Chevrolet's new headquarters. The dealership had been at the Broadway location for thirty-six years, starting with a single building of 15,000 square feet and a handful of employees. The new building had taken a year and a half to complete. In February 1968 the move-in began, and a grand opening was set for April 4.

"We have planned our location on Murfreesboro Road in relation to the Interstate network so we will be little more than ten minutes' drive from any place in the city," Haynie told newspaper reporters. "It will also be convenient for out-of-town customers to reach our place of business."

The eight-acre, state-of-the-art complex consisted of a gleaming new-car showroom with room for thirteen automobiles, a service department capable of handling 137 cars at a time, a rental car and leasing department, a parts department that stocked over $200,000 worth of inventory, a body repair shop, and a special section for commercial and light truck sales and service. An expansive used car lot with a separate building housing an office and lounge was surrounded by plenty of parking spaces so people could examine the inventory on hand.

The building itself covered two acres, with windows lining the showroom on three sides and occupying the lowest level facing Murfreesboro Road. The glassed-in executive offices for Haynie and Bill Powell and a third officer not yet named were on this level, as were glass-partitioned cubicles for salesmen. The main floor also contained a large sales meeting room, conference rooms, and a combination switchboard and reception desk.

Guest parking for new car sales had been problematic downtown, but now it was possible to drive right up to the new car showroom to see the latest models.

Capitol Chevrolet was a big operation. The leasing office, human resources, title clerk, comptroller, finance and insurance departments, and the truck sales manager's office were located on the second level along with the service department check-in. Two large double doors allowed cars coming from the direction of downtown Nashville to pull in to register for servicing. On the opposite side were two matching doors for cars to exit. The customer lounge was located on this level as well as the cashier's window and service manager Charlie McCaffrey's office. Cars were driven from the check-in up to the next level where they would be worked on. Also on the third level were the parts department, the service work area, and the body shop.

Haynie was elated at the way the building had turned out—the plush carpets, the gleaming glass, and when you walked into the showroom, you were hit with the unmistakable new-car smell. He watched his son saunter about, talking to employees, always a smile on his face. Haynie beamed with pride. Life couldn't be better. Every hope and dream he ever had was now coming true.

The Grand Opening of the new headquarters of Capitol Chevrolet on April 4,1968, attracted local dignitaries and top executives from General Motors. Haynie, second from left, grasping the arm of his friend, Gov. Buford Ellington, third from left. Billy Gourley is second from right. *Courtesy of Billy Gourley*

***

By 6:00 a.m. on Thursday, April 4, 1968, the day of the grand opening, a crowd had gathered outside the imposing new building. Haynie had arranged for the first 300 visitors through the door to receive a miniature replica of the best-selling 1968 Chevrolet Camaro. On so many occasions in the past, he had managed to draw crowds to the showroom for openings. This day promised to be the biggest of all.

The opening ceremony was scheduled for 11:00 a.m. Haynie was in his element. His close friend Governor Buford Ellington was set to cut the ribbon. High-ranking executives from the General Motors Chevrolet Division had flown in from Detroit, Cincinnati, and Louisville. The city of Nashville was sending the head of the Chamber of Commerce.

By 10:30, photographers and reporters from the *Nashville Banner* and *The Tennessean* began to arrive. The ribbon cutting ceremony was set to launch a three-day-long grand opening celebration that would extend through Friday, April 5, and Saturday, April 6, with tours of the building taking place from 8:30 a.m. until 10:00 p.m. each day.

A tent was set up outside, but a few minutes before 11:00 a.m., a flash of lightening followed by a loud clap of thunder startled the crowd. The skies opened, and rain pelted the tent. Everyone rushed inside. Over a hundred people crowded into the main showroom for the official ceremony. Guests scattered into other parts of the building. As rain continued to pour outside, E. M. "Pete" Estes, a vice president of General Motors and general manager of the Chevrolet Motor Division headquartered in Detroit, delivered a speech describing the new facility as "one of the best in the country."

"We're certainly impressed and very proud of this dealership," he said.

Governor Ellington came rushing in at the last minute, an assistant in tow holding an umbrella. In his remarks before cutting the ribbon, the governor described his seventy-two-year-old friend as a man "young enough to dream and old enough to have a vision for the future." Haynie made a few remarks, thanking everyone for making his dream come true, that it was his proudest day as a Chevrolet dealer, and he looked forward to a bright future. He joked that he hoped this expensive new building would help him sell a lot more cars. The audience laughed.

The sun came out just as the ceremony concluded. Governor Ellington said he could pose for a picture but told Haynie he had to leave immediately afterwards for the State Capitol to deal with growing unrest in Memphis. He explained that Dr. Martin Luther King Jr. had returned to the city for what Ellington hoped would be a new, peaceful march for striking garbage workers after the one the previous week had disintegrated into chaos. There had been rampant looting and vandalism along the march route. Ellington said he had to be ready to send in the National Guard if violence broke out again.

All afternoon, people toured the new facility. Shortly after 6:00

p.m., as a few visitors continued to stroll through the building, congratulating Haynie and talking with Bill Powell, two newspaper reporters who were still on the premises began rushing out to their cars. Word spread quickly that Dr. King had been shot in Memphis. An hour later, news came that he was dead.

By 8:00 p.m., gunfire rang out in the northern section of Nashville, near Tennessee State A&I, an all-Black technical college. Rocks were thrown at police who had rushed to the area, and someone hurled a Molotov cocktail through the window of a liquor store.

In Nashville's Black communities, there had been longstanding resentment toward the police and civic and political leaders who, for years, had ignored the appalling conditions in their neighborhoods. Now, despite Dr. King's persistent message of non-violence, tensions exploded. Nashville Mayor Beverly Briley asked Governor Ellington to send in National Guard troops.

By 2:00 a.m. on the morning of April 5, convoys of jeeps, trucks, and armored personnel carriers began rumbling along Broadway, past the former buildings occupied by Capitol Chevrolet, en route to north Nashville. Hal Hardin, a third-year law student at Vanderbilt, could hear gunfire from his room near the campus. The city seemed to be exploding.

For the next two days, 4,000 National Guard troops camped in Centennial Park in the shadow of the Parthenon. Despite their presence, riots continued, and north Nashville was sealed off.

Miles away from the turmoil, the celebration at Capitol Chevrolet continued, with hundreds of visitors filing through the building as if nothing had happened. As far as Haynie was concerned, all was well. The three-day extravaganza had been a great success. His long-time dream was off to a rousing start.

After the grand opening, Haynie and Josephine settled back into their routine with Josephine finalizing plans to honor a very special bride-

Haynie and Josephine Gourley at a gala opening. *Courtesy of Billy Gourley*

to-be. Every Christmas morning for years, the Gourleys had stopped in for breakfast at the home of Mary and Dick Braden. The Bradens' daughter Lisa was the same age as Billy Gourley. She was, in fact, the first girl he ever kissed, and the two had been pals since childhood and even dated for a while.

On Wednesday, April 17, Haynie and Josephine joined several other couples in giving a formal dinner-dance in honor of Lisa and her fiancé, Vince Foster from Hope, Arkansas, who decades later would meet a tragic end during the Clinton Administration. The two were to be married the following Saturday at St. Henry's Catholic Church. The elegant party was held in the penthouse apartment belonging to Skeeter and Dr. Addison Scoville atop Windsor Towers near MBA and included a seated dinner and dancing. Haynie loved this sort of thing—a lively party with close friends and dancing with Josephine until the wee hours. He couldn't have been happier. At seventy-two, he was having the time of his life.

After many years, Haynie had given up his box at the Iroquois Steeplechase, but he and Josephine still enjoyed the parties surrounding the event. On Saturday morning, May 11, they attended a pre-Steeplechase brunch given by their longtime friend Dot Dubuisson at her home on Chickering Road in Belle Meade.

The coveted invitation to the 1968 Swan Ball had arrived at the Gourley home. The Spanish-themed gala was to be held on June 8. It promised to be yet another spectacular ball. Josephine couldn't wait. There were plans for a life-size *papier maché* bull in the main hall of the Cheekwood mansion, and young men dressed as toreadors would be opening car doors at the valet drop-off. Reporters from *Women's Wear Daily* and *Vogue* were flying down from New York to cover the event. Not to miss out, Josephine returned their reservations the minute they arrived. This would be their sixth consecutive Swan Ball. The gala was only a little more than three weeks away. Josephine and Haynie wouldn't miss it for the world.

Haynie was now managing to squeeze in a round of golf at least twice a week. He especially looked forward to his Friday foursome. They had played the Belle Meade course for years now. Josephine kept up her dizzying schedule. Many of Billy's friends were getting engaged now that they had graduated from college. Hardly a day went by that Jo didn't attend a luncheon or tea, mostly for prospective brides.

Haynie and Josephine also relished getting to see their grandson Bill Bainbridge, now one-and-a-half and toddling about. Little Bill also was a delight to his Uncle Billy who had fallen for this newest member of what Billy Gourley referred to as his "loving Christian family."

***

Almost everyone in town knew it was a given that Billy Gourley was the heir apparent to Capitol Chevrolet. With his friendliness and good looks, Billy continued to draw the attention of the local newspapers. The previous Christmas, when Billy was among eleven popular young men asked to join the Bachelors' Club, composed of recent college graduates not yet married, *The Tennessean* ran a large photo spread of him shopping for presents at a local mall. Billy was described as "tall, tanned William H. Gourley Jr. who works for Capitol Chevrolet Company, plays golf in his spare time, and loves to water ski and 'goof around.'"

Despite all the racial strife in Nashville, as far as Billy could see, there was nothing but good things on the horizon for him. Unlike some of his friends who were struggling with what steps to take next, Billy's life was mapped out for him. He couldn't have been happier, knowing he had a secure future to look forward to at Capitol Chevrolet.

CHAPTER [9]

On a Monday in early May 1968, Billy took his own car to the new body shop for repairs. He received permission from Haynie to borrow one of the demonstrators to use while his car was being worked on.

The next morning when Billy arrived at work, the new car sales manager Jimmy Allen, a longtime family friend and protégé of Haynie's, came to Billy's cubicle and asked him to come with him. Allen led Billy outside and across to the new office on the used car lot. Bill Powell was waiting for him, along with Frank Wright, the used car manager.

There was silence for a moment as Billy looked at the three men lined up.

"Why did you take that car home?" Powell asked abruptly.

Billy was stunned by the question and Powell's harsh tone. It took a moment for Billy to understand what Powell was talking about. Billy explained that his car was in the shop, and Haynie had told him he could borrow one of the demonstrators.

"Well, you are not supposed to take them home," Powell said sternly.

"I didn't know, Mr. Powell," Billy said. "I asked my father if I could use the car, and he said it was fine. I see salesmen taking the cars all the time, so I thought it would be okay."

"Well, it's not okay," Powell said. "You shouldn't have done it. Go get the car and bring it here, and don't ever do it again."

Billy felt humiliated by the way the incident played out, especially in front of the two other managers. Billy told no one at the time, not even his father, but it would soon come out and add fuel to a flame that had begun to ignite.

By the week that began May 20, 1968, business at the new headquarters of Capitol Chevrolet surpassed all expectations. Volume was up, and the new space was already translating into more sales and service.

Memphis was still reeling from the aftermath of the assassination of Dr. Martin Luther King Jr. a month and a half earlier, yet the Tennessee Automobile Dealers' Association convention was to go on as scheduled in the city.

The Gourleys and Powells had taken trips together to Miami and Biloxi, Mississippi, and had enjoyed each other's company. On Monday, May 20, the two couples left to attend the convention in Memphis, riding in Haynie's 1968 black Cadillac. Bill Powell drove, with the men in the front seat and Helen and Josephine in the back.

At the convention, there were meetings during the day for the dealers and activities and tours for the wives. On Tuesday night, the Gourleys and Powells attended the closing banquet. At one point during the evening, Bill Powell danced with Josephine, and Haynie led Helen Powell around the floor. All seemed well on the surface.

But Haynie heard something in Memphis that greatly alarmed him.

During the course of a conversation with two other dealers whose sons were exactly Billy's age—one a Chevrolet dealer from Waynesboro, Tennessee, and the other a Ford dealer from Morristown—Haynie learned that the two men had already made their sons executives in their businesses and had set them up to take over their dealerships.

"You need to buy back your stock," they warned Haynie, after hearing that he was no longer the sole owner of Capitol Chevrolet. "You don't want anything to happen to you and have your son get cut out of the business."

"The way it is now," the Chevrolet dealer told him, "the second largest stockholder would become the dealer, not your son."

For months, Josephine had been concerned about Billy Gourley's experiences at the dealership under Bill Powell. Her son was going to work every day at Capitol Chevrolet, but Josephine saw no progress in Billy's upward trajectory in the company. Josephine was upset over what she perceived as Powell's unfair treatment of Billy. She was worried that Powell was dragging his feet in grooming Billy to become an officer. She accused Powell of not carrying out her husband's and her wishes to accelerate Billy's position at the dealership to executive status. Powell was too slow, she believed, and seemingly was making no move to train Billy and prepare him to attend the Dealers' Sons School in Detroit.

"He should be an officer by now," she had complained.

Haynie, too, had been disappointed with the lack of progress in Billy's training. Just before the move to the new headquarters, Haynie had again approached Bill Powell about making Billy an officer and providing him with one of the three new executive office spaces. Bill Powell had rejected the idea.

"He's not ready yet," Powell had said. "He's got to learn the business first."

Billy himself had gotten up the nerve to ask about the possibility of becoming an officer and had received a flat no from Powell. At the move-in, Powell assigned Billy one of the new-car sales cubicles, and Haynie had acquiesced.

***

The Powells and Gourleys returned to Nashville around noon on Wednesday, May 22. The trip to Memphis changed everything. At dinner that evening at the Gourley home, Haynie told Billy and Josephine about his conversation with the men, how their sons were already executives at their dealerships.

After they finished dinner, Haynie asked Billy to phone Powell to see if he could come over to talk.

Within minutes, Powell appeared at the Gourleys' front door.

"What's wrong now?" Powell asked, brushing past Billy as he stepped into the wide entrance hall. Billy was taken aback at his tone of voice. Powell sounded exasperated.

Powell sat down at the dining room table, not saying a word. There was an awkward pause.

Josephine broke the silence. "Bill, we have called you down here to talk to us. My Haynie has the heaviest heart about your attitude toward my son, and my son has the heaviest heart. Something has got to be done."

Haynie spoke up.

"I want Billy to be an officer in the company. He's been working at Capitol since he was fourteen years old. You know this is my dream, what I've worked for. You know this is why I wanted a new building. I've lived for this. I had a hard time growing up. I had a horrible life. I don't want Billy to have the sort of life I had. And I want him to have this business."

Haynie paused for a second, then continued.

"At the convention, I talked to two other dealers, and their sons were about Billy's age, and they already had managerial positions at their companies. They agreed with me that my son should be in the Capitol Chevrolet Company. I think he's ready to make some mistakes. I think he should be put in as an officer, not with more pay, but I want him to be an officer."

Josephine chimed in. "He wants to be an officer in the company, but he is scared of it, because he doesn't think you want him to be."

Powell turned to Billy. "Are you physically scared?"

"No, sir, I am just scared to try because I think you don't want me to be an officer."

Pointing a finger at Billy, Powell said, "What you need is the skin of an elephant."

There was an awkward silence. Billy was stung by Powell's words.

Haynie began again. "Bill, Billy Gourley has a big interest in this business..."

Powell snapped back, interrupting Haynie. "Well, he doesn't have any more interest in it than I do."

"They just told me about the car incident, about Billy taking home a car," said Josephine. "I don't think Mr. Gourley would have gotten mad."

Powell looked at Haynie and said, "Well, maybe the best thing for me to do is to get out."

More silence. To Billy's astonishment, Haynie said in a calm voice, "Bill, I think you're right. We'll always be friends. I'll do everything I can to help you get another dealership. I'll call the Chevrolet Motor Company, and we'll talk it over. You'll go out the way you came in, and of course your payment, your monetary value will be the same."

Powell did not respond. He pushed his chair back and stood up.

"Has my son ever been impudent to you in any way?" Haynie asked.

"No," Powell answered, as he headed to the front door. Billy followed him and said good night. Powell said nothing, closing the door behind him.

Early the next morning, Thursday, May 23, Haynie called Billie Dee Boyer, the switchboard operator at Capitol Chevrolet, and asked her to cancel his Friday afternoon golf game with his regular foursome. "Tell them something has come up, and I'll explain it to them later."

Haynie hung up and dialed Sam Fleming who was already in his office downtown.

"I'd like to see you as soon as possible," Haynie told Fleming.

"I'm pretty well committed starting about 9:30 this morning," Fleming answered. "If you can come right now, I'll be glad to see you."

"I have my hat on. I'm on my way."

Within thirty minutes, Haynie was sitting across from Sam Fleming in the Third National Bank's executive offices downtown.

"Can you let me personally or let the company borrow $200,000?" asked Haynie, explaining that he wanted to buy back the interest that Powell owned in Capitol Chevrolet.

Fleming was shocked. He had heard that Powell was an excellent manager. Fleming had made the original loan to Powell and had understood things were going well at the dealership.

"I would like to know what has brought about this change of heart," said Fleming.

Haynie said he had no ill feelings toward Powell in any way, but went over the events of the night before, telling Fleming that he wanted

Billy to become an officer in the company and citing what the dealers at the Memphis convention had told him about their sons.

"Bill told me he thought it was wrong to bring Billy in and that it wasn't good for the company and that if I insisted, he would just drop out," Haynie explained.

Fleming listened and then said, "Of course, I'll make the loan, either individually or to the company, whichever you decide."

Haynie thanked Fleming, saying he would get back to him to get things moving. He picked up his hat and left.

When he arrived at his office at Capitol Chevrolet, Haynie phoned John Glenn, his accountant and treasurer of the company, and asked him to draw up an agreement to buy back Bill Powell's stock.

Haynie had now begun the process to right a situation that had gone unexpectedly wrong. He wanted a swift solution.

That same morning around 8:15 a.m., Josephine Gourley telephoned Thomas Jackson in Louisville, Kentucky, zone manager for the Chevrolet Motor Company, to tell him what had happened. Jackson often stayed at the Gourley home on his trips to Nashville and was considered a good friend of the family.

"Well, Jo, I could see it coming on opening day of the new building," Jackson said. "Haynie's already called me and told me, but I knew about it last night from Bill Powell. He said he had been accused of mistreating Billy, and he wanted me to come to Nashville to talk to everyone. I'm flying down this morning."

Jackson's flight from Louisville touched down a little after 11:30 at Nashville's Berry Field. Harold Summers, district manager for Chevrolet in Nashville, met Jackson's plane. The two men then drove to Capitol Chevrolet to meet with Powell and Haynie.

It was nearing noon, so Haynie suggested they all go to the Hilton Hotel at the airport for lunch. Summers drove, and on the way over the four men talked about how things were going with the new building, avoiding any mention of the events of the night before.

Once they were settled at a table, Jackson spoke first. "I was a little amazed to receive a telephone call like this because the dealership is operating very nicely, and I thought the two of you were making great headway together. I hate to see any disruption or separation between you as partners."

Haynie said nothing, but Powell replied that it looked like he would have to leave Capitol Chevrolet because of the misunderstanding.

Jackson told Powell that he had been an excellent dealer along with Haynie and that Chevrolet did not want to lose him.

"We don't have anything open in this section right now, but I would be happy to call other managers to the south of us to try to locate you another Chevrolet dealership," Jackson said.

Jackson then explained that before any change could be made in the franchise, he would have to get it all on paper. Approval must come from Detroit, he said, not from "our end," meaning Nashville's zone headquartered in Louisville, Kentucky.

"All we can do is recommend," Jackson said.

When the four men returned to Capitol Chevrolet, they sat down in Bill Powell's office. Once again, Jackson expressed his regret at the break-up. He turned to Haynie and reminded him that no money should change hands until they had approval from Chevrolet.

"This could take a while to work its way through Detroit, but I'll get it started immediately," Jackson said, still speaking to Haynie.

Haynie and Bill Powell agreed they would continue to operate as usual until an agreement could be drawn up.

Before Jackson and Summers left, Jackson placed a call to Cincinnati, asking Billie Dee Boyer to get the time used and let him know of the long-distance charges. The party in Cincinnati, where Chevrolet had regional headquarters, was not in. Jackson left a message for the supervisor.

The delay in getting the ball rolling was about to change everything.

PART [II]

"There is no such thing as justice—in or out of court."
— Clarence Darrow, 1936

CHAPTER [10]

The next morning, Friday, May 24, 1968, after kissing Josephine goodbye, Haynie backed his car out of the driveway and headed off to work. Since 1948, he had driven straight down Harding Road which became West End Avenue, passing the Parthenon on the left and the campus of Vanderbilt University on the right. Merging onto Broadway, he went by Union Station, once a busy train station, its decline already in progress. Downtown had changed. The once glorious Maxwell House Hotel, which had dominated the corner of Fourth Avenue North and Church Street for almost a century, had burned on Christmas Day 1961. And now several businesses were moving out to the edge of town, leaving the once-thriving area desolate.

But every morning since the move, Haynie had taken a new route. He was always in high spirits as he drove off to the new building. This morning he had been especially exhilarated, knowing he had made the right decision. Josephine knew he hated to lose Powell, but now Haynie could be assured that Billy would not be cut out of the business and that it would stay in the family, as he had always planned on. He loved having his son right there with him. Now he would be free to move Billy into the third executive office.

Soon after leaving Belle Meade, Haynie made a right onto Woodmont Boulevard and crossed over Estes Road, where he had bought his first home. He reached the traffic light at Hillsboro Road. On the righthand side at the corner stood Woodmont Christian Church, designed by Edwin Keeble and almost identical to the architecture of Haynie's own beloved Vine Street Christian Church. The soaring thin spire, one of "Keeble's needles," was so distinct that it had become a sort of landmark. To Haynie's left was Woodmont Baptist Church, making this intersection instantly recognizable to Nashvillians in that part of town as the "church corner."

Haynie continued straight, crossing Granny White Pike and Franklin Road. At this point, Woodmont Boulevard became Thompson Lane. Just after he hit Nolensville Road, Haynie made a left onto Foster Lane. At the intersection of Foster Lane and Murfreesboro Road his grand new building loomed atop the hill straight ahead. He had told Billy he didn't think he would ever tire of seeing this splendid sight.

Haynie drove by the used car lot and up to the second level where he entered the service department and parked in his usual spot in one of the service lanes. As soon as he got out of his car, a service representative jumped into the black 1968 Caprice and whisked it away to be washed and the interior blown clean. This happened like clockwork every day. His car was waxed at least once if not twice a week. Haynie had always insisted that the cars he drove be kept immaculately clean, a habit he had formed way back in the 1920s.

At a little after ten o'clock, Hamilton Wallace Jr. was sitting in his office on the service floor when Haynie stuck his head in. Wallace had been hired by Bill Powell to head a new leasing department at Capitol Chevrolet. He had started on the sixth of May, so he had been on the job for only a couple of weeks.

From a prominent Belle Meade family, Wallace had come to Capitol from another well-known successful dealership, Beaman Pontiac.

"Ham, I want you to know this," Haynie began. "Bill Powell is going to be leaving us. I love the boy like a son, but we've had a feud and a misunderstanding about the way he's treated Billy, and we think, both he and I think, it's best that we sever our relationship. He's going to be leaving, and I am hoping you will stay on with us and help along with this lease program and build this thing up."

Wallace was taken aback at this news. Before he could respond, Buddy Rich, one of the employees from downstairs, came into the office to say that John Sloan was in Haynie's office waiting for him. "We'll talk later," Haynie said, excused himself, and left.

Haynie went downstairs to his office to greet Sloan, a longtime friend and the president of the Nashville-based Cain-Sloan department stores. Sloan had just purchased a car from Capitol and was meeting with Haynie to talk about some adjustments he needed. Another friend of Haynie's, Jimmy Tupper, was out in the showroom, also waiting to see him.

For Billy Gourley, May 24 was turning out to be a typical Friday morning. He arrived at work around 7:30 a.m. and was looking forward to finalizing the sale of a new car to one of his high school buddies. He had not given much thought to the meeting two nights before when Powell had come to his parents' home. He had seen Thomas Jackson and Harold Summers the day before but had not talked with his father about what the men said. He figured Haynie would tell him in good time.

Around 10:20 a.m., Billy was on the showroom floor talking with a customer when he saw Haynie walk into his office where John Sloan was waiting. Billy then went back to his desk to finish some paperwork.

After Sloan left, at about twenty minutes before eleven, Haynie stopped by Billy's glass cubicle. Billy stood up and walked over to his father.

"Bill Powell wants to go for a ride and talk things over," Haynie said. "I'll let you know what he says when I get back."

The dealership's receptionist, Billie Dee Boyer, was a youngish grandmother who wore her blonde hair piled atop her head in a tall beehive and was known for her big round sunglasses. Calls in and out of the dealership and within the building ran through her switchboard. "Miss Billie," as she was called by most of the employees, answered incoming calls and then plugged in the number of the employee or department for the transfer. She had been hired by Haynie in 1962 and was now getting used to her setup in the new building. When Haynie arrived every morning, he would let her know where he was on the premises in case any calls came in for him.

A little before 10:45, Haynie rang Boyer and asked her to place a call to Thomas Jackson in Louisville. She had done this so many times through the years that she knew the number by heart. But before the call went through, Haynie rang back, asking her to cancel the call, that he would make it later.

A minute later, Haynie walked up behind her desk in the middle of the showroom.

"Miss Billie, I'll be back in about fifteen minutes." She turned her head to the left and said, "All right, Mr. Gourley."

Out of the corner of her eye she saw Bill Powell standing at the foot of the stairs, waiting for Haynie. She watched as the two men started up the steps together.

In the service department, several of the service writers were standing at their desks, filling out work orders for customers' cars; others were leaning against their desks chatting back and forth. Haynie's black four-door, top-of-the-line Caprice had been returned to the floor, freshly washed and shiny. The full size, boat-like '68 sedan was roomy, measuring eighteen feet long and six-and-a-half-feet wide, and took up a good deal of space in the service lane.

Around a quarter to eleven, one of the service writers, Meacham Clark, was at the desk nearest the entrance doors. He was busy writing up a service order for a customer when he glanced up to see Haynie's car pulling away. He noticed that Haynie was in the passenger seat, then looked back at what he was doing.

Shop foreman George Crawford had come to work at Capitol Chevrolet in 1962. It was his job to oversee the mechanical work on cars on the next level up. At 10:45, he came down the stairs to the service check-in desk and saw Haynie and Bill Powell come out from the door by the cashier's window and walk over to Haynie's car. He heard Bill Powell ask Haynie who should drive. Crawford chuckled to himself, knowing what Haynie would say. Mr. Gourley always had someone else do the driving. Bill Powell walked around and got into the driver's seat, and Haynie slipped into the passenger side. As Crawford continued across the service lanes, he saw Haynie's car exit through the righthand door and disappear.

Another service writer, Chuck Williams, also saw Haynie's car leave. He then walked over and climbed into Haynie's Cadillac, which had been brought in the day before, and drove it to the new-car department to have it washed.

According to his watch, it was ten minutes before eleven o'clock when truck sales manager James Walter Hughes received a call about delivering a new truck to Baltz Brothers Meat Packing company on Elm Hill Pike. Hughes picked up a dealer's tag from his desk and was walking outside to the parking lot opposite the back entrance to the service department when Haynie's car glided past him. Bill Powell was driving, and Haynie sat in the passenger seat. Hughes watched as the two men pulled out onto P'Pool Avenue heading in the direction of Elm Hill Pike a half-block away. Hughes turned around and walked back inside where he retrieved the keys to the new truck.

When he came back out, Hughes put the license tag in the truck window and drove out of Capitol Chevrolet, crossing Murfreesboro Road and pulling into a Shell service station where he asked for four gallons of gas. He waited a few minutes for the attendant to work the pump and then go inside for a ticket to charge to the company account. The attendant came back out, Hughes signed his name, and headed back to the dealership.

***

At about the same time James Walter Hughes received the call from Baltz Brothers, Charles Edward Donnelly was standing in line at the

Krystal on Murfreesboro Road. When it came his turn, he ordered a large coffee to go. The big burly man climbed back into his delivery truck, taking sips of his coffee as he drove along. He worked for Time Trucking Company, and today he had a load of paper to deliver to an ad agency that produced calendars. He turned onto Arlington Lane and came to a stop sign where the road ended at Elm Hill Pike. He looked both ways. To his left he saw a black Chevrolet slowing down to cross the railroad tracks. He immediately recognized the car and the two men inside. Should he wait for them to pass, or should he go ahead of them since they had practically stopped at the railroad tracks? He made a snap decision and pulled out. He glanced in his side mirror to see the car come up close behind him. Maybe he should have waited, knowing he was about to make a left turn and could hold up traffic.

As he approached Spence Lane, Donnelly put on his blinker. A paving crew was working at the intersection. He was relieved when a flagman waved him on to make his left turn, so he didn't have to make the men in back of him wait after all. As he made his turn, he saw the black Chevrolet continue straight, heading on down Elm Hill Pike.

Donnelly then pulled up to the loading dock at the Francis & Lusky Advertising Agency where workers used jacks to lift the heavy paper out of the truck.

Two minutes after Donnelly made his turn, a short, thin Black man with dark skin finished making a dynamite blast at a construction site where he was leveling the earth to lay pipe for a new Kroger warehouse. He climbed into the company pick-up truck and drove over the bumpy ground to the construction trailer located on a small rise overlooking Elm Hill Pike at Massman Drive. Here, he stopped to have lunch. Sitting in the truck, he pulled out the two sandwiches his wife had packed for him that morning. As he was eating, he looked up to see a black car pull over and stop under some trees by the side of Elm Hill Pike, adjacent to the H.D. Lee Company. The workman was only a couple of hundred feet away. Watching the activity around the car, he was bewildered by what he saw. He recognized the sounds he heard, but he couldn't make sense of any of it. In all, the black car stayed parked for around ten minutes. Then it started moving forward. It pulled into a driveway by a rock wall, backed out into the road, and headed in the opposite direction toward town. As the car passed by the workman, he noticed that the passenger was slumped forward in his seat. The car picked up speed.

The man in the pick-up lived thirty miles away. He did not own a television and had never read a newspaper. As only one of two Black workers in the company, he kept mainly to himself, so he told no one about the bizarre incident that had just unfolded in front of him.

At least twelve minutes had passed since Charles Donnelly had watched the black car go through the intersection of Spence Lane and Elm Hill Pike. He was standing on the loading dock at Francis & Lusky waiting for his receipt when he saw the same car coming from the opposite direction. Traffic had slowed because the road had been reduced to one lane. Donnelly noticed that the passenger, whom he knew well, was hardly visible. His window appeared to be down. Donnelly didn't think much about it and went on to his next delivery.

Less than two minutes after Donnelly saw the black Chevrolet come back through the intersection of Elm Hill Pike and Spence Lane, Walter Hughes drove in the back gate at Capitol Chevrolet. He had just climbed down from the Baltz Brothers' new truck when he was startled by the sound of tires squealing. He looked up to see Haynie's car speed past him, headed for the building. Powell was at the wheel, but there was no sign of Haynie.

Inside the service area, Meacham Clark and Chuck Williams were standing at their desks during a lull in new check-ins. George Crawford, the service shop foreman, had come back down and was on his way over to service manager Charlie McCaffrey's office when he heard a car coming in at a high rate of speed, horn blaring.

Everyone looked up at once. By the time Chuck Williams could get out the words "What fool is blowing his horn?" the men saw Haynie's car careening around the corner, barely missing the side of the lower door and skidding violently to a stop next to the water cooler.

Mouths flew open, and all eyes were drawn to the driver's side as the door opened. Everyone watched in astonishment as Bill Powell emerged from the car, stood up, then crumpled to the cement floor.

It took a moment for the scene to register, but George Crawford rushed to Powell and tried to lift him up. Then Charlie McCaffrey and Chuck Williams ran over and gripped Powell under his arms; the three men struggled to bring him to his feet. It wasn't working. He was so heavy they only managed to drag him a few feet. People started running over, seemingly materializing out of nowhere, crowding around the scene. Powell was moaning. Everyone was asking what happened.

When they reached the back of Haynie's car, Powell stopped a moment, pulled himself up and spread out his right hand on the lid of the trunk. George Crawford took note of this gesture. Even in the chaos of the moment Crawford thought it strange.

Dragging Powell, they managed to get him to McCaffrey's office.

"Call the police, call an ambulance," Powell shouted as soon as they cleared the door.

George Crawford ran to Meacham Clark's desk and started fumbling with a phone book. Clark came up behind him and said, "Just call the switchboard and have them call." Crawford dialed Miss Billie and told her to call the police and an ambulance.

Everyone was still shouting for Powell to tell what happened.

"Damn nigger shot me," growled Powell, staggering as the men held onto him, finally getting him over to the opposite wall.

As they laid Powell on the floor, he began describing how a Black man jumped into the car at a four-way stop on Elm Hill Pike. Everyone who heard him immediately thought of Fessler's Lane, located right around the corner toward town from Capitol Chevrolet and the only four-way stop on Elm Hill Pike.

Then, Powell abruptly sat up and yelled, "Get Haynie." The men looked at each other. No one had seen Haynie.

Powell pointed to the car.

George Crawford and Chuck Williams ran back out and were joined by one of the young employees named Rogers. The passenger window was blown out, with jagged shards of glass clinging to the edges of the frame. They opened the door to find Haynie wedged face down in the floorboard. At first, they couldn't budge him, but the men grabbed his arms and were finally able to free him from his awkward position.

They laid him out on the concrete floor. Crawford grabbed him under his arms, and Williams picked him up by his legs. Rogers put his arm under Haynie's back for support. Haynie, unlike Powell, was totally limp and quiet; his head lolled backwards. He weighed a good bit less than Powell. The men carried him to the other end of the service lounge where they laid him on a bench.

Crawford and Williams went back over to Powell. Williams saw blood on Powell's left pants leg, bent down, and removed Powell's tie, making a tourniquet above his knee.

Several men asked again what happened. Powell, grimacing as he spoke, said he and Mr. Gourley were stopped at a stop sign, and "a colored man opened the back door and jumped into the car."

"The man said, 'Give me all your money.' Mr. Gourley reached into his coat pocket for his wallet and said, 'Here, James,' or something like that, 'you can have everything I've got,' and the man started cursing and yelled, 'Don't go for your gun,' and then he started shooting."

Hamilton Wallace had not heard the commotion and was sitting at his desk filling out papers to lease a car to his first cousin, John Bransford Jr. Capitol's housekeeper Hettie Grady came into Wallace's office. "Mr. Ham, there's been an accident," she said breathlessly. Wallace assumed there had been a fender bender and took no notice and continued with what he was doing. She came back a minute later and said, "No sir, Mr. Powell's hurt bad."

Wallace and Bransford jumped up and ran across the hall to Mc-

Caffrey's office. Wallace noticed that Haynie's car was parked in a different place.

In the service lounge, Powell was sitting on the floor, leaning against the wall. The room was crowded; everybody was talking at once. Wallace saw the three men come in carrying Haynie. Wallace bent down and asked Powell what happened.

"We came to a stop sign," Powell said, "and a colored man leaped in the back seat, demanded money, and when Mr. Gourley reached in his coat for his wallet, the man started cursing and cut loose with a gun and shot me and Mr. Gourley."

Wallace pulled some cushions off a sofa to put under Powell.

"Where were you hit?" Wallace asked.

"I think in the stomach," answered Powell.

A crowd was gathered around Powell, but no one was near Haynie as he lay still on the bench across the room. Powell overheard Chuck Williams say an ambulance would not do Mr. Gourley any good, that he was already dead.

Bill Powell shouted, "No, he can't be dead. Get him to a doctor quick. He will be all right."

***

Downstairs in the showroom, Billie Dee Boyer received the call from the service department and fumbled with a phone book for a moment when one of the salesmen, Tom Darnell, walked up. "Just call the operator." Boyer put the call through, and the operator said she would send the police and an ambulance right away.

Boyer looked over at Billy Gourley, sitting in his cubicle. "Somebody needs to tell him," she thought, then dialed his phone.

"There's been an accident, and your dad's been hurt," she said, trying to keep her voice calm.

Billy jumped up, rushed across the showroom, and flew up the stairs. He noticed his father's car sitting in the wrong place and then burst into the service manager's office. Bill Powell was sitting on the floor against a wall with several people crowded around him. Billy then saw his father lying alone on a bench across the room.

"What happened, what happened?" Billy shouted. Powell started the story of the Black man jumping into the car at a four-way stop. At that point, sales manager Jimmy Allen took Billy's arm, pulled him away from the bench where his father lay motionless, and led him out of the room.

"Your dad was shot in a robbery," Allen said, putting his hand on Billy's shoulder. "Billy, he's dead."

Billy felt cold wash over him. He looked at all the people gathered around Powell.

"Did anybody call an ambulance?" Billy asked, pulling away from Jimmy Allen and heading back to his father.

Both ambulances arrived at the same time. The driver and a young attendant hopped out with a stretcher. Bill Powell shouted, "Take Haynie first." Several employees rushed over to help.

Haynie was put on a stretcher and pushed into the back of one of the ambulances, a dark blue, low-slung Cadillac. Billy ducked his head and climbed in with his father.

"Take him to Vanderbilt Hospital," Billy said to the driver as the attendant closed the doors. "That's where his doctors are."

The driver started in the direction of Vanderbilt and then called back to Billy. "If it was my daddy, I'd want him taken to General. It's a lot closer."

Billy gave him the go ahead to turn around. Jimmy Allen's words rang in his head. It all seemed so surreal.

As they sped toward the hospital, Billy knew deep down that his father was dead, but told himself no, that Haynie always pulled it out in the end.

Billy felt numb. "This can't be happening," he thought to himself. "This is just a bad dream. I'll wake up, and he will be okay."

After the first ambulance pulled away, George Crawford and several men struggled to carry Bill Powell to the other ambulance. His bulk kept the stretcher off-balance and made it difficult to steady. They were finally able to wrestle around and keep Powell from falling off.

From the back of the ambulance, Powell called out, "Please, somebody ride with me." Hamilton Wallace climbed into the ambulance. Powell told the driver to go to Vanderbilt Hospital.

"Please don't drive so fast and get us killed," Wallace shouted at the driver.

In the ambulance, Powell handed Wallace his wallet and asked him to give it to his wife and to please locate her and tell her what happened before she heard it on the news and had an accident herself.

The ambulance arrived at the emergency entrance to Vanderbilt Hospital where Wallace rushed to check Powell in, then tried to get in touch with Helen Powell. He called several of her friends but was unable to reach her.

Wallace spied Josephine Gourley surrounded by several people. He did not go over to her, feeling that since he was the only person available to give information to the hospital, it was his duty to stay with Powell until he was checked in.

Back at Capitol Chevrolet after the ambulances left, Chuck Williams stood in one of the service department lanes. He was bothered by something. He had twice listened to Powell's account of the incident and twice had seen him gesture to show how Haynie had reached into his coat pocket for his wallet to hand over to the robber.

Countless times, Williams had run errands for Haynie, mostly to pick up gifts for Mrs. Gourley, to buy her Russell Stover candy for Valentine's Day or a wedding anniversary. Williams knew one thing for certain. Haynie had never kept a wallet in his coat pocket. Without fail, he would reach into his back left hip pocket to pull out cash to give to Williams.

At General Hospital, Haynie's motionless form was carried into the emergency room. Billy tried to call his mother. At that moment, Josephine Gourley was at Vanderbilt Hospital. The Belle Meade police had received a call and had gone to the Gourley home to pick her up. Several people were still gathered around her at the emergency room doors when someone came out and said her husband was at General Hospital. A patrolman from Metro police who had answered a call on his radio and had gone directly to Vanderbilt Hospital volunteered to drive Josephine to General Hospital.

When his mother arrived at the emergency room, Billy could hardly say the words out loud. Haynie was dead. He had been shot in a robbery, Billy told his mother. Josephine was stricken. He saw the hope in her expression turn to pain. Someone came out with a brown envelope containing the contents of Haynie's pockets and handed it to Billy. Neither he nor his mother went in to see Haynie.

Dr. Morse Kochtitzky, a friend of Haynie's and a member of Dr. Tom Frist's group, was making rounds at the hospital. He offered to drive Billy and his mother back to the Gourley home. As they left General Hospital, Billy turned to see two of his longtime buddies, Joe Ledbetter and Ben Gambill, standing by the emergency room door, watching as Kochtitzky's car drove away.

***

Hal Hardin, a third-year student who was about to graduate from Vanderbilt Law School, was working a part-time job as an investigator in the Nashville district attorney's office. He liked to joke to his friends that he felt like the comic strip character Dick Tracy because he had been assigned a gun and his own car, complete with two-way radio and siren.

Around noon, Hardin was riding with George Curry, an investigator with the district attorney's office, when a call came over the radio that there had been a shooting on Elm Hill Pike. The two rushed to the road within minutes but could find no police activity. They were headed back toward downtown when another call came in that a body had been taken to General Hospital. No other information was given.

Hardin and Curry turned around and drove to the hospital. The two were shown into the room where Haynie had been taken. Hardin knew of Haynie Gourley and had seen him before. Now, directly in front of him, the popular Nashville businessman lay on a steel table in the hospital's morgue. Hardin gazed at the body while someone explained what had happened—that Mr. Gourley and his vice-president Bill Powell at Capitol Chevrolet had been at a four-way stop on Elm Hill Pike when a Black man jumped in the back seat of Mr. Gourley's car and held them up at gunpoint. When Mr. Gourley reached for his wallet, the gunman cursed, and yelled, "Don't go for your gun," and started shooting wildly, killing Mr. Gourley and wounding Bill Powell in the left calf. Bill Powell was rushed to Vanderbilt Hospital in another ambulance.

Haynie's shirt had been removed, and it was obvious there had been blood, but it had been cleaned off. Hardin stared at the wounds—one just below Haynie's ear at the jawline, one to his lower neck near the collar bone and another to the left side of his chest.

Something seemed wrong to Hardin. The angles and the trajectory of the bullets made no sense. A bullet lay on the table. The men were told that it had fallen out of the back of Haynie's coat but had not entered his body. Hardin noted how bruised Mr. Gourley was around the wounds to his head and neck, but not around the chest wound. That also seemed odd.

Hal Hardin and George Curry left the hospital, but Hardin could not shake the sight of Haynie Gourley lying on that cold steel table, his stout belly exposed, white as a sheet.

***

Around noon, Sherman Nickens, a homicide detective in the Metro Police Department, was directing traffic at the corner of Fourth Avenue and Church Street in downtown Nashville. Charlie Hunter, an investigator with the district attorney's office, parked at the intersection, and, dodging cars, ran over to Nickens.

"General Shriver wants you to go to Vanderbilt Hospital right away," said Hunter.

Nickens demurred. He regularly took on these off-duty extra jobs to supplement his policeman's salary. He was busy working the heavily congested intersection when Hunter arrived.

"I can't just leave right now," Nickens said.

"Forget this. You need to get over to Vanderbilt."

Nickens reluctantly left his post and headed to the hospital, still dressed in his patrolman's uniform. When he arrived, he found Bill Powell in the emergency room. Hunter had given Nickens a quick account of Powell's story.

Nickens had been thinking on the way to Vanderbilt Hospital. With the situation in Nashville as volatile as it is, how is it that a Negro has the nerve to get in a car with two white men in broad daylight, especially one as powerfully built as Bill Powell and the other pretty big himself?

Something didn't ring true. Never in his dozen or so years on the police force had he heard of anyone pulling off a robbery by jumping into a car on a busy road and holding somebody up at gunpoint.

When Nickens arrived at the hospital, he gave orders to an emergency room staffer not to clean Powell's hands. He asked the nursing assistant to wrap them in plastic until the police could run some tests. He had to cover all his bases.

Without speaking to Powell, Nickens left for Capitol Chevrolet.

CHAPTER [11]

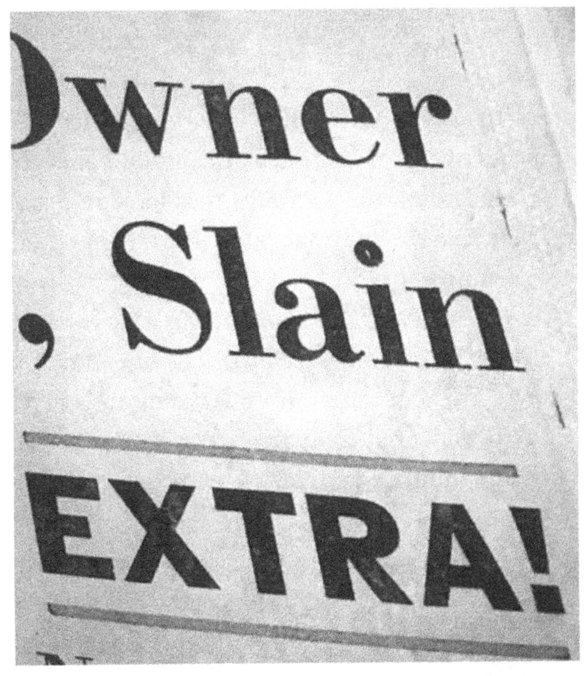

Detail of headline on front page of the *Nashville Banner*, afternoon of May 24, 1968. *Nashville Public Library, Special Collections, Banner Newspaper Collection*

There were two major newspapers in the Tennessee capital—the morning paper *The Tennessean* and the afternoon *Nashville Banner*. Although both papers shared the same building, were printed on the same presses, were distributed by a common agent, and had a consolidated classified ad department, they had different owners and were cutthroat competitors when it came to breaking news. They were also miles apart on editorial viewpoints, *The Tennessean* being known as the liberal paper, leaning toward Democrats, while the *Nashville Banner* was staunchly conservative and overwhelmingly Republican. Regardless of their political leanings, most Nashvillians subscribed to both papers.

One of the best-known disagreements between the two rivals occurred in the mid-1960s when Daylight Savings Time was being fiercely debated across the country. *The Tennessean* was for the change, but the *Nashville Banner* was adamantly opposed. The clock the two newspapers shared atop their jointly-occupied building had two faces, pointing in opposite directions. Both newspapers were defiant. *The Tennessean* side showed Central Daylight Savings Time while the *Nashville Banner* stubbornly kept its clock set to Central Standard Time.

On Friday, May 24, 1968, it was the *Nashville Banner* that had the jump on the shocking news.

From the moment word was received that Haynie Gourley had been murdered, reporters and photographers flew into action. This was a huge story—one of the city's best-known citizens murdered in broad daylight on a busy road. When the news broke on radio and television, the whole of Nashville was transfixed.

James Stahlman, owner of the *Nashville Banner*, was a close friend of Haynie's and a fierce competitor of *The Tennessean*'s liberal editor John Seigenthaler, who was at the moment on a leave of absence to manage Robert Kennedy's presidential campaign. Because the shooting took place in the morning hours, Stahlman's afternoon paper had the advantage.

It took no time for the *Nashville Banner* to start the presses rolling. People were clamoring for details. For only the second time in its ninety-two-year history, the newspaper was about to run a second Extra edition. The first occasion was on November 22, 1963, when John F. Kennedy was assassinated and now on May 24, 1968, with the murder of Haynie Gourley. The regular edition had already been printed without the breaking news. But by 3:00 p.m., the paper came out with an Extra edition with explosive headlines that screamed, "Haynie Gourley, Owner of Capitol Chevrolet, Slain." People stormed newspaper stands, grabbing up copies, and newsboys were sent out hawking the editions, with both Extras selling out quickly.

Nashville had begun what would be an unprecedented obsession with a high-profile crime that would grip the city like nothing else had ever done.

***

David Allman, who was assigned to the patrol division of the Metropolitan Police Department, was near the intersection of Nolensville Road and Polk Avenue—about two-and-a-half miles away from Capitol Chevrolet—when he received radio orders a little after 11:00 a.m. to proceed to the dealership. The code given indicated that an automobile accident with personal injuries involving a drunk driver had occurred.

When Allman arrived at Capitol, he found a chaotic scene. Dozens of people were crowded around a black car. Others milled about in the service department. One of the employees gave Allman a description of Bill Powell's account of what happened. The officer asked everyone to back away so he could secure Haynie's car until the police identification unit arrived. Allman peered through the back window and could see a hat, a pair of glasses, and a billfold on the back seat. He opened the back door and picked up the wallet and handed it to another officer who had just walked up. Allman saw only an Esso gas card, but the other policeman pulled out two one-hundred-dollar bills that had been folded up and tucked into in an inside compartment in the wallet. Carney Patterson, a salesman at Capitol, saw the policeman pull the money out. The killer had gotten nothing.

Any evidence the car held was already contaminated. Photographers from *The Tennessean* arrived and began snapping pictures of the car's interior. Finally, the identification unit from Metro police turned up. An officer lifted fingerprints from the car doors. His was a futile task. The door handles had already been touched dozens of times since the car came barreling into the service department. What baffled those who examined the car was why there was a bullet hole in the back of the front passenger seat, about eighteen inches down from the top. This made no sense, given Powell's story. A chalk circle was eventually drawn around the hole, and later, the seat would be torn apart to reveal a bent metal support rod. Another year would pass before any official explanation was offered, but for the moment, it appeared that someone had shot into the seat where a bullet might have reached a front-seat passenger.

A few minutes past noon, Patrolman Frank Galbaugh of the Metro Police Department was at Vanderbilt Hospital investigating a narcotics case when he was told to go to the nearest phone. On the line was a police dispatcher who instructed Galbaugh to locate a shooting victim, William Powell, who had just been brought in, to see what information he could obtain from the victim.

Galbaugh found Powell in one of the emergency rooms, lying on a hospital bed that had been raised to a thirty-degree angle. The policeman asked the two physicians present if he could question the patient, providing he was willing. Entering the room, Galbaugh told Powell he hated to disturb him at this time, but if he felt like talking, he would like to find out some more information pertaining to the incident. Powell said he would be happy to cooperate.

Galbaugh listened as Powell described how he left Capitol Chevrolet with Haynie Gourley and was driving down Elm Hill Pike. "I got to the stop sign at Spence Lane, and there was a truck parked on the side of the road."

Powell said he slowed down. With a slight chuckle, he told Galbaugh he knew the police would probably have given him a ticket because he didn't come to a complete stop at the stop sign.

At this point, Powell said a Black man jumped into the back seat of the car and demanded money. Powell described how he continued rolling through the intersection and how Mr. Gourley reached into his coat pocket for his wallet. The man cursed, calling Mr. Gourley a son-of-a-bitch and shouted, "Don't reach for that damn gun," and then started shooting.

Powell told Galbaugh he realized Mr. Gourley had been hit and leaned over to help him. Powell said that when he reached for Mr. Gourley, the assailant struck his arm with some object which he thought was a weapon. Galbaugh asked when and how he was shot in the leg. Powell said in all the confusion he really didn't know.

Galbaugh listened to the story and took notes. He asked to see Powell's forearm and saw a red place midway between his elbow and wrist. Galbaugh looked closely at the red mark. It was not bleeding and appeared to be a scrape. Galbaugh noticed it had a square shape.

When Powell was asked if he was able to describe the man who jumped into the car, all he said was that he would never forget his eyes, that instead of being white, they were cloudy and yellow-looking.

Galbaugh asked what the weapon looked like. Powell said he never saw one, but that it was loud and sounded like a shotgun. From Powell's description of the shooting, Galbaugh assumed that Haynie Gourley had never gotten the wallet out of his coat, and that, according to what Powell was telling him, Haynie was shot the moment he made a move toward his coat pocket.

All through the interview, Galbaugh was struck by the fact that Powell was talking in a very loud, forceful voice. Galbaugh thought it odd; it seemed as if Powell were giving a speech and trying to drive home a point to win over his audience.

Something else Powell said bothered Galbaugh. He knew the intersection well where Powell claimed the man had jumped into the car. Powell had made a big deal about rolling through the stop sign. He'd even made a joke about it.

The trouble was that there was no stop sign on Elm Hill Pike at Spence Lane and never had been.

A little before noon, Homicide Detective Ernest Castleman, an eighteen-year veteran of the Metropolitan Police Department, was at the police station downtown when he and Detective Joe Dodson with the Criminal Investigation Unit learned there had been a shooting and received orders to proceed to the intersection of Elm Hill Pike and Fesslers Lane. When they arrived, they saw nothing out of the ordinary.

Then, a call came with orders to go to Vanderbilt Hospital to interview Bill Powell, a shooting victim.

When Castleman and Dodson arrived, Galbaugh had left, and Powell had just been wheeled from x-ray back to the emergency room. He was surrounded by several people, including his wife Helen, his sister-in-law Roberta Witherspoon, and Bill Trickett, a Pontiac dealer and close friend of Powell.

Castleman did most of the talking. The questioning took place in a room next to the emergency room admitting office. Powell told the officers how a "colored man" had jumped into the car with him and Mr. Gourley as he pulled up to the intersection of Elm Hill Pike and Spence Lane. Powell did not mention a stop sign but said he had to slow down behind a truck that was turning left, and that's when a man got into the car, pulled a gun, and demanded their money.

Powell continued. "Mr. Gourley said, 'You can have it all, James,' or something to that effect and started to reach into his coat pocket to get his billfold.

"As soon as Mr. Gourley made a move," Powell said, "the male colored started to shoot. I don't know how many times he shot, and I didn't know which way he went after he left the car."

Powell described the man as being around thirty, or a little older about six feet tall. The whites of his eyes, he said, were "yellowish and real glassy." Powell said the man was dark skinned, that he had on a black shirt, and was wearing a "really old" dark hat and a dark-colored jacket. Powell lowered his voice and said the man called Mr. Gourley a son-of-a-bitch when he demanded money.

"When Mr. Gourley was shot, he slumped over in the seat and cried out, 'Oh,'" Powell said. Powell described how he kept on driving for a few feet with the gunman in the car and made a sudden U-turn in the middle of Elm Hill Pike. He told the officers he grabbed Mr. Gourley to try to hold him up and was driving with one hand and holding Mr. Gourley with the other. As he made the turn, the gunman jumped out of the car. Powell said he did not see where he went. When the gunman was gone, Powell said he drove as fast as he could back to Capitol Chevrolet.

"I almost had a wreck," he added.

Castleman asked Powell to explain exactly where the incident happened.

"If you'll get me a piece of paper, I'll draw you a map," answered Powell.

A nurse produced some paper, and Powell sketched out the route, starting at the back of Capitol Chevrolet, then coming onto P'Pool Avenue and making a right turn onto Elm Hill Pike. Powell's drawing showed that he made a U-turn immediately after passing through the intersection with Spence Lane. He drew arrows to indicate his route from Capitol Chevrolet to Spence Lane and back.

Route To Death Scene

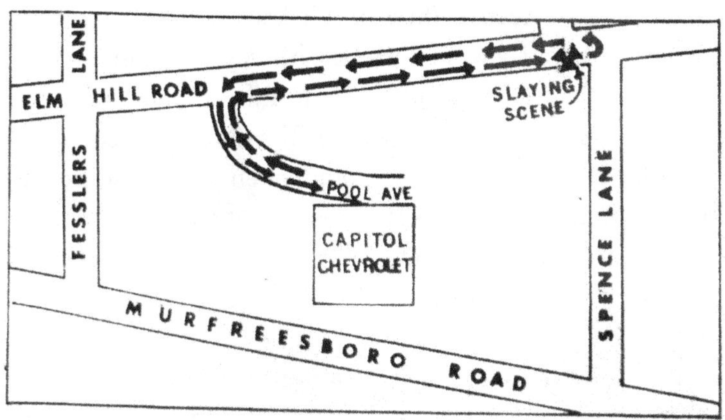

Artist's rendering of a map drawn by Bill Powell on the afternoon of the murder, May 24, 1968. *Nashville Public Library, Special Collections, Banner Newspaper Collection*

Several aspects of Powell's story troubled Castleman. He tried to picture how a man could get out of a moving car without falling, not to mention being able to close the door behind him.

According to the map Powell drew, the incident had to have taken place only minutes after the two left Capitol Chevrolet. Powell said he never stopped the car and that he "drove 80 miles an hour" back to the dealership. That meant he would have made it back to Capitol Chevrolet less than five minutes after they left for the ride.

Castleman would soon learn that Powell was gone for close to fifteen minutes.

Once police learned where Powell said the shooting took place, patrolmen rushed to the intersection of Elm Hill Pike and Spence Lane where they found a work crew repaving the road. The men, employees of Globe Construction Company, told police they had not noticed a black Chevrolet at the intersection, nor had they seen a Black man on foot. The workers told police that much earlier that morning, however, a red Mustang with four "Negroes" inside kept passing through the intersection, with loud, throbbing music blasting from inside the car.

When homicide detective Sherman Nickens arrived at Capitol Chevrolet, his first directive was to have the black Caprice moved to the intersection of Spence Lane and Elm Hill Pike. Bloodhounds from the state prison were brought to the scene. The car doors were opened and the dogs let loose in hopes they could catch a scent in the back seat and follow it into the scrubby land beyond. It would not take long for the district attorney's office to realize that the investigation had already been bungled by police carelessness. Nothing about the car had been preserved.

There would be many more glaring mistakes by the police that would significantly reduce the chances of finding Haynie Gourley's killer.

Crews from WLAC-TV were quick to arrive at the scene, and two news cameramen, Lou Penuel and Robert Bosworth, drove past the intersection of Spence Lane to Massman Drive, which crossed Elm Hill Pike more than a half mile further down from the spot Bill Powell said he had made a U-turn. The two men found shattered glass on the right-hand shoulder of Elm Hill Pike under some trees next to the H.D. Lee Company building.

After Patrolman Dodson left Vanderbilt Hospital he drove straight to the intersection of Spence Lane and Elm Hill Pike where he found a crowd of people gathered around the black Caprice. Assistant Chief Donald Barton and several other policemen were at the scene.

Dodson parked his police vehicle and began knocking on doors of houses near the intersection. No one was home except for an elderly Black woman. She said she had not seen or heard anything unusual.

Dodson then got back into his patrol car and began driving slowly down Elm Hill Pike, well past the point where Powell had shown on his map that he made the U-turn.

When Dodson reached Massman Drive, he saw the TV camera crew and another police officer under some trees on the right side of Elm Hill Pike. Dodson parked and went over to the crew standing over broken glass they believed could have come from Haynie's car. The two officers gathered the glass to give to the forensic team.

Dodson recalled the drawing Powell had made. This location was well over a half mile past where Powell said he had turned around.

Dodson was puzzled. Why was the glass here? Massman Drive was not even on the map Powell drew. Powell was adamant that he made a U-turn just beyond Spence Lane. The drawing he made showed a distance of only a few hundred feet past the cross street. The glass should have been close to that intersection, not way down at Massman Drive.

It would be a year before this mystery was explained.

CHAPTER [12]

Around 11:25 a.m., Dr. T. E. Simpkins was leaving Goodlettsville, Tennessee, after visiting one of his patients when he received a police radio call to go directly to General Hospital's emergency room.

Dr. Simpkins, a surgeon who had been practicing medicine in Nashville for thirty-four years, had for the past thirteen years served as medical examiner for the Metro government. His role in any murder investigation was to determine the cause of death.

A bespectacled graying man with a bristly mustache, Dr. Simpkins had graduated from David Lipscomb College, attended Vanderbilt University, and received his medical degree from the University of Tennessee.

Before he arrived at General Hospital, Simpkins had not been told the name of the deceased. When he walked in, he immediately recognized Haynie Gourley as the man who lay on a gurney in one of the emergency rooms.

Dr. Simpkins ordered the body moved into another room and laid out on a steel table to begin his exam.

He first determined that Haynie was five feet eleven inches tall and weighed 180 pounds. His initial findings were that Mr. Gourley had been shot three times in the left side. He sustained a bullet wound between the left ear and the jawbone. The entry point showed evidence of seared edges. Dr. Simpkins concluded that a gun had been held to his head and fired. That same bullet exited his lower face on the right side, fracturing his right jaw.

A second contact entry wound was present in the upper shoulder area. Again, Dr. Simpkins determined that the muzzle of the gun had been pressed against the body. There was no exit wound for this bullet, which Dr. Simpkins would remove later that afternoon during the autopsy.

Haynie had also been shot in the side of the chest, but this time the gun was likely fired from one to two feet away. This bullet also remained lodged in his body.

On the table where Haynie lay, Dr. Simpkins discovered a bullet. He speculated that it had dropped from Haynie's clothing. The back of Haynie's coat and shirt appeared to have been ripped by gunshot, but the skin was not broken. The bullet holes in the clothing were between Haynie's shoulder blades. It appeared that he had been shot in the back, but there was no wound, a curious finding that had no explanation at first glance but would become obvious later.

Dr. Simpkins determined that at least two of the shots were fatal—the one that had entered the collarbone area and the one that had entered the chest on the left side. The bullet that passed through the head quite possibly could have been fatal; it had done major damage, but Dr. Simpkins said his findings on that particular wound were inconclusive.

Later in the afternoon, Dr. Richard Callaway, a resident in pathology at General Hospital, assisted Dr. Simpkins with the autopsy. The examination revealed the path of the bullets. The bullet that entered the left shoulder passed downward through the section between the lungs that contains the heart, esophagus, and trachea. This bullet also pierced the large vein coming from the lower part of the body into the heart at the level of the diaphragm, went through the liver, and bisected the lower portion of the right kidney, almost severing the organ. The bullet finally lodged in the upper hipbone.

The second fatal bullet entered Haynie's body between the ribs on the left side of the chest, passed through the upper lobe of the left lung, penetrated the left part of the pericardium, the sac surrounding the heart, then entered the right ventricle of the heart. It next cut through the dome of the liver and lodged at the lower point of the rib cage on the right side.

The third bullet—the one not present—entered just below the left ear, fractured the angle of the left mandible, passed through the base of the tongue, and exited the right side, fracturing the jaw.

Dr. Simpkins concluded that of the two contact shots, the one to his collarbone area was fired from behind Haynie, from above the level of his shoulder. In the other instance, the gun had been held to his head just below the ear, execution-style.

***

From his hospital bed, Bill Powell continued telling Capitol employees and friends who came to his room the same account he'd given at the dealership, although the stop sign at Spence Lane was no longer mentioned. Instead, he now said he had slowed down behind a bread truck that was making a left turn when the assailant jumped into the car.

Powell's story remained the same throughout the early afternoon.

"I thought he had shot me in the stomach," insisted Powell, whose wound was in the fleshy part of his left calf. He described how he had swung at the gunman. Powell showed those present the red mark on his right arm.

Powell then explained that he made the U-turn just past Spence Lane and headed back to Capitol Chevrolet, driving 80 miles an hour while reaching across the front seat in an effort to hold Mr. Gourley upright. "I wasn't able to hold him. He just slumped to the floorboard."

***

Billie Dee Boyer was still at the reception desk when she learned someone had made the decision to close the dealership at 2:30 p.m. Erline Cockerham, private secretary to Haynie and Bill Powell, stopped by Boyer's desk at 2:00 p.m. Boyer told Cockerham she did not have a ride home. Boyer's husband was out of town for the day and couldn't be reached. He was due to pick her up at four-thirty.

"I'll take you home," said Cockerham. "But let's go out to see Mr. Powell and Mrs. Gourley first. Is that all right?"

"Of course," Boyer replied.

When the two women arrived at the hospital parking lot, Boyer watched as Cockerham reached into the back seat of her car and grabbed Powell's gray suit jacket.

When they got out of the car, Cockerham held up the coat, shook it, and then brushed it off with her hands.

"I thought I would bring him his coat. He might need it." She threw the jacket over her arm, and the two women went into the hospital, stopping at the receptionist area to ask for directions.

When they reached Powell's room, Cockerham told him she had brought his coat and gave it to his wife Helen, who was standing beside his bed.

When they asked Powell how he was doing, he said he had a sore arm where the Black man had hit him. Once again, Powell told his story. He quoted Haynie as having said, "James, you can have everything I've got," when the man demanded money.

What Billie Dee Boyer remembered most about Powell's story was that he kept repeating, "I will never forget the killer's eyes."

After about ten or fifteen minutes, Boyer and Cockerham left the hospital to visit Josephine Gourley at her home.

***

Tennessee Bureau of Investigation agent William E. Coleman, a twenty-one-year veteran of the TBI, started with the agency when it was first created. Coleman was in the vicinity of Elm Hill Pike when news of the shooting came over the state police radio. He first went to Capitol Chevrolet where he met Detective Bill Larkin of the Metro Homicide Division who gave him an account of Bill Powell's story. Coleman was immediately struck by the fact that the car had not been preserved as it should have been. Any evidence it might have contained had now been contaminated.

Coleman peered through the back door window of the car and noticed that the black carpets on the back floorboard appeared to be clean. He was looking specifically for any kind of dusty substance on the floor mats from the repaving project underway at the intersection at Spence Lane and Elm Hill Pike where the killer had allegedly jumped into the car. There should have been at least flecks of gray dust left by the man's shoes, but he saw nothing.

With Detective Larkin, Coleman carefully inspected the car and found a bullet hole in the back of the front passenger seat, to the right of center, about ten inches down from the top of the seat.

This struck Coleman as strange. Haynie's wounds, he understood from Larkin, were on the left side of his neck, shoulder, and chest. Had the gunman also shot into the back of the seat? And why?

After leaving Capitol Chevrolet, Coleman drove to Elm Hill Pike and Spence Lane.

At the intersection, Coleman stopped, got out of his truck and stepped out onto the road where Powell said the man entered the car. Oily crushed rock and dust from the paving project readily stuck to the bottom of his shoes. When he climbed back into his truck, the grimy dust adhered to the floor mat. Yet, he was sure there had been no signs of any kind of construction debris on Haynie's back floor mats. They had appeared perfectly clean.

At about 5:30 that afternoon, Agent Coleman drove to Vanderbilt Hospital to interview Powell. His wife Helen was present in the room along with Charlie Hunter, chief investigator for the district attorney's office.

Coleman listened as Powell described how he had been forced to slow down because he was behind a truck that was turning left onto Spence Lane from Elm Hill Pike. Powell said nothing about a stop sign.

Powell had also changed another detail. He told Coleman that Mr. Gourley reached into his left rear pants pocket for his wallet, not his coat pocket as he had claimed earlier at Capitol Chevrolet and afterwards in the emergency room at the hospital. As Mr. Gourley made a move to retrieve his wallet, the man fired two shots, Powell said. He told Coleman that after the second shot was fired, he reached for Mr. Gourley and received a lick on the arm from the assailant. Powell said he made an abrupt U-turn in the middle of the road, just past the intersection, at which time the gunman opened the door and leapt out while the car was still turning. Powell said he didn't believe the Negro even fell.

Coleman, like the policemen who had been at the hospital earlier in the afternoon, wondered how the man had managed to jump out without falling, while at the same time closing the heavy car door in the middle of a sharp turn.

When Coleman asked about the right passenger-side window being broken out, Powell said Mr. Gourley's head "might have hit the glass when I made the U-turn." Coleman thought to himself, "Wouldn't Powell have heard the glass shattering, and wouldn't the glass have been in the middle of the road?"

Powell once again said he drove back to Capitol Chevrolet at a high rate of speed, maybe 80 miles per hour, while holding Mr. Gourley up.

Elm Hill Pike was a heavily traveled, two-lane road that crossed over railroad tracks. Coleman wondered if Powell had tried to cross double yellow lines and pass any cars in his way. It seemed unlikely that the road would have been completely empty at that hour. Even without traffic, the 80-mile-an-hour speed did not sound plausible.

Coleman asked Powell if he owned a gun. He said that he did not. Helen Powell corrected him, reminding him that he had a shotgun for hunting.

"But I don't own a pistol," Powell quickly volunteered.

Coleman then asked Powell why he and Mr. Gourley were out for a drive, and Powell answered that they were taking a ride to discuss Powell's leaving the company. Powell admitted to Coleman that he and Haynie were dissolving their partnership, that it would come out anyway, but that there was no ill will at all between the two men.

Coleman wanted to know exactly what was said as they were riding down Elm Hill Pike toward Spence Lane. Powell answered that they were just riding along, talking about how the area had built up. Powell told how Mr. Gourley pointed to the H.D. Lee Company and said he didn't even know that building was there.

Coleman was confused. Powell had just told him that he had made the U-turn shortly after passing Spence Lane, close to the Baltz Brothers Packing Company which was on the left side of Elm Hill Pike. The H.D. Lee Company was a good half mile past Spence Lane on the right at Massman Drive. Why would Haynie Gourley be pointing to a building if it wasn't even in sight?

Something didn't add up, but Coleman kept quiet and made a mental note.

As he continued to talk, Powell said the assailant was wearing a hat pulled down over his eyes and then, almost in the same breath, said that what he remembered most about him were his eyes, that he had peculiar-looking eyes. Powell told Coleman he didn't think he could identify the man, but that he couldn't forget those eyes.

Powell also said he had not even seen a gun, that he had only heard two shots, and that he thought the second shot had hit him because he

Metro Homicide Detectives Bill Larkin, seated, and Sherman Nickens were assigned to head up the Gourley murder case. *Nashville Public Library, Special Collections, Banner Newspaper Collection*

felt an immediate sharp, burning pain in his stomach.

As Powell talked, Coleman tried to picture how the gunman managed to shoot between Powell's legs. Powell was a hefty man. His legs would have taken up the space under the steering wheel. How had the killer made that shot to the inside of his left calf?

Coleman could not make sense of it.

***

By mid-afternoon, Detectives Sherman Nickens and Bill Larkin were officially put in charge of the case. Nickens, in his early thirties, was known for his street smarts and already had a reputation of cozying up to government officials while at the same time schmoozing with the unsavory characters he investigated. He had worked homicide for three years. Nickens was trim, had a receding hairline, and was generally considered to be a nice-looking man. When not in a police uniform directing traffic, he dressed in a coat and tie. By contrast, Larkin was short, plump, and taciturn, with a slack jaw, especially noticeable when next to the smooth-talking Nickens. He usually dressed in a white shirt, open at the collar, and dark, ill-fitting trousers, giving him an unkempt look.

Later that afternoon, Nickens returned to Vanderbilt Hospital. When he walked in and saw Bill Powell, he had a fit. Powell had been completely cleaned up, "like a newborn baby." There had been no plastic put on his hands. In fact, a nurse technician told Nickens the first thing Powell did on arrival was wash his hands. There was now no need for a paraffin test to determine if Powell had recently fired a gun. Any trace elements would have already been washed away.

***

News of the murder of Haynie Gourley and the wounding of Bill Powell spread quickly and had everyone in the city talking. The story dominated the six o'clock television newscasts. A killer was on the loose. Given the high-profile victims, both prominent in the business community and popular residents of Belle Meade, police knew they would face intense pressure to find the killer quickly. An all-points bulletin was issued for a Black man, about six feet tall, wearing dark clothing and possibly an old hat. He was to be considered armed and dangerous.

Several hours after the slaying, a man fitting the murderer's description was spotted in a neighborhood near downtown. Acting on a tip, the police picked up twenty-seven-year-old Lorenza Perry, a custodian at Hickman Elementary School. Perry was arrested and taken to the Metro jail where he was already facing charges of assault and battery filed earlier that day by his wife. The police revealed no details and kept Perry isolated from other inmates.

Metro detective Ernest Castleman returned to Vanderbilt Hospital that evening, this time to show Powell several photographs of possible suspects fitting the description he had given police. Powell picked Lorenza Perry out of the group, saying that he bore a resemblance to the gunman more than the others. He asked to see him in person.

Ballistic tests on a slug found in Haynie's body indicated that he had been killed by a .38-caliber pistol. Perry did indeed own a gun—a .38 caliber stack-barrel Derringer. Perry led police to his apartment and turned over his weapon. At least five bullets had been fired from the gun that killed Haynie Gourley and wounded Bill Powell. Perry's Derringer, however, was capable of holding only two bullets at a time. Moreover, Perry claimed he had been at work around the time of the murder. Several students confirmed his alibi, saying they had seen Perry at the school around 10:45 a.m. In addition, there was no evidence that Perry had been on Elm Hill Pike at any time that day. To everyone's great disappointment, Perry was released. Police vowed they would not rest until the killer was caught.

This was little comfort to a city on edge.

***

Billy and his mother arrived back at the Gourley home around noon. Henrietta Green was waiting for them. She already knew. Billy folded the tiny woman in his arms. He could feel her sobbing.

Word of Haynie Gourley's murder spread like wildfire throughout the city. Cars were already parked up and down Belle Meade Boulevard. The scene inside the house was chaotic. People began lining up to get in the front door.

James Cook, Haynie's best friend, was waiting in the living room, along with several of Josephine and Haynie's closest friends.

Traffic only increased with the exhaustive television coverage and the *Nashville Banner*'s two Extra editions. By late afternoon, the street was blocked. The Belle Meade police had to re-route traffic for residents to get through. Billy and JoAnn's friends came, but so did strangers, many of them appearing at the back door, each with a story of how Haynie Gourley had helped them in some way.

Henrietta Green went to the kitchen to receive the food that began arriving by mid-afternoon. By six o'clock, casseroles covered with tin foil, boxes of cookies, brownies, pies, cakes, country ham, deviled eggs, potato salad, pimento cheese sandwiches, fried chicken, and a dish of banana pudding took up every available space on the counters, all typical of the food people in the South brought when someone died.

Red wooden crates of Coca-Cola were stacked in the corner of the breakfast room. Gallon jugs of sweet tea and lemonade sat in a cooler filled with ice. One of the cooks from a nearby neighbor came in with two pans of homemade rolls and stayed to help Henrietta set the food out on the dining room table.

Billy stood at the back door, where strangers walked up and knocked hesitantly. He heard over and over the same words: "You don't know me, but Mr. Gourley was so kind-hearted, and he helped me through a bad time. Never asked me to pay him back." One woman held a little girl in her arms and handed Billy a bag of Hershey's kisses, saying Mr. Gourley had not charged her when her transmission went out.

That night after everyone left, Billy went to his room and paced the floor. His mind was muddled by shock and grief and disbelief, still thinking that somehow this was all a bad dream and that he would wake up, and it wouldn't be true, that nothing would have changed.

His father was his best friend, someone he thought would be there long into the future. Haynie had been in such good health, enjoying life, his family, and friends. He was so proud of the new building, but he'd only had a few short weeks to revel in his accomplishment.

Billy began to go over the events of the day. He had more questions than answers. Why did Bill Powell drive back to Capitol Chevrolet instead of heading straight to nearby General Hospital, wasting precious time that might have saved his father's life?

Haynie had told Billy that Bill Powell wanted to go for a ride and talk. Why do that? They could have met anywhere in the building and not be overheard. Bill Powell had an office; Haynie had an office with an eight-foot-long directors' table. Their offices were both private; there were conference rooms and meeting rooms. There was no need to leave the dealership.

And it didn't make sense that a robber would shoot an old man with white hair, but barely wound a six-foot-four, 240-pound man who was only forty years old. Why would anyone pull off a brazen armed robbery in broad daylight and not take the money? With all the racial tensions in the city, how would a Black man have the audacity to get into a car with two white men, no matter what their size? That just didn't happen, wouldn't happen.

Another thing ate at Billy. Capitol's new-car sales manager Jimmy Allen had been a protégé of Haynie's and a longtime close friend of the family. Years before, Allen had been in a terrible accident, his car hit by a train. Haynie got him to the best doctors and literally saved his life. This raised a real question mark. Why didn't Jimmy come straight to the house to see his mother? He was the very one Billy thought would be the first in the door. Did he stay away because he knew something, or did he not want to alienate Powell and lose his job?

Billy picked up the brown paper envelope he'd been given at the hospital. He opened it and poured the contents on top of his dresser.

He was hit by a fresh wave of grief when he caught a familiar whiff of his father's Juicy Fruit gum.

He picked up both cufflinks. The clasp of one was broken off. He tugged at the other one, twisting it hard. It stayed intact. This made no sense. If his father had been shot dead immediately, how did the cuff link get broken?

When he finally crawled into bed, he was drained and exhausted, but his mind was racing. He felt a mixture of anger and disbelief and overwhelming, gut-wrenching sorrow. Someone like Haynie, so kind to everybody, did not deserve to die the way he did.

Billy kept going over the facts. He tried to make sense of Powell's story. Nothing added up.

Then it hit him. Hit like a brick. It all seemed so obvious.

The key was the timing. Bill Powell was about to lose his job and his 25% interest in Capitol Chevrolet. He would have to uproot his family to find another dealership where he could make the kind of money Capitol was paying him. He had to act fast. He might have had only days left before he had to sell his stock back and get out of the business for good.

Billy hoped it had been quick, that Haynie never knew what hit him. He would find out later that was not what happened.

***

Saturday, the twenty-fifth of May, the day after the murder, was a cloudy, sultry day, the air thick with humidity. Billy did not discuss his suspicions with anyone. He was only concentrating on the preparations for the funeral. The family had to pick hymns, call pallbearers.

That morning, Josephine and her two children rode out to Mt. Olivet Cemetery where she purchased six burial plots. Dating from 1856, Mt. Olivet was Nashville's most prestigious cemetery and the resting place for many famous Tennesseans—United States senators, Tennessee governors, Nashville mayors, founders of universities, Union and Confederate generals, a Supreme Court justice, John Overton, one of the founders of Memphis, Thomas Ryman who built the Ryman Auditorium, Tennessee whiskey distributor George Dickel, various titans of business, and several owners of 19th century plantations.

Ironically, the tranquil place on a gentle knoll where Haynie Gourley would be buried was on Lebanon Pike between Fesslers Lane and Spence Lane, only a three-minute ride from Elm Hill Pike where Haynie had met a violent end.

Belle Meade Boulevard remained clogged all day Saturday as friends came to reminisce about Haynie and offer their condolences. They gathered in the living room talking in low murmurs, hugging Josephine and JoAnn as they came and left.

Throughout the house, there was the bustle that follows a sudden death. The doorbell rang constantly, with telegrams pouring in from all over the country. Every few minutes, a florist arrived with flowers. Wreaths and large arrangements on stands lined the walls of the main rooms. Baskets of potted green houseplants filled the back terrace. All through the house, the subtle scent of eucalyptus had been replaced by the cloying perfume of carnations and lilies. There was a phone call every minute for Josephine.

Both newspapers, the morning *The Tennessean* and the afternoon *Nashville Banner*, carried expressions of shock and grief over the murder. The comments came from business associates, city and state officials, and friends who described Haynie as an "outstanding businessman and citizen" and a "fine gentleman."

"The tragic death of Haynie Gourley is not only a personal loss to me but also to the economic life of Nashville and Tennessee," Gov. Buford Ellington was quoted in *The Tennessean* as saying. "Mr. Gourley was an outstanding citizen, a fine gentleman, and I trust the party responsible for his death will be apprehended and brought to justice."

Nashville mayor Beverly Briley described Haynie as one of Nashville's outstanding businessmen "who has contributed a lot to the atmosphere of the community and will be missed by his many friends, associates, and employees."

"He was the kind of businessman who commanded the respect and admiration of the business community," said Edward J. Shea, executive vice president of the Nashville Area Chamber of Commerce. "Equally admired was his interest in and his service to the community—his loss will be keenly felt by his legion of friends and the community."

Harry Sadler, president of Harry Sadler Chevrolet Co., stated:

"The depth of shock and sorrow which the death of Mr. Haynie Gourley has brought to me and others who knew him so well cannot be measured in words. To the sadness which we feel that a life so full of brilliance, courage, strength, and promise has been ended at the height of his career, must be added the deep and lasting regret of our community over the tragic manner its end came."

***

Josephine Gourley did not want to prolong the ordeal of the funeral and burial.

Haynie's service was held at Vine Street Christian Church at two o'clock Sunday afternoon, May 26, just over forty-eight hours after he was slain. The current pastor, Dr. Wayne Bell, and Dr. Roger Nooe, the longtime former pastor of the church, both of whom knew Haynie well, officiated.

The church was packed. The list of twenty-six honorary and sixteen active pall bearers read like a Who's Who of Nashville: bank presidents, the governor of Tennessee, the owner of the *Nashville Banner*, prominent physicians, plus General Motors executives from Detroit. One of the two men who helped Haynie acquire his own dealership, James K. Dobbs of Memphis, now head of several nationally known businesses including the Dobbs House, served along with James Reed Jr. and James Reed III from rival Jim Reed Chevrolet.

Also included was Morse Kochtitzsky, the doctor who, two days before, had driven Haynie's shocked and devastated wife and son away from the hospital where Haynie Gourley, to the great disbelief of all who knew him, had been declared dead on arrival.

For days after the funeral, friends and well-wishers continued to come to the Gourley home. Sympathy cards and more telegrams poured in from all parts. Billy was still numb with grief. All the hours seemed to run together. Billy's aunt from Texas stayed on to be with his mother. Josephine was inconsolable and mostly remained in bed, saying over and over, "I've lost the love of my life." Lawyers and insurance men came and went, dealing with the necessary mechanics of a death in the family.

"It just seems like something like this could never happen to us," Billy confided to a friend. "I wish I would wake up and things would just continue like they've always been."

The Gourleys' housekeeper Henrietta Green took Haynie's death as hard as anyone. She kept up a good front as people crowded into the house, but, in Billy's words, "She was just crushed." Her health began to decline soon after Haynie's death. She had no particular illness but passed away a year later. Billy always thought she died of a broken heart.

CHAPTER [13]

Jerry McFarland and Bobby Timms from Lebanon, Tennessee, search Mill Creek for a weapon, May 30, 1968. © *The Tennessean – USA TODAY NETWORK*

On Elm Hill Pike, an intensive manhunt was underway. Metro police and homicide detectives told reporters they hoped to discover that the assailant had dropped his weapon as he ran. But it was as if the man had vanished into thin air. There was no sign of the battered hat Bill Powell said he wore. There were no witnesses who saw a man getting into the car at Spence Lane. No one had seen the U-turn or the gunman opening the door, shutting it, and then keeping his balance to run away.

On Sunday, May 26, as the funeral cortege made its way to the cemetery three miles away, police were using mine detectors borrowed from the U.S. Army at Fort Campbell, Kentucky, to search the area around Spence Lane. But nothing was found in the overgrown weeds and brush along the edges of Elm Hill Pike.

Homicide Detective Sherman Nickens said he'd never seen a case with no clues whatsoever. The more he contemplated Powell's story, the more skeptical he became. He was becoming convinced that the police were looking in the wrong place for the killer.

On Monday, Asst. Metro Police Chief Donald Barton reported that nothing much had changed since the start of the investigation on Friday after the shooting. He also said that at this time, no one had been cleared. Some readers, particularly residents of Belle Meade, saw his statement in the newspaper and wondered if it had a deeper meaning.

On the Tuesday following the murder, James Cook, one of Haynie's best friends, was having lunch with his son, Jimbo, Billy Gourley's "little brother" in the SAE fraternity at Vanderbilt. The two families had been close for years. Upon reading that Bill Powell would never forget the eyes of the assailant, James Cook, who owned a printing company and had long been one of Haynie's golfing buddies, told his son, "Yes, I bet Bill Powell will never forget those eyes. But they weren't some stranger's eyes; they were Haynie's."

***

On the Monday after the murder on Friday, the front seat covers of Haynie's car, along with articles of clothing worn by the two men, were hand carried by Metro police detective Ernest Castleman to the FBI's Washington, D.C. laboratory. Castleman traveled by plane and returned on Tuesday evening. Oddly, no seat covers or floor mats were taken from the back seat where the alleged assailant might have left evidence.

"I guess it will be two or three days before we find out anything," Castleman told reporters, referring to the FBI response. "They are only allowed to release a report in writing."

Meanwhile, police investigators received a ballistics report from the TBI lab, which determined that the bullets that killed Haynie had been fired from a slightly used weapon, most likely a .38 caliber Smith & Wesson.

The slugs were identified by TBI ballistics expert Robert Goodwin as being 200-grain, lead, blunt-nosed bullets with a copper coating, the type of ammunition usually only available to police or law enforcement officers. Goodwin found the rifling marks on the bullets to be exceptionally clear. If the gun could be found, it would be an easy match.

A possible break in the case came on May 28, four days after the murder. Metro detectives questioned two white men who wished to remain anonymous. The men claimed they had seen a late-model automobile stopped at the intersection of Spence Lane and Elm Hill Pike at about the same time as the murder.

One of the unnamed witnesses said he saw a man leaving the car. The lead was followed up, but apparently the alleged sighting never happened.

The detectives were right back where they started.

***

Recovering at Vanderbilt Hospital, Bill Powell now assumed the duties of chief executive at Capitol Chevrolet. On Tuesday, May 28, four days after the shooting, he issued a statement saying that the dealership was open for business and would "continue operating just as it had in the past."

Powell let it be known that he was cooperating with police and offered to lead officials on a ride to point out the route he and Mr. Gourley had taken. He readily answered all questions, but he was now beginning to make even more changes to his original account of the slaying. The variations in Powell's story of a Black man jumping into the back seat as the car slowed at Spence Lane where it crossed Elm Hill Pike seemed to be shifting to fit what the police uncovered or by what was printed in the newspapers.

Powell was consistent, however, in saying the assailant shot Mr. Gourley the moment he made a move, but there was still no explanation given as to how Haynie's wallet wound up in the back seat.

On Wednesday, May 29, Bill Powell kept his promise to retrace the death route. A three-car caravan was organized which included Powell's attorney Cecil Branstetter, his physician, Dr. Douglas Riddell, District Attorney Thomas Shriver, and Detectives Sherman Nickens and Bill Larkin. Powell, clad in pajamas and a yellow robe, was brought out of the hospital in a wheelchair around 5:00 p.m. Branstetter drove the first car, and Powell sat in the passenger seat.

Before the ride commenced, Cecil Branstetter had Detective Sherman Nickens frisked to make sure he was not wearing a wire. Nickens was taken aback. He said nothing but resented Branstetter's taking this action.

Branstetter drove, and Detective Bill Larkin rode in the back seat with Nickens who took notes as Bill Powell carried on a running commentary. Nickens noticed that Powell talked continuously and quite breathlessly as they covered the route. Nickens thought Powell seemed a bit too eager.

Powell continued his uninterrupted narration as Branstetter drove further down the road. Powell pointed out where the man jumped into the car at the intersection of Spence Lane and Elm Hill Pike and where the shooting took place just beyond. Powell then told his fellow passengers how he drove further on down Elm Hill Pike than he had first said to make a U-turn.

Both in his original description of where Powell said he made the U-turn and in the drawing he made for Ernest Castleman in the emergency room on the day of the murder, Powell had not mentioned Massman Drive. During this retracing, however, he said he was no longer sure where he made the U-turn, that perhaps it was further down toward Massman Drive than he first thought. This new revelation contradicted Powell's original account of how long the gunman was in the car since Massman Drive was over a half-mile past Spence Lane.

The trip produced no new clues. Powell stuck to the latest version of his story, that the killer jumped into the car as it slowly rolled along behind a truck making a left turn at the intersection of Spence Lane and Elm Hill Pike. He also kept repeating over and over, "I'll never forget his eyes."

Detective Nickens, however, was acutely aware of the changes from Powell's original story. He did not make notes on the trip about his own thoughts, but Powell's observations only added to his suspicions.

The police were back at the scene every day for a week, searching for clues. On Thursday, May 30, after the ride with Powell, they concentrated on an area further down Elm Hill Pike.

Nickens and Larkin led a team of police officers who spent three hours meticulously searching a fifty-foot-wide swath on either side of Mill Creek. The stream ran under a bridge on Elm Hill Pike near the spot where Bill Powell was now saying the assailant had disappeared. Using metal detectors and wooden probes, they searched the dense weeds and scrubby growth along the creek banks and in the creek itself.

The last day of the search was on Friday. The nearly three-hour hunt turned up nothing but mosquito bites, and the police reluctantly admitted there were no new developments in the case.

To reporters from the newspapers, Nickens and Larkin expressed hope that the killer had thrown away the gun he used, but Nickens emphasized it was only a vague hope. Nickens reiterated that he had never seen a case with absolutely no clues. The investigation appeared to be going nowhere.

***

Day after day, the front pages of both newspapers continued to be dominated by the Gourley murder. The few known facts were re-hashed, but there were no new leads on a suspect and no new information. However, there was no let-up in the speculation about what happened, especially among Belle Meade residents.

On May 31, a week after Haynie's murder, Capitol Chevrolet placed an ad in *The Tennessean* and the *Nashville Banner* offering a $5,000 reward to "anyone giving information leading to the arrest and conviction of the murderer of our president, Mr. W. Haynie Gourley." The Nashville Automobile Dealers Association had already announced a $5,000 reward.

The City of Belle Meade added $2,000, bringing the total to $12,000 for the capture leading to conviction of the killer of Belle Meade resident Haynie Gourley.

After an eight-day stay, Bill Powell was released from the hospital. On his way home, he and his wife Helen stopped by to see Josephine and to express their sympathy. The meeting lasted only a few minutes. Josephine Gourley was there with her sister from Texas, but she was in bed and too distraught to talk.

Billy returned to work before Bill Powell had recuperated from his flesh wound. When Powell came back two weeks after the murder, he did not talk to Billy about his father or offer any explanation or description of what happened on May 24. There was no further mention of training Billy for the eventual takeover of Capitol Chevrolet. Billy was unaware of the dealings Powell was making with the Chevrolet Motor Company, assuring that Billy's family would have no further claim on the business his father had started thirty-six years before.

Haynie's dream for his son appeared to have died along with him.

CHAPTER [14]

On June 5, thirteen days after Haynie's death, the doorbell rang at the Gourley home. JoAnn Bainbridge was there with her mother. Henrietta Green answered the door.

Four somber-looking men in suits stood under the front portico. The spokesman, Chevrolet zone manager Thomas Jackson from Louisville, asked to see Josephine. In the back stood Bill Powell. Henrietta led the men into the living room and asked them to wait while she let Mrs. Gourley know they were here. Henrietta noticed that the tall man had stepped into the den off the main hall. The other three took a seat in the living room. When Josephine came out, followed by JoAnn, the men stood up. Josephine recognized William Clark from Cincinnati and Capitol Chevrolet accountant John Glenn. She knew why they had come.

Upon Haynie's death, his portion of the shares in Capitol Chevrolet had passed through his will to Josephine, making her the majority owner of the corporation with 75% of Capitol Chevrolet's stock.

"Josephine, I can't tell you how heartbroken I am over Haynie. He was a great friend of mine," Clark, sitting forward on the edge of an easy chair, began, adding that they had come to help her with the transition.

"Bill, I am too heartbroken to talk about business," Josephine said.

Undeterred, Clark read her Paragraph Three from the 1966 contract Haynie had signed, explaining that Powell was named co-franchisee, which meant he was to take over the business in case of Haynie's death.

"It's customary when a dealer dies, his widow sells," said Clark.

"Even in the case of murder?" Josephine asked.

"I don't know," Clark said. "I've never had these dealings."

Jackson spoke up, telling of an experience he had with a murder, when a dealer was killed by a taxicab driver.

Thomas Jackson had been an overnight guest in her home countless times and a good friend for decades. Josephine had also known William Clark for years. Now they sat before her, with a look of pity, but determination.

"If you were my sister, I would advise you to sell," Clark said.

John Glenn remained silent. He was holding a manilla folder. He did not mention that he had already drawn up a new contract between Bill Powell and the General Motors Corporation and that, for all practical purposes, Josephine and her family were already out of Capitol Chevrolet.

"I am in no shape to make any decisions," she told the men.

Clark and Jackson insisted she had no choice, but she told them again that she was too heartbroken to make a move.

"The love of my life is gone," she said, tears welling in her eyes. "I will not do it."

With that, the men rose to leave, saying to let them know when she was ready to sell, advising again that she should get this over with. She did not respond.

Henrietta saw the men to the door. Bill Powell came out of the den and joined them. He had stayed out of sight the entire time.

***

Nashville could not get enough of the Gourley case. With every day that passed, an article about the murder appeared on the front page of both daily newspapers, even when there was nothing new to report.

But three weeks after Haynie's death, the city awoke to news of a horrific crime that sparked fear throughout the neighborhoods on the south side of town and knocked the Gourley story off the front pages.

Around 2:30 a.m., on Saturday, June 15, Barbara Bolte, twenty-three years old and seven months pregnant, was asleep on the living room sofa of her home at 4943 Edmondson Pike, about eleven miles from the alleged scene of the Gourley slaying. She was awakened by a noise and opened her eyes to see a tall, thin Black man standing over her, holding a butcher knife.

The man wore rubber gloves, and without saying a word, began stabbing her in the upper chest and throat. She put up a violent struggle and instinctively threw her arms up in an attempt to ward off the blows, badly slicing her hands. Then, he threw her to the floor and brutally raped her. Loss of blood and the sheer ferocity of the assault caused her to lose consciousness. She had not heard the man grab her eighteen-month-old daughter Dera from her crib and, holding her by her feet, slam her against the wall, cracking her head open and inflicting grave injury

She was also unaware that her husband, John Bolte, twenty-seven, a shop apprentice, lay dead in a pool of blood on their bed at the back of the house. He had been nearly decapitated by a blow from a double-bladed woodsman's ax.

When Barbara Bolte regained consciousness seven hours later, she managed to crawl to the kitchen and call police. Several of the same detectives who were searching for leads in Haynie's murder responded to the call. When they arrived, they found John Bolte in the couple's bedroom. An ax lay beside the bed, and bloody footprints led from the bedroom into the living room. The handle of a knife was found on the bloodstained couch, and a broken blade lay on the floor. The house had been ransacked.

Homicide investigator Ernest Castleman interviewed neighbors, but no one had heard the attack or seen anyone enter the house. Barbara Bolte described the assailant as being about six feet tall, weighing between 130 and 150 pounds, wearing dark trousers, a gold pull-over V-neck shirt, and gray socks. The investigator quoted Mrs. Bolte as saying the intruder was a Black man with a thin moustache. He was not wearing shoes when he attacked her.

Immediately upon reading the news of the Bolte slaying, the public feared that Haynie Gourley's killer was still on the loose, now terrorizing white people in the middle of the night. Residents locked their doors. The entire city was on edge.

The Nashville newspapers wasted no time in suggesting a possible connection of the Bolte murder to Haynie Gourley's death. Every article about the Bolte case that appeared in *The Tennessean* also contained references to the Gourley murder. Despite the grisly slaying of John Bolte, it was Haynie Gourley's murder that was still foremost on people's minds.

On June 29, a letter to the editor of *The Tennessean* complained that more extensive coverage had been given to the murder of Haynie Gourley because of his wealth and position in Belle Meade society, while the Boltes were people of modest means and received much less attention. The writer accused Governor Buford Ellington of offering a reward for Haynie's slaying, but not for the murder of John Bolte.

In truth, Gov. Ellington had nothing to do with the rewards. They had been put up by Capitol Chevrolet, the Automobile Dealers Association, and the City of Belle Meade.

Still, the contrast in the interest in the murders was obvious. *The Tennessean* continued to mention the Gourley case in every single article it printed about the monstrous attack on the Bolte family.

***

There was huge buzz when artists' renderings of the suspects in the Gourley and Bolte murders appeared side by side in the newspaper and on television. The sketch made at Powell's direction showed a man with a wide face and light-colored eyes who appeared to be older than Mrs. Bolte's attacker.

Powell said he thought the two men resembled one another, even though Mrs. Bolte was sure the man who raped and stabbed her had a thin mustache and was wearing a hearing aid in one ear.

Anna Faye Kraft, an employee of the Tennessee Department of Employment Security located in a building on James Robertson Parkway downtown, picked up a newspaper and looked at the drawing of the assailant in the Bolte case. She recognized the man immediately and phoned police. James Thomas Jefferson had made frequent visits to her office, seeking employment. After the highly publicized sketch was disseminated over television and in the newspapers, Jefferson's name was also given to the police by two hearing aid centers.

Police searched for Jefferson for a week with no luck. On Monday, July 1, Jefferson showed up at the employment office. Keeping her cool, Anna Faye Kraft picked up the phone and called the police to ask if they were still looking for the man from the newspaper, saying that he was on the premises.

Metro Police Lieutenant Bobby Hill and two other officers arrested Jefferson without incident outside the Tennessee Department of Employment Security building. Jefferson, wearing a hearing aid, had in his possession eleven Buffalo nickels "in good condition," part of a coin collection missing from the Bolte house. He claimed he got the nickels at a Charlotte Avenue drive-in market while playing pinball.

After Jefferson was taken into custody, his shoes were removed and his feet compared with casts taken at the crime scene.

"They were similar," Captain Mickey McDaniel of the Metro police department said.

The next day, the twenty-seven-year-old father of three, who already had a prior record for burglary and for passing bad checks, sought bond before Judge Allen Cornelius. Jefferson, of 337 21st Ave., N., was charged with the murder of John Robert Bolte, two counts of assault with the intent to commit murder, and the rape of Barbara Bolte.

Jefferson denied being the attacker and said he was with his girlfriend the night the murder occurred. He claimed he went to her home on Friday, June 14, and did not leave there until about 9:00 a.m. on Saturday, after the Bolte murder was discovered. He told the court he had never been to the Bolte residence and did not know the Bolte family.

At police headquarters, Barbara Bolte picked Jefferson from a lineup as the man who raped and stabbed her and left her to die.

Judge Cornelius announced that enough evidence had been presented to "justify presumption of guilt and to justify this court in denying him his bond," and Jefferson was bound over to the grand jury.

Powell insisted that he should be allowed to see the Bolte killer in a line-up. He said he was "fairly certain" this was the same man who entered the car and wounded him and killed Haynie Gourley.

Jefferson was scheduled to appear in a lineup in front of Powell, who was now referred to in the newspapers as president of Capitol Chevrolet Company. Police hustled to have the lineup ready on the day of Jefferson's arrest, but the event was postponed because Jefferson's lawyer, Avon Williams, could not be present.

Another viewing was set up, but again, Williams was not available, and the lineup was put off a second time.

Finally, Richard Speight, an assistant in the district attorney's office, announced that Jefferson was only considered a suspect in the Gourley slaying because he bore a resemblance to a sole eyewitness's description.

Speight said there was also the consideration that Jefferson's photograph had been all over the newspapers and television, which would affect the integrity of a lineup. Speight announced there was no evidence to show "any connection whatsoever" to link Jefferson to the Gourley slaying and that there were no further plans for a lineup.

"Certainly, if we have any suspect—on a traffic violation or otherwise—who bears a resemblance to the description Mr. Powell gave," Speight told reporters, "we want Mr. Powell to look at him. But we have no present plans for a lineup."

***

Every day when Billy Gourley came to work, he would look at his father's empty office, and a lump would form in his throat. He remembered how safe and happy he had felt, having his father always there, proud to see him greeting friends and putting a hand on their shoulders. Haynie knew every one of his employees and treated them the same, asking about their families. It made no difference whether they were mechanics or the top salesmen of new cars, he kept up with all of them.

There was a deep void in Billy's world. The path had been bumpy when Bill Powell was in charge of his training, but at least he knew where he would end up. Now, nothing was clear. He kept coming to work, hoping to gain experience toward obtaining another dealership at some point. He couldn't believe that all Haynie's plans he'd worked toward all his life were gone in a matter of moments. His father's lifelong dream was for Billy to run the dealership and keep it in the family name. He could now only watch as Bill Powell yukked it up with customers. Even Sherman Nickens, the homicide detective in charge of finding his father's killer, would come into the showroom, and the two would appear to be joking around. Billy was stung by these encounters. He felt at sea, not knowing quite what to do in what seemed more and more like a hostile work environment where his presence did not count.

Billy was now living in an apartment in the Green Hills section of Nashville. Alone in his room at night, he would obsess about the gun. That was the key to solving the case. Where was it? If the killer had been some random crook, would he have tossed his gun, to be found and connect him to the crime? But wouldn't it be more dangerous to keep the weapon where he lived? If the police were to discover it, and it matched the bullets, there would be no doubt of his guilt.

What bothered him most was sales manager Jimmy Allen. Billy couldn't let go of the idea that he must know something. Allen used to pal around with Billy all the time. Before the murder, he had even let him have a party at his house. Now, he ignored Billy. They never talked, even about selling cars. Billy still could only think of two reasons for his coldness: that he didn't want to alienate Powell and jeopardize his job, or that Jimmy Allen knew who the killer was.

***

One morning in mid-July, not even two months after his father's death, Billy was at his desk in his cubicle which opened onto the new-car sales floor near the corner of the showroom. He glanced to his left to see the huge glass doors slide open and an employee back a shiny black 1968 Caprice onto the showroom floor. Billy gasped. The scene seemed to unfold in slow motion.

The employee, a young man Billy did not recognize, kept backing in until he came to a stop in front of Billy's cubicle. He maneuvered the car a little so it would point slightly toward the front of the showroom. Billy was staring straight at the car his father had died in. The front and back license plates with the number 58 had been removed, but Billy knew the car. He was stunned. This was the first time in Capitol Chevrolet history that a used car had been refurbished and put on the floor to be presented as new. Billy realized that only Powell could have ordered the restoration. The placement of the car seemed intentional. Powell must have known the effect it would have on Billy. But no one came over to talk to Billy or mentioned anything about the car.

For two weeks, the car sat in front of Billy's cubicle, only a few feet from his desk. Billy watched as potential buyers circled the Caprice, looking inside, opening the doors, and climbing into the driver's seat.

After two weeks, the car sold. The subject never came up with Powell, who had not come near Billy's cubicle while the car was in place.

Billy was astounded that anyone could have been so thoughtless. He knew his own father would never have done something so cruel. It made him miss Haynie even more.

CHAPTER [15]

The afternoon was hot, pushing 90 degrees, typical of late August in Nashville. It was quitting time for Henry Arthur Lewis. He had just finished smoothing out a portion of ground where his employer, Walton Construction Company, was laying a two-inch gas pipe along the 1100 block of Elm Hill Pike near the I-40 overpass, a stone's throw from Capitol Chevrolet. He would have to wait until more pipe was delivered the next day to finish the job. He climbed down from his front-end loader, crossed the two-lane road, and began walking east along a scrubby ditch about fifteen feet from the edge of the pavement.

The lean, balding, soft-spoken father of eight often looked for glass soda bottles while he was on construction sites. One of his sons liked to take the bottles to a country store near their home in Lebanon, Tennessee, to exchange for coins for his piggy bank.

Lewis hadn't found a lot of bottles lately, but he'd uncovered a perfectly good fire extinguisher someone had tossed out. As he walked the shallow ditch across from the Mount Zeno Kindergarten, something white on the ground caught his eye.

He climbed onto the bank and bent down to get a better look. It was a gun. The muzzle of the barrel was lodged in the dirt. The white pearl-clad handle was suspended in the air at a slight angle. Still bending down, Lewis grasped the handle and pulled the gun out of the hard, weedy ground. He inspected the weapon, turning it over carefully in his hands. The end of the barrel was packed with dirt. There was rust on some of the metal, but Lewis was delighted because it looked like he could salvage the gun. He opened the cylinder and found five spent shells; the sixth chamber was empty.

Lewis took the gun and walked back across the road. It occurred to him that just to be on the safe side he should empty the shells before he got into his car to drive the thirty-one miles home. In front of the Mount Zeno Kindergarten where he'd been working, he stopped at a pile of backfill dirt ready to be pushed into the trench where more pipe would be laid the next day. He opened the cylinder and dumped out the empty cartridges. They fell and scattered onto the freshly dug earth.

When Lewis arrived home, he placed the gun on the kitchen table, took some sandpaper, and attempted to remove the rust. With a piece of stiff wire, he punched the half inch of dirt out of the end of the barrel. Next, he used steel wool to buff the rusted parts.

Lewis's wife walked in and asked what he was doing. He explained how he had found the gun stuck in an embankment on Elm Hill Pike and that he intended to clean it up and see if it worked.

His wife's reaction was immediate.

"Henry, that's the road that Chevrolet man was killed on. I heard it on the news. I'm almost sure that's the road he was killed on."

"Well, I don't know," Lewis said, then added in an attempt to calm his wife, "I haven't been watching the news close enough. I don't think it is."

"If that were to be the gun, I don't want it in my house," she said sternly.

"Well, I don't think it is." Lewis said again.

After supper, his wife kept asking him to get rid of the gun. He began to think it wasn't worth making her upset, and if she was right, he did not want to get involved in any murder case. He agreed to take the weapon to his brother's house. Lewis was disappointed. He had been thrilled with the find.

The next day, he drove to 1400 Depot Street in Old Hickory where his brother lived and gave him the gun. His brother stuck the pistol in a drawer in a back room.

Lewis never mentioned the pearl-handled gun to anyone and soon forgot about it.

***

The late summer days dragged on with no new developments in the investigation. The reward money sat uncollected.

There were rumors of a shake-up in the police department because of a general lack of efficiency in solving crimes. Word was that Nashville Mayor Beverly Briley was putting pressure on the detective division to make changes, citing specifically the lack of movement in the Gourley murder case and in the mugging death of a prominent Nashville pharmacist. Although even the slightest lead had been followed up in the death of Haynie Gourley, with no clues and with Bill Powell as the only eyewitness, there was not much to go on.

After James Thomas Jefferson was arrested on July 1 for the Bolte murder and police could find no way to connect him to the May 24 shootings, another month passed with no progress. Police questioned dozens of people, but no arrests were made. Once again, the investigation into Haynie Gourley's slaying was at a dead end.

***

Out of the blue, on August 31, there was a potential development in the case. An East Nashville nineteen-year-old named Gerald James Wingard, had been arrested for the August 17 murder of James Holt, a grocery store employee. Holt, thirty-seven, was walking home from work when he was ambushed and gunned down as he entered a gate leading to his trailer in a mobile home park. He died of a bullet to the heart.

Holt's billfold, which contained an unknown amount of cash,

was missing. Witnesses heard a shot and saw four youths running from the area.

An anonymous tipster called police to say Wingard was also the killer of Haynie Gourley. Rumors started flying that a suspect had been arrested in connection with Haynie's death. Wingard was held without bond at the Metro jail.

On Saturday morning, September 7, Metro police officer Arnold Hendricks, patrolman Carl Harrison, and Lt. Malcolm Akin drove to Capitol Chevrolet to see Bill Powell. Hendricks was one of the officers who had arrested Wingard for the Holt slaying.

The policemen brought with them six photographs, including one of Gerald Wingard. Powell went through the photographs and stopped at Wingard.

Gerald James Wingard
Remains in jail

"That looks like him," Powell said. "I'll never forget those eyes."

That afternoon, Homicide Detective Sherman Nickens arranged for Wingard to appear in a lineup to be viewed by Powell. After talking with his client, Powell's attorney Cecil Branstetter decided not to accompany him to the police station.

Five men were in the lineup. Number Three was wearing an old hat. Powell asked that the hat be placed on Number One. When he saw the man wearing the hat, he immediately said, "That's him."

Powell signed a paper declaring that he had positively identified Number One—Gerald James Wingard. Several officers from the police department witnessed Powell's identification. At last, it seemed that Haynie Gourley's killer had been found.

***

"Youth, 19, Identified as Slayer of Gourley," screamed the front-page headlines of *The Tennessean* on the morning of Tuesday, September 10.

To everyone's astonishment and relief, the article revealed that automobile dealer William Powell had made a positive identification, naming Gerald James Wingard, 19, of 1000 N. Fifth St., as the gunman who wounded him and killed his business partner, W. Haynie Gourley, on May 24, 1968.

The line-up on Saturday had been followed by a closed-door meeting at police headquarters on Monday. This time, in the presence of Cecil Branstetter and District Attorney Tom Shriver, Powell again positively identified Gerald James Wingard as the man who jumped into Haynie Gourley's car and proceeded to shoot.

Sherman Nickens and the other officers who had been present at the line-up on Saturday and who also attended the Monday meeting, verified the results—that Bill Powell had picked Gerald James Wingard out of the line-up and had stated again that he was positive that Wingard was the killer.

But the euphoria over the identification was short-lived.

Wingard, despite called-in tips to the contrary, denied any knowledge of the Gourley slaying and the wounding of Powell. Wingard swore that he had not even been in Nashville on May 24, 1968. He told police he had been at a Job Corps center in California from April 24 until June 1.

To back up her son's story, Wingard's mother, Mrs. Essie Baker, corroborated his claim. She gave Metro detectives her son's checkout slips, which were signed by his Job Corps supervisors on May 30, 1968. Her son, she said, remained in California until June 1, when he was sent back to Nashville.

Reporters tried to reach Bill Powell for comment before the news broke on Tuesday afternoon that the man Powell had positively identified could not have been the killer. When the press tried to obtain a statement from Powell, they were told he was in Cincinnati on Chevrolet business and could not be reached.

On Wednesday, *The Tennessean* ran a front-page article confirming that Gerald James Wingard had been at the Parks Job Corps Center in Pleasanton, California, on May 24, 1968, the day Haynie was killed. Attendance records showed that Wingard did not leave the premises from the time he arrived April 24 until he was terminated on June 1. A morning roll call on May 24 had confirmed his presence.

Assistant Chief Barton and Homicide Detective Sherman Nickens both asserted that Powell had made a positive identification in their presence. Powell was asked several times at the line-up on Saturday and again at the closed-door meeting on Monday, September 9, at Metro police headquarters, if he was certain about the identification. Powell told police emphatically that Wingard was the man. He said once more that he could not forget the killer's eyes.

But now police knew something for certain. Wingard did not kill Haynie Gourley or wound Powell. He was not even in Nashville on Friday, May 24, 1968. He had an iron-clad alibi. He was 3,000 miles away.

There was immediate backpedaling by Powell when he learned Wingard was in California on the day of the murder.

After meeting with his lawyer Cecil Branstetter on Saturday, September 14, a week after the line-up, Powell called newspaper reporters from both dailies to his home in Belle Meade to explain himself. It was the first time he had spoken directly to the press since the day of the murder some three months earlier.

Powell was defiant. He insisted that he had told police at the lineup at headquarters on September 7 he was only "reasonably positive" that one of the men in the lineup was the murderer.

"I didn't mean to say I was positive beyond any doubt," he told reporters. "I thought there was enough similarity between the suspect in the lineup and the murderer that I was justified in saying the two were the same man."

He continued his denial. "I would never have said I was absolutely positive because I didn't want to make a mistake. If the man I identified is not the man who did the killing, then there is someone out there who looks just like his twin."

Powell said he was taken into an office near the lineup room and asked if he was certain this was the man. "I replied that I was not certain. The policeman said, 'Don't worry about that. We've already got this guy on one murder. He looks like a Sunday School teacher but he's capable of doing it.'

"About this time, the other officers, including assistant police chief Barton, came into the office. I asked him if I could see the man accused in another Nashville murder. I had seen this man's picture in the newspapers and on TV and thought there were some similarities.

"I was told there was a court order prohibiting this, and Barton wanted to know whether or not I was certain about my identification in the lineup.

"I said I was certain this was the man, but that I just wanted to see the other man for my own peace of mind.

"I know this sounds kind of screwy. I was reasonably convinced Wingard was the man, and in a way I wasn't."

When detective Sherman Nickens heard Powell's claim that he had not been sure about Wingard, he was apoplectic. Nickens had been at the lineup on Saturday and at the meeting at police headquarters on Monday. On both days, Powell had said that without a doubt, Number One in the line-up—Gerald James Wingard—was the "Negro" who had jumped into the car at Spence Lane and Elm Hill Pike.

Powell's statements at his home now directly contradicted what he told police at the Monday meeting. Powell's lawyer Cecil Branstetter had accompanied him to that meeting and had heard his client say that he was positive Gerald Wingard was the killer.

But at Powell's called press conference, Cecil Branstetter defended his client's claims that he never made a positive identification. "As attorney for Mr. Powell, I feel it improper for Mr. Powell or myself to make any statement as to what went on in that meeting. Such statements should come from public officials such as Thomas H. Shriver, the district attorney."

On Saturday, September 14, an article appeared in the paper about some behind-the-scenes shenanigans by certain Metro police concerning Wingard.

Metro patrolman Arnold Hendricks was reprimanded for reportedly suggesting that Gerald James Wingard be charged with the murder of W. Haynie Gourley simply because Wingard already faced another murder charge.

"We've already got this Negro on one count, why not fry him on two?" Hendricks was overheard saying before it was discovered that Wingard had been in California at the time of the slaying.

"That's what they said I said," Hendricks argued. "Somebody misheard me. What I actually said was we already have this subject on one charge. Mr. Powell has picked him out of the lineup. We have eyewitnesses in the other case, and it appears he is going to be the one in this Gourley case, too."

CHAPTER [16]

After the line-up debacle, the Gourley case once again seemed to be going nowhere. Thomas Shriver, whose full title was District Attorney General and who had been elected two years before, remarked to newspaper reporters that he believed there was someone out there who was not coming forward.

And no one did until a Williamson County man named John Barros surfaced late in September 1968. Barros turned over two bullets to the Metro Police. Upon examination, the bullets, a distinct type not easily found on the retail market and used mostly by police, were an exact match to those taken from Haynie Gourley's body. Shockingly, Barros claimed he had found them in one of the automobiles that had been brought to the car cleaning business he formerly operated with Bill Powell and two other automobile dealers.

This should have been sensational news, but the discovery of the matching bullets never made the papers, and police were mum on the subject.

John Barros did not just materialize out of the blue. He had a contentious history with Bill Powell that had reached a boiling point. In the late winter of 1968, Barros, a slight man with a receding hairline and glasses, was running a business called Holiday Car Clean-Up Center, which cleaned and prepared new and used cars for sale. Barros counted Capitol Chevrolet and several other automobile dealers in Nashville among his clients. He had invested $18,000 in equipment, and his venture had proved lucrative very quickly.

But on April 23, 1968, Barros was summoned by Bill Powell to Capitol Chevrolet's new headquarters at 600 Murfreesboro Road.

Barros thought he had been asked there to discuss the cars he was servicing for the dealership. Instead, Barros was blindsided by Powell's announcement that he and two other dealers had decided to operate their own clean-up business and that Barros's services were longer needed.

Barros was stunned. He had been assured by Powell and the other dealers he serviced that they would continue to patronize his business.

At that meeting, Powell offered to purchase Holiday Car Clean-Up Center for $8,000, ten thousand dollars less than Barros's initial investment.

Holiday Car Clean-up Center was located at 1219 McGavock Street in a building Barros rented for $425 a month. Three years remained on his lease.

Bill Powell moved his newly formed business—Automobile Clean-up Center, Inc.—to a vacant building leased to Capitol Chevrolet for $1,000 per month. Powell and the other dealers agreed to keep Barros on as manager. Barros, feeling cornered, reluctantly accepted.

Shortly thereafter, on June 1, 1968, the building Capitol was leasing burned to the ground. After what turned out to be a suspicious fire, the new corporation borrowed $20,000 from Commerce Union Bank, and Barros was told he was personally obligated for $5,000 of the loan. Instead of using Barros's leased building on McGavock Street, the business was relocated to 1410 Lebanon Road. Barros was furious and confronted Bill Powell. The two argued and could not come to an agreement.

On September 12,1968, during the week of the line-up fiasco, Powell phoned Barros and told him either to buy the three dealers out, or that he, Powell, was going to liquidate the business.

On September 26, 1968, Barros filed a $250,000 lawsuit in Chancery Court against William E. Powell of Capitol Chevrolet, Beryle Waller, owner of Waller Buick Company, and E. J. Preston of Preston Lincoln-Mercury. The lawsuit sought damages for forcing Barros out of his car cleaning business.

Barros alleged that Powell told him someone from Capitol was coming to take inventory and that he should "get out right then and there, and if he couldn't take his personal belongings with him, to throw them over the fence and get them the next day."

Beryle Waller called a locksmith who came and changed the locks to the building. When Barros asked Waller what the dealers expected to pay for his interest in the business, Waller answered, "You don't have a damn thing coming."

"This was nothing more than a conspiracy on the part of the defendants to defraud complainant out of his business by force, coercion, and threats, and he was in fact forced into the position of either losing his entire investment by this high-handed and conspiratorial threat or else concede to the defendants' demands," the suit charged.

The complaint also alleged that Powell's move was engineered for the sole purpose of bailing Capitol Chevrolet out of an expensive lease which had nineteen months remaining.

When asked by reporters about the case, Bill Powell responded: "I haven't seen the allegations and really don't know what the suit is all about. All I know is he just resigned as manager, and we did offer to sell him the business. I've never squeezed the man out of anything."

In only a matter of days, Barros was back in the news, this time with a bizarre story, but one that raised hopes in solving the Gourley case.

Barros told newspaper reporters he had received an anonymous phone call. The male voice on the line said he had in his possession the weapon that killed Haynie Gourley.

"If you want the gun," the caller said, "put $150 in an envelope in the back of your mailbox tonight. Do not call the police." Barros followed the caller's instructions and the next morning retrieved a .38 caliber Smith & Wesson pistol from exactly where the caller said it would be. The envelope with the money was gone.

Barros delivered the gun to Metro Police Chief H. O. Kemp. Despite high hopes that the murder weapon had at last been found, the .38 revolver was examined by the Tennessee Bureau of Criminal Investigation which determined that the mailbox gun was not the weapon used to kill Haynie Gourley and wound Powell.

Given tensions over the lawsuit with Powell, Barros volunteered to take a lie detector test to substantiate his claims about the matching bullets he turned in to police and the gun in his mailbox.

Barros never showed up for the test, however, and the matter soon quieted down. In addition, no court date was ever scheduled to hear Barros's lawsuit.

Nothing would be heard from Barros again until the spring of 1969 when he would make even more fantastic claims.

***

On Thursday, October 17, after a three-week lull with no news, the Gourley murder was back on the front page of *The Tennessean*. Once again, hopes rose for a break in the case. Another .38 caliber Smith & Wesson pistol had been discovered the day before in Brown's Creek, not far from Murfreesboro Road. Willie Gammage, thirteen, and his brother, Melvin Gammage, eleven, were playing near the water when they found the gun. The youths' mother turned the weapon in to juvenile authorities who handed it over to Metro police.

The pistol was registered to Erwin Klotwog, a former policeman who had quit the force only a few months before the discovery. Klotwog said he had loaned the revolver to his brother Gershon Klotwog, who, in turn, said the gun was stolen from his truck while parked at his place of business, Gus Furniture Company at 820 Fifth Avenue South.

Gershon Klotwog told police that the pistol was loaded and in a holster when it was stolen and that he had sawed off the four-inch barrel to two inches, making it a snub-nosed pistol. The Klotwog gun was capable of holding six bullets, the same as the weapon that killed Haynie Gourley, but TBI agents determined that this was not the gun that killed Haynie Gourley.

Although this story appeared to be over and have no meaning in the case, the term "snub-nosed" had appeared in bold type in articles in both the *Nashville Banner* and *The Tennessean*. Detective Bill Larkin began telling the press that police were searching for a snub-nosed pistol in the Gourley murder, and the information appeared over and over in print.

District Attorney General Thomas Shriver had often been quoted as saying he was convinced that somebody out there must know something. Shriver was right. A Nashville man was, in fact, harboring a secret. Only days after Haynie's murder, he had been questioned by police. He answered specific questions truthfully but volunteered nothing. His entire future could have been at stake had he confessed what he knew.

When he saw Larkin's statement in both daily newspapers that Haynie Gourley was killed with a snub-nosed pistol, the man breathed a sigh of relief. Maybe he wasn't involved after all. He decided to keep quiet.

***

Around the first of November 1968, the detective team members who had been working the Gourley slaying were ordered to return to their regular duties. Police officials announced they had reached a "stone wall" in the Gourley case. There were no more leads to check out, no one else to question. The case ran cold.

CHAPTER [17]

There had been seventy-five murders in Nashville in 1968. Only a handful were random in a city with a population of almost a half-million. Two of the killings by strangers dominated the headlines—the Gourley murder on May 24 and the brutal ax slaying of John Bolte on June 15. The August ambush of grocery worker James Holt, for which James Gerald Wingard was arrested, likely only made the papers weeks later because the teenager had been positively identified by Bill Powell as the man who had jumped into Haynie's car. Otherwise, the Holt murder might have been just another statistic buried in the back pages of the newspapers.

By far, it was the murder of Haynie Gourley by a phantom killer that captured the public's imagination. Stories about the murder and investigation had taken up thousands of words in both Nashville daily newspapers and generated continuous coverage on television.

Even so, no one had come forward with any useful information. Police were no closer to arresting the person who held a gun to Haynie Gourley's head and pulled the trigger than they had been on the day of the murder. Despite five months of intense searching and interviewing the same construction workers on Elm Hill Pike over and over, there were no new leads and no one else to question. As far as anyone knew, Bill Powell remained the only witness to the crime.

In the district attorney's office, the eight-inch-thick file on the Gourley murder was gathering dust. Occasionally, Sherman Nickens would visit Powell at Capitol Chevrolet, acting as if they were good buddies. On the sly, Nickens staked out Powell's house some nights, watching his comings and goings, but his efforts did not bear fruit.

By the early winter of 1969, the newspapers and television stations had mostly gone quiet on the subject. An occasional article with a headline like "Mystery Remains in the Gourley Case," or "Killed on 'Happiest Day,'" would pop up on the front page. Then nothing.

***

For as far back as Billy Gourley could remember, his parents had celebrated New Year's Eve at the Belle Meade Country Club. But the arrival of 1969 brought only uncertainty and sorrow to the Gourley family. Josephine cried a lot but did not discuss the case with her son.

Billy Gourley kept showing up at Capitol Chevrolet, but he was largely marking time, hanging on so he wouldn't entirely lose contact with the automobile business. By his own admission, his performance was lackluster. He spent his working hours grieving for his father, picturing how it used to be, thinking back on how proud Haynie had been of the new building, how happy he had been to have his son in the business. In his spare time, Billy threw himself into charitable causes, but nothing helped the pain he felt. He couldn't accept that his father was gone forever. After all these months, it still felt like a bad dream, one that he would wake up from and everything would be okay.

By March 1969, ten months had passed since Bill Powell said he would never forget the eyes of a Black man who, in broad daylight, at a time when racial tensions in Nashville were at a height, jumped into a moving automobile occupied by two white men and proceeded to shoot one dead and wound the other.

At least three times as far back as the fall of 1968, there were rumors that a grand jury was about to convene in the Gourley case. Each time, the public was disappointed, and grumblings erupted about the ineptness of the police investigation.

But early in March 1969, reports began to circulate that the Davidson County grand jury was about to take up the Gourley case. Both Metro Police officials and District Attorney Thomas Shriver denied any such plans. Still, the speculation persisted.

On Wednesday, March 19, 1969, both newspapers announced that the Davidson County grand jury had convened, meeting on the mezzanine level of the sixth floor of the courthouse in downtown Nashville.

The development came after what one police official described as "one of the most exhaustive murder investigations in Nashville history, yet one that had failed to yield a single concrete clue."

When the news broke, District Attorney Thomas Shriver declined to say whether the grand jury would be hearing evidence against any one person. Shriver would only say that the grand jury would return one of three findings. They could return a "true bill," meaning they found sufficient evidence to warrant a trial. Or they could make a "presentment," an informal statement in writing indicating that a public offense was committed, which would also be subject to trial.

The third option would be a "no true bill" if the grand jury found insufficient evidence and no probable cause to hand down an indictment. In that case, no action would be taken, and there would be no trial.

Nashville was once again obsessed with the mysterious Gourley murder and continued to come up with theories about what happened on May 24, 1968. Chatter was especially rampant in Belle Meade society, with speculation concentrating on the only witness to the crime, Bill Powell.

Questions abounded, however. Could a former Vanderbilt football star, a devoted husband and father, a respected member of the community and a church deacon, shoot a man in cold blood? With the National Guard clampdown following the assassination of Dr. Martin Luther King Jr. only six weeks before the murder, what Black man would have the nerve to jump into a moving car with two powerfully-built white men in the middle of the day at a busy intersection?

An editorial in *The Tennessean*'s opinion pages expressed frustration at the lack of progress in solving the case by publishing a challenge to the grand jury:

> "The community is deeply concerned at the pace in which the investigation has moved in the past ten months.
>
> "Thousands of police hours have been spent investigating the mysterious murder, which took place in full daylight at a relatively open and visible location. Honest and able officers worked tirelessly for leads. Hundreds of persons have been questioned. Rewards totaling $12,000 have been offered for the arrest and conviction of the killer of Mr. Gourley.
>
> "The failure of enforcement agencies to solve the case is regrettable in view of the current crime situation in the community. When a case of this magnitude goes unsolved for so long, it raises questions concerning self-confidence of the enforcement agencies and rouses questions of public confidence.
>
> "The D.A.'s office and grand jury should redouble their efforts to track down the killer and bring him to justice before the cause of firm, impartial law enforcement suffers a setback in the community."

District Attorney Thomas Shriver predicted the grand jury probe would be lengthy and could run over into the following week. Josephine Gourley was due to be the first witness. Just before the proceedings were to begin, however, a grand juror approached one of the reporters from *The Tennessean* and began commenting on the case. The juror gestured toward newsmen gathered in the hall. "I think we're making a mountain out of a molehill on this thing. A lot of money has been spent, and I think that a man has to go by his heart and soul—that's what we would have to go by since we don't have that kind of money." This statement caused a delay of four hours as Josephine Gourley sat on a wooden bench.

After Shriver had ascertained that the jurors could proceed without bias, Josephine Gourley, grim and unsmiling, wearing a tailored navy-blue dress, walked up the steps to the grand jury room. A photographer snapped her picture. She turned around and said in a soft voice, "I wish you wouldn't use that. My heart is too heavy. It won't be a good picture."

Her testimony lasted over an hour.

Photographs of each day's parade of witnesses appeared on the front pages of both *The Tennessean* and *Nashville Banner*. Among them were Metro policemen, construction workers at the alleged scene of the crime, and Capitol Chevrolet employees who had witnessed the moment on May 24, 1968, when Bill Powell came hurtling at high speed into the service area of the dealership with Haynie Gourley dead on the floorboard beside him. Reporters and TV news crews hounded witnesses for comments as they emerged from the jury room. Once again, papers on newsstands quickly sold out. The three broadcast stations ran segments rehashing details of the murder. The public had again immersed itself in the unsolved, high-profile crime, following every twist and turn of the supposedly secret grand jury probe. Trying to guess whether an indictment was imminent became a sport.

A heretofore unknown witness, truck driver Charles Donnelly, emerges from the Grand Jury room, followed by Detective Sherman Nickens. © *The Tennessean – USA TODAY NETWORK*

Five witnesses followed Haynie's widow, including the disgruntled John Barros. On Thursday and Friday, several police and homicide detectives were called to testify. Other witnesses included a technician from Vanderbilt Hospital who was present when Bill Powell was first admitted to the emergency room and had seen Powell wash his hands.

The most intense speculation from the public centered around a mystery witness who had not appeared in any previous media accounts. On Friday morning at 8:30 a.m., a tall, heavy-set man with glasses and a double chin, dressed in a light-colored jacket, open collared shirt, and dark pants, walked up the stairs to the courtroom. When he emerged from the grand jury room, a reporter stopped him.

"Did you see Mr. Gourley's car on the day of the murder?" the reporter asked.

"Yes," answered the man, but that was all he would say before he disappeared into the elevator.

Shriver refused to say who had found the witness, only that he was a person heretofore unknown to the district attorney's office or to Metro police detectives. People were quick to latch onto the possibility that he might just be the key to solving the baffling murder.

The grand jury session stretched into the next week, with Billy Gourley testifying on Monday along with more Capitol Chevrolet employees.

Metro Police Lieutenant J. W. Irvin revealed that he had told the panel how he had acquired two bullets of the same type, brand, and caliber that killed Haynie Gourley. He said he was told the bullets were found in a car being serviced at the Auto Cleanup Center, Inc., and stated they were given to him by John Barros, who at the time was the manager of the car cleaning company doing work for Capitol Chevrolet.

Robert Goodwin, ballistics expert from the TBI, showed jurors some 200-grain, .38-caliber ammunition of the same type and brand as the bullets removed from the body of Haynie Gourley and which exactly matched those found in a car at the clean-up company tied to

Bill Powell.

The grand jury probe lasted nine days, longer than any session in recent years. All in all, thirty witnesses testified.

***

Thursday, March 27 was a cloudy, chilly day in Nashville. Billy Gourley sat at his desk at Capitol Chevrolet, his stomach in knots. At noon, after a suspenseful week of hearing bits and pieces of testimony leaked from the grand jury room, he learned that the thirteen-member Davidson County grand jury had handed down an indictment: William E. Powell, forty-one, president of Capitol Chevrolet, was charged in the murder of his business partner W. Haynie Gourley.

Criminal Court Judge Allen R. Cornelius Jr. dispatched two court officers to Capitol Chevrolet headquarters to take Bill Powell into custody. The two were sworn to secrecy and ordered by Cornelius not to discuss even the fact that an indictment existed before Powell was arrested and brought to the courthouse.

About three hours later, Powell, dressed in a dark suit and striped tie, appeared in front of Judge Cornelius on the sixth floor of the courthouse. To avoid newsmen who had camped out at the courthouse, Powell walked up the back stairs to the courtroom.

Judge Cornelius set the bond at $5,000 and announced that Powell's arraignment would be held later.

Donning a light tan trench coat and dark gray hat, Powell, accompanied by his lawyer Cecil Branstetter, walked across the street to Metropolitan Police headquarters where he was fingerprinted and released after posting bail.

When queried by reporters, Branstetter said Powell had offered to appear before the grand jury but was not called.

Branstetter added in a sharp tone, "If they wanted the truth, Mr. Powell volunteered to give it to them."

Powell made no comment.

James L. Winfree, an agent with the United States Fidelity and Guaranty Company, posted the bail bond and drove Powell and Branstetter away from police headquarters.

***

The next morning, all of Nashville knew. A large photograph on the front page of *The Tennessean* showed Bill Powell walking through a corridor, rubbing his hands moments after he had been booked and fingerprinted at Metro Police headquarters. The headline across the top read: "Powell Indicted by Jury in Gourley Murder."

Bill Powell was going to stand trial for killing Haynie Gourley.

On Friday, March 28, 1969, the day after the indictment and a day before his twenty-fourth birthday, Billy Gourley handed in his resignation to the Human Resources department at Capitol Chevrolet. The past ten days had been unbearable. His future, once comfortably on track, was now even more up in the air. Bill Powell, he believed, had robbed him of the person he loved most in the world. Even though he was relieved by the grand jury's decision, he knew the days ahead would be fraught with tension, anxiety, and uncertainty. All his father's plans he'd worked for all his life were gone in a matter of moments. Walking out of the dealership that day, Billy had no idea if he would ever again enter the building that had been his father's pride and joy and the culmination of his longtime dream for his only son.

As soon as the news of Bill Powell's indictment hit the papers, John Barros sprang back into action, renewing his lawsuit against Bill Powell and the other two Nashville car dealers.

The damage suit was almost identical to the one Barros filed in September 1968. This time, the suit was filed in Circuit Court. Barros was again seeking $250,000 in compensation, claiming the three men had intentionally defrauded him out of his business by "force, coercion and threats."

Barros told reporters that the $20,000 loan taken out by Powell's corporation from Commerce Union Bank in September 1968 was still outstanding.

Another name from September 1968 cropped up after the indictment was handed down.

Gerald James Wingard told his lawyers in mid-March 1969 that before he appeared in the lineup in front of Powell in September 1968, a man dressed in jail clothing had visited him in his cell. The man, he said, offered him $1,000 if he would admit to killing Haynie Gourley.

Wingard said he had never told anyone about the alleged offer because his parents had advised him to remain silent. Wingard said the mystery man had stayed only a short time, and he never saw him again.

Charlie Hunter of the district attorney's office said that Wingard had volunteered to submit to a lie detector test, but the test was inconclusive. A second test was ordered but never administered. If someone had tried to buy off Wingard, it would never come to light.

Not surprisingly, on April 2, Bill Powell's attorney, Cecil Branstetter, asked the criminal court to set aside his client's indictment for murder. The motion to dismiss charged that District Attorney Thomas Shriver and Metro Detectives Sherman Nickens and William Larkin encouraged Powell's indictment by refusing to follow leads which corroborated Powell's account of the slaying. Instead, the motion said, they doggedly pursued "every possible lead" they thought would produce either evidence or publicity material to discredit Powell.

The plea called out incompetence on the part of the police, pointing out that on the day of the slaying Nickens and Larkin moved the death car back to a place near the scene of the crime "for the benefit of photographers." It further said that they later allowed photographers to take pictures as they ripped apart the seat of Haynie Gourley's car, destroying evidence.

Judge Cornelius postponed the arraignment of Bill Powell to allow Shriver time to respond to the eight-page plea, giving him until April 15 to file his answer.

***

Just hours before Branstetter's plea was filed, John Barros contacted Metro police. He claimed that a volley of gunshots had been fired into his automobile from a passing car. Photographers from the *Nashville Banner* rushed to the scene and photographed Barros and his shot-up car.

Barros said the terrifying incident happened as he drove along Berrys Chapel Road in a remote rural area near his Williamson County home. He claimed two men in a dark-colored car came up from behind and passed him, opening fire. A bullet that pierced his windshield, showering him with glass, barely missed him. Another slug broke out the left rear window and another struck the front fender.

Barros hinted that the shooting could be revenge for the lawsuit he filed against Bill Powell and for his testimony in front of the grand jury which resulted in Powell's indictment.

Barros was scheduled to meet with Shriver in his office but when he failed to appear, DA investigator Charlie Hunter was sent to Barros's house. Barros told Hunter to go away. Barros later showed up at Shriver's office with his lawyer. After a lengthy meeting, Barros returned home and was scheduled to report to the DA the next day to take a polygraph test and sign a written statement. However, Barros's attorney flatly refused to allow his client to be subjected to a polygraph test, saying it was "premature."

Reporters waiting outside Shriver's office asked Barros if he had reported the shooting incident to the Williamson County authorities since it allegedly occurred outside Davidson County. His attorney answered, "That's my job. We are certainly going to be sure the incident is reported to the proper authorities, and we are hopeful that adequate provisions will be made to afford Mr. Barros the protection he deserves as a citizen."

Shriver, who was already suspicious of Barros's motives and his truthfulness, never heard from Barros or his attorney again.

In the meantime, Shriver made a controversial announcement: The Gourley family had hired their personal attorney, John J. Hooker Sr., to act as special prosecutor to assist in presenting the State's case at the trial. The Gourleys gave no reason, but everyone knew it was because of Tom Shriver's inexperience. Shriver was thirty-six years old and had been district attorney for only two years. He was well liked but he was known to be a weak trial lawyer. By contrast, Hooker, at sixty-five, had forty years' experience and was famous for his courtroom oratory and persuasive arguments.

Powell and Branstetter vehemently objected to Hooker's appointment. On April 17, Branstetter filed a motion asking Criminal Court Judge Allen R. Cornelius Jr. to bar Hooker from participating in the case.

Branstetter was blunt, accusing Josephine Gourley of "nefarious motives" in the hiring of Hooker.

"The family of W. Haynie Gourley has no hope of taking the Chevrolet dealership from the defendant except by proving him guilty of the murder of Mr. Gourley," Branstetter said. "The widow and family of Gourley therefore have a pecuniary interest in assuring that this defendant will be convicted of murder."

Branstetter's motion also said: "Immediately upon the death of Gourley, the defendant became and now remains the sole owner of the Chevrolet dealership, in which neither the family nor the estate of William Haynie Gourley, or the corporation, Capitol Chevrolet, shares any ownership."

Gourley sympathizers were outraged. Haynie had spent thirty-six years working hard to build up the business and had every intention of keeping it in the family. Much of the public viewed Powell as having stolen the dealership from the Gourleys by murdering Haynie Gourley before the papers necessary to buy back Powell's stock and a new contract could be completed.

Regardless, Branstetter further complained that as a special prosecutor Hooker would act both on behalf of the State and of Gourley's widow.

"Eminent though he be, John J. Hooker Sr. cannot serve two masters. He should be barred from any further participation in the case."

Branstetter further accused Shriver of summoning a grand jury when there was no evidence that Powell had anything to do with Haynie Gourley's murder, further proof that the Gourley family "has a financial interest in seeing Powell convicted on murder charges."

Cornelius ultimately ruled that attorney John J. Hooker Sr. could participate in Powell's trial "in the role of an assistant to Shriver."

Branstetter's efforts to quash the grand jury indictment had failed. On Wednesday, April 30, 1969, William E. Powell was arraigned on charges he murdered William Haynie Gourley. He entered a plea of "not guilty."

When Judge Cornelius set a trial date of July 14, Branstetter raised objections, arguing that the publicity around the indictment would mean Powell could not get a fair trial with the court date so soon. Furthermore, he argued there were twenty other first-degree murder cases that had been pending for more than a year.

Cornelius would not budge. "They are all set or will be set this term," he said.

Branstetter made three more motions to have the indictment quashed, all of which Judge Cornelius overruled.

Then, Branstetter blurted out, "Mr. Powell enters a plea of not guilty, because he is not guilty."

This setback for Powell did not stop Branstetter. On May 16, he gave notice to Shriver and Hooker that he had asked the Tennessee Court of Criminal Appeals to dismiss the indictment against Powell, saying the two State's attorneys had violated Powell's "basic, fundamental, constitutional rights."

On Tuesday, June 17, the Court of Appeals ruled against Branstetter's motion. Powell's options had run out. The trial would go on.

To counter the Gourley family's move of hiring their personal attorney as special prosecutor, John Tune, a well-known Nashville lawyer and friend of Powell's, recommended Powell recruit Tune's father-in-law Jack Norman Sr. to assist with his defense.

The veteran criminal lawyer, widely known throughout the South, had agreed to sign on if Branstetter's appeals were denied. The ruling by the appeals court meant that the two most famous lawyers in Tennessee would be pitted against each other. Nashville was enthralled by the possibility of this dramatic match-up.

When Hooker learned of the ruling, he canceled a trip to Europe on the Queen Elizabeth II in order to participate in the trial.

The July 14 date left little time for either side to prepare. One of Branstetter's first steps was to issue a subpoena to WLAC-TV to turn over the footage shot at Capitol Chevrolet the day of the murder. Television crewmen had filmed a police officer examining Haynie's billfold just after the crime.

"It shows that the billfold was empty—meaning that the gunman could have taken money and fled—and it also shows that police obscured any fingerprints that may have been on it," Branstetter pointed out. However, Branstetter was well aware that the wallet was later found to contain credit cards, photographs, and two 100-dollar bills, all intact.

On Tuesday, June 24, Cecil Branstetter and District Attorney Thomas Shriver appeared before Judge Cornelius in a fiery exchange over items requested by the defense.

In one especially heated moment, Branstetter accused Shriver of "character assassination" when Shriver quoted Gerald James Wingard, once identified in a lineup by Powell, as saying Cecil Branstetter offered Wingard $1,000 to say he killed Haynie Gourley.

This angry exchange did not bode well for the upcoming trial.

CHAPTER [18]

As July 14 approached, Nashville was riveted. Such was the obsession in the city that Nashville television stations requested permission from Judge Cornelius to broadcast the trial. WSM-TV, the NBC affiliate, planned to televise the trial live, while the ABC station WSIX-TV said it would record portions of the proceedings for delayed broadcast. CBS affiliate WLAC-TV was also considering televising excerpts from the trial.

Judge Cornelius had strong reservations about any television coverage. "I am concerned about the Supreme Court's ruling in the Billy Sol Estes fraud case, where a conviction was overturned because of television coverage." He added, "I am concerned, too, with the Samuel Sheppard case, in which a conviction was overturned because of prejudicial publicity by the news media."

Never before had television stations been allowed to broadcast while court was in session in Davidson County. However, according to television officials, this trial was too sensational not to be covered in full. Jud Collins, news director for WSM-TV, said his station could televise live from the courtroom without disrupting the proceedings.

"We have had our engineering people look at the courtroom and draw up a plan which would provide for building an enclosure to isolate the camera," Collins said. "There would be no cables to trip over, and no bright lights or sound. We feel this trial is of tremendous community interest. At the same time, there are only about sixty seats in the courtroom. Not many people will be able to see the trial, and television, if permitted, could bring it to the public."

Powell was approached by representatives of the television stations. He said he had no objection to any fair news coverage which would get the whole truth to the public.

Branstetter complained that Shriver and Hooker were "all for it," because everything that was being said by TV and radio and newspapers was biased against his client.

Judge Cornelius told the television representatives that he would take the matter under consideration.

A week before jury selection was to begin, rumors were rampant. A news story broke on Tuesday, July 8, revealing that a Metro patrolman, Howard D. Kirkland, had been hired by "a friend of Mr. Powell's" to work in his off-duty time in an effort to uncover information police had overlooked in the investigation of the case. According to an article in *The Tennessean*, Kirkland was being paid for his services and reimbursed for expenses incurred on trips around Tennessee and to at least one other state. However, Cecil Branstetter denied that Kirkland was working for Powell in any "official" capacity.

"I have talked to him and given him some of the same leads given to other policemen and the district attorney and his staff," Branstetter told reporters. Branstetter claimed that Kirkland's involvement in the case "is nothing more than that of a policeman interested in finding out who killed Gourley."

Shriver originally accused the policeman of a conflict of interest. Later on, Shriver would welcome Kirkland's detective work. His probes, in fact, would change the course of the trial and hand the state a crucial witness.

***

With the city sweltering in temperatures hovering near 100 degrees, the upcoming trial was all Nashville could talk about. Newspapers sold out, and ratings for television newscasts were off the charts.

This was not just any murder trial. It had all the elements of a crime novel—a high-society killing, a former college football star accused of murdering one of Nashville's most prominent citizens, and a multi-million- dollar business hanging in the balance. Depending on the outcome of the trial, one of two families would own Capitol Chevrolet Company. The other would lose it forever.

The stakes couldn't have been higher.

***

The front page of the Sunday, July 13, 1969, edition of *The Tennessean* dramatized the obsession gripping the city:

> "Not since Clarence Darrow and William Jennings Bryan squared off in Dayton has a Tennessee trial so engrossed the public as that which starts tomorrow."

Speculation dominated conversations at dinner tables across the city as people pored over stories about the once-charmed lives of the Gourley family, their prominence in the community, and their unimaginable loss.

In Belle Meade, everyone had a theory about what really happened. Friends and college buddies of "Big Bill" Powell fiercely denied that he could have ever murdered anyone. Nashville was divided, but by far most people believed that the former Vanderbilt football star had shot his boss in cold blood. Even residents of the less prosperous northern and eastern sections of the city, many of whom had bought Chevrolets from Haynie Gourley going back years, weighed in on the side of the Gourley family.

When a thirty-something graduate of Fisk University heard the news of Haynie's murder, he recalled a big event in his life. "My father took me downtown to get my first car, and Mr. Gourley himself showed us around. I knew he was giving us a special deal. He was the nicest man. I hated what happened to him."

The anticipation surrounding the huge match-up between two legendary attorneys eclipsed anything Nashville had ever seen.

John J. Hooker Sr., special prosecutor for the State, and Jack Norman Sr., co-counsel for the defense, were far and away the most celebrated lawyers in Tennessee. Both had important national ties, and both had appeared on the national stage. In their mid-sixties and two years apart in age, Hooker and Norman were old friends who had appeared as adversaries or co-counsel in at least 100 cases. They were often on the same side, but when pitted against each other in the courtroom, all bets were off.

The two attorneys shared fame in Tennessee and beyond, but their lifestyles could not have been more different. At sixty-five, Hooker was a portly, elegant man with a taste for bespoke suits, the pants of which he wore high on his considerable waist, and crisp shirts made to order in London. Described by one attorney as a "courtly gentleman," he lived in high style in a historic stately brick mansion on his 350-acre farm, Hooker Hill, in the rolling hills between Brentwood and Franklin, Tennessee. He and his wife Effie were surrounded by servants and fine china and crystal and gleaming silver. Hooker was known for his lavish Christmas parties, gathering top Nashville attorneys, judges, and businessmen and their spouses to feast on roast prime rib, fried quail, and country ham from Hooker's own smokehouse, and to drink free-flowing liquor fashioned into any drink his guests desired.

Hooker could often be found riding wildly over the picturesque fields of his farm in his Cadillac. It was not an unusual occurrence for him to get stuck in mud on these adventures. James, his devoted man-Friday, who did everything for him from acting as chauffeur to fixing his drinks, would often have to bring a tractor to pull him out.

Young lawyers flocked to Hooker, and he was an obliging guru and storyteller. With his rich, modulated voice, he would hold them spellbound with endless stories of celebrity friends and courtroom encounters, peppering his commentary with stern lectures on the purity of the law. Love of the law was Hooker's hallmark, and he held an "almost religious belief" in its sanctity.

Hooker represented many prominent families in Nashville along with top national and international businesses, including The Coca-Cola Company, Greyhound Bus Lines, and Marshall Field's. He was the attorney for the Jack Daniel's Distillery in Lynchburg, Tennessee, which meant his friends President John F. Kennedy and his brother Robert Kennedy would receive crates of the famous whiskey at Christmastime.

Davidson County was a dry county, and word was that Hooker supplied his favorite Nashville restaurant, Jimmy Kelly's, with an endless supply of Jack Daniel's secreted through the back door

The most notorious local case involving Hooker began in the early morning hours of April 6, 1963. Hooker's client, socialite Gene Beasley Wilson, married to financier and sports car enthusiast John B. Wilson, had been out with her husband at a party on Chickering Road in Belle Meade.

The couple returned to their Harding Road mansion at 2:00 a.m. Gene went to the room of her twenty-year-old son, who had arrived in town earlier that evening. Exactly what happened next is unclear, but Gene, frantic, called her personal physician Dr. W. J. Cove to come immediately. The doctor drove up the winding drive and met the police and *Nashville Banner* reporter Larry Brinton in the back parking area.

Rushing upstairs, they found John Wilson sprawled on the floor between the twin beds in her son's room. Bright red blood covered the front of his white shirt and formed a pool next to his lifeless body. A bloody samurai sword with a twenty-inch blade lay on the carpet at the foot of the bed.

Next to arrive was Gene's lawyer, John J. Hooker. Hooker led Gene out of the room. When she came back in, she told the police that she had gone in to talk to her son. She said her husband barged in and began his usual berating of his stepson. In an effort to defuse the situation, Gene hopped up on the other twin bed and took the sword off the wall and began flailing around, imitating the famous swashbuckling motions of actor Douglas Fairbanks. She plunged the sword into a decorative pillow, and when she drew it back out, her husband lunged at her, impaling himself on the sword.

Hooker accompanied Gene downtown where she was booked on a murder charge.

The slaying was discussed over and over in Belle Meade circles. The theory was that she had covered for her son, the real killer. The sword, the medical examiner found, had been plunged straight into Wilson's chest, not at a downward angle from the height of the bed. Police also observed when they arrived, the bed where she claimed to have wielded the sword was perfectly neat and not disheveled as it should have been. Despite the incriminating evidence, Hooker prevailed, convincing the district attorney that it had been a terrible accident.

Hooker gained national fame in another highly publicized case. He was hired by Bobby Kennedy, who was serving as United States Attorney General under his brother's administration. The younger Kennedy had long wanted to prosecute Teamsters Union president Jimmy Hoffa. Kennedy said he needed someone "older, overpowering and incorruptible" as prosecutor. He called on Hooker.

When Jacqueline Kennedy heard of her brother-in-law's choice, she asked why he picked a Southerner. Bobby answered that if a lawyer could get charges dismissed against a woman standing over her husband's body holding a bloody sword, that's the kind of attorney he needed to go after Hoffa.

***

In the fall of 1963, a jury tampering case against Hoffa got underway. In his closing argument as prosecutor, Hooker's histrionics reached new heights. Letting his voice fade to a raspy whisper, he literally knelt in front of the jury box, pleading, "I hope you won't think I'm irreverent but I'm on my knees to ask God for justice and that justice be done in this case."

Because of all the media publicity, the Hoffa trial was moved to Chattanooga in 1964. After seven weeks of raucous courtroom drama, Hoffa was convicted on three counts. The defense argued for a new trial, claiming that before their decision was handed down, some of the jurors had been seen drunk in the middle of the night at the downtown Read House hotel where they were staying during the trial.

But the defense's tactic did not work. Bellhops came forth admitting they had been offered suitcases full of cash to confirm the allegations of drunkenness. On March 12, 1964, Hoffa was sentenced to eight years in prison and fined $10,000. Kennedy, at the time still serving as U.S. Attorney General under President Lyndon Johnson, had at last exacted his revenge on Hoffa, and John J. Hooker Sr. had gained even more national fame.

Equally as famous as Hooker and possibly even more colorful, Jack Norman Sr. was a legal giant and old-fashioned theatrical courtroom performer. He had been known to cry during closing arguments and make the jury cry as well.

With dark bushy eyebrows and grizzled white wisps of hair encircling his balding head, Norman, sixty-three, was often seen in summer wearing white linen suits with white buckskin lace-up shoes and a white fedora-shaped straw hat with a black band to match his tie. He had a bulldog-like presence due to a blunt nose, jowly cheeks, and stocky build. He was seldom seen without a lit cigar hanging out of one cor-

Defense attorneys for William E. Powell: Jack Norman Sr., with his signature cigar, and Cecil Branstetter. *Courtesy of Hal Hardin*

ner of his mouth. His piercing scowl intimidated anyone who met him for the first time, but he was privately known to have a heart of gold.

Norman was born to modest circumstances, growing up on Second Avenue South in a downtown Nashville neighborhood known as Varmint Town. He worked his way through college and held three jobs while at Vanderbilt Law School. After graduation, with no family background or social connections, his job applications were rejected by top Nashville law firms.

In 1926, Norman rented a desk in a downtown Nashville office to start his law practice and quickly became known as a fierce and effective fighter for his clients, who were often from the underbelly of society. Norman was powerful and articulate in the courtroom and was said to practice law "by ambush." His motto was, "There's just one side to a lawsuit, and that's mine." One district attorney called him "the most effective courtroom lawyer I have ever seen."

Norman was known for his brashness, striding back and forth in front of the jury with a yellow legal pad in one hand and waving his glasses around with the other. So exceptional was his reputation that lawyers would sometimes close their offices to attend court and watch him in action.

As a defense attorney in criminal cases, Norman was known as a "vicious attack dog" and an "incendiary orator." His closing arguments could hypnotize juries. He would alternate between whispers so low the jury had to lean forward to hear him and explosions of rhetorical thunder so loud the din would shake the courtroom.

He was as eloquent as Hooker and just as well known for holding jurors spellbound. He also had a knack for befriending them in a subtle way to sway them to his side. His most famous trick was to stick a long needle in the end of his lit cigar and leave it on an ashtray when a prosecution witness was on the stand. The burning ash would be supported by the needle and thus become longer and longer without falling off. The jurors would soon lose their concentration due to this fascinating scene playing out on the defense table.

Norman and his wife Carrie had five children whom they raised at Red Gables, a twenty-room Tudor house on Ensworth Avenue in

Nashville. In the mid-fifties, Norman sold the estate to the organizers of a new private school and purchased a building in Printers Alley, at the time a down-at-the-heels slice of downtown Nashville. He converted the ground floor of a former tin-works factory into his law office. In 1958, he and his wife moved into living quarters on the top floors where they entertained many high-profile guests, including Jack and Jacqueline Kennedy.

Like Hooker, Norman was a staunch Democrat and active in the party on a national level. On November 21, 1963, Norman was taking a deposition at the Veterans Hospital in Nashville when an announcement came over the loudspeaker, "Mr. Jack Norman, the White House is calling." Larry O'Brien, a member of President Kennedy's inner circle, was on the phone, confirming that the President would help Norman's son Seth with his candidacy for president of the Young Democrats. O'Brien told Norman that the President would phone him upon his return from Dallas. The call never came. The next day was November 22, 1963. Seth Norman did, however, end up winning the election.

Norman was devoted to philanthropic Masonic and Shrine causes and personally brought the Shrine Circus to Nashville. He produced the attraction for thirty years. His son, Jack Norman Jr., also an attorney, worked at the circus where he met his first wife, Duina Zacchini Norman, a trapeze artist and member of The Flying Zacchinis. Duina's father, Edmundo Zacchini, was known as the Human Cannonball. Duina herself was shot out of a cannon along with her sister when their father was overseas serving in the U.S. Army during World War II.

Norman worked mostly criminal cases, defending some of the most violent offenders, many of whom couldn't pay. He developed a secret strategy, one he was about to use in perhaps the most famous trial of his career, and one that had helped him win the bulk of his cases.

In one of his rare losses, Norman represented Thomas Osborne, the Nashville lawyer accused of jury tampering in the Hoffa case. Osborne was sent to prison, and the score stood 1-0 in favor of his sometimes rival, John J. Hooker Sr.

The Powell murder trial presented Norman with a chance to even the score. Norman had the advantage of experience, having been involved in many more criminal cases than Hooker, who had spent most of his time in civil courts.

As the outside temperature rose in Nashville, the stage was set for a blistering confrontation between the two legal legends.

At the prosecution table, Hooker would sit with thirty-six-year-old District Attorney Thomas Shriver. Tall and gangly, with black-rimmed glasses, a long face, and thick dark hair, Shriver was not a forceful speaker and had little courtroom experience. He graduated from Vanderbilt Law School and was the son of a prominent judge. In his pastime, he enjoyed repairing antique clocks, playing the guitar and mandolin in a hillbilly band, and restoring antique cars. He could often be seen in his neighborhood driving a vintage convertible roadster. In his courthouse office, he was seldom seen without a lit pipe.

Assistant District Attorney Hal Hardin brings a suitcase containing Haynie Gourley's clothes to court. They were not, however, entered into evidence. *Nashville Public Library, Special Collections, Banner Newspaper Collection*

Twenty-seven-year-old Assistant District Attorney Hal Hardin would have the third seat at the prosecution table. Hardin graduated from Vanderbilt Law School and was employed by the Job Corps in St. Louis as a supervisor of some 200 women corps members. Shriver asked Hardin to return to Nashville to aid in the trial. A devoted protégé of John J. Hooker Sr. and strikingly handsome, Hardin was tall, with thick black hair and blue eyes. His good looks would soon become a topic of conversation among many young women who attended the trial.

Bill Powell's defense team was headed by his personal lawyer, Cecil Branstetter. Tall, graying at the temples with a straight patrician nose and furrowed brow, he was known to possess a brilliant legal mind. Branstetter was stationed in England during World War II and awarded a scholarship to Oxford University. He graduated from Vanderbilt Law School, where, among other top honors, he served as editor of the law review. At forty-eight, Branstetter already had a stellar reputation as one of Nashville's top labor lawyers and a fiery litigator.

In the early '60s when Jimmy Hoffa was looking for someone to represent him in Nashville, he was given three names: John J. Hooker Sr., Jack Norman Sr., and Cecil Branstetter. When Branstetter learned that jury tampering was involved, however, he declined to represent Hoffa.

In 1951, Branstetter was elected to the Tennessee General Assembly where he spearheaded the passage of a bill allowing women to serve as jurors. He was also known as a "father of the Metropolitan Government," having served on the charter commissions which consolidated the City of Nashville and Davidson County into one entity. By the time he was hired by Bill Powell, Branstetter was noted in *The Tennessean* as "one of the finest lawyers in the South" and a man of "steely integrity."

Presiding over the trial was forty-eight-year-old Judge Allen R. Cornelius Jr. Cornelius had only been on the criminal court bench for one year, after having previously served ten years as a general sessions court judge where he heard mostly civil suits. Cornelius wore glasses, was tall and thin, and had prematurely white hair. He was well regarded among attorneys as a fair and principled judge.

However, many secretly wondered if Cornelius had enough expe-

Judge Allen R. Cornelius Jr. © *The Tennessean – USA TODAY NETWORK*

rience to control the legal giants who would soon be squaring off in his courtroom in the most publicized murder trial in Nashville history.

***

With the trial set to begin just days away, the temperature continued to climb into the high 90s with no relief in sight. But thoughts of the oppressive heat were overshadowed by rumors of new evidence in the Gourley murder case.

On Friday, July 11, three days before the start of the trial, Powell, Branstetter, and Jack Norman Sr. were spotted in the Elm Hill Pike area where Bill Powell claimed he and Haynie Gourley had been shot.

When queried by reporters, Branstetter said the visit to the crime scene was to gather information on distances, take measurements, and try to determine how the road and terrain had changed in the year since the shooting. Despite Branstetter's answer, speculation continued that

Powell's team possessed new clues, even though nothing specific had been printed in the paper or appeared on the evening news.

On that same Friday, Powell lunched with several business associates and discussed hiring a new employee. He was calm and relaxed and made no mention of the upcoming trial. During all his previous court appearances, Powell had been unfailingly polite to reporters and listened quietly as the attorneys wrangled over points of law and even insulted each other. But he was being watched closely by the police and investigators, all looking for cracks in his seemingly untroubled façade.

There was another development having to do with media coverage of the trial. Jack Norman was vehemently opposed to the proposals from the three major Nashville television networks to broadcast the trial live.

"To give criminal trials over to the entertainment field is the last step toward the ridiculous," Norman said.

Branstetter told reporters: "It does to some extent make actors out of the witnesses. You might have voluntary witnesses who want to testify just to get on TV. That's already started."

Branstetter was referring to a Columbia, Tennessee, businessman who had asked for $25,000 to testify about what he saw and heard at the shooting scene. Shriver's office investigated the man's story, which was completely discredited.

Judge Cornelius finally ruled that no television cameras or newspaper photographers would be allowed in the courtroom during the trial. Instead, Tom Little and Charles Bissell, cartoonists for *The Tennessean*, would depict courtroom scenes. The public would have to be satisfied with the artists' renderings of the major players—the Gourley and Powell families, the judge, attorneys, and witnesses.

Hearing about this ruling, Larry Brinton, the ace crime reporter at the *Nashville Banner,* came up with an idea, given the intense interest in the trial. It would be difficult to pull off, but he proposed to publisher and owner James Stahlman that the newspaper hire court stenographers to transcribe every word of the trial, which would be published daily in its entirety. This way, the public would be able to keep up with courtroom proceedings. All of Nashville and the hundreds who would try for one of the sixty-four seats in the courtroom would know exactly what was going on inside Courtroom 611 by reading the complete transcript in the newspaper. Brinton held out little hope that Stahlman, a staunch fiscal conservative, would agree to such a proposition.

But Brinton was wrong. Stahlman said yes, and Brinton thought he had pulled off a coup for the *Nashville Banner*. Brinton was stunned when Stahlman announced that he had made a deal with his rival John Seigenthaler, editor of *The Tennessean*, to share the expense of hiring extra personnel to record every word of the trial. Stenographers would change out every ten minutes, and runners would rush the bits of transcript back to the papers to be loaded onto the printing presses. Both newspapers would print the transcript from the previous day's proceedings, including all testimony, all arguments before the judge, and any testimony given while the jury was out of the courtroom.

The move was unprecedented. Never before had either newspaper attempted such a colossal undertaking. When the trial started, people grabbed up newspapers as soon as they hit the stands. It was not an uncommon sight to see downtown office workers with their heads buried behind open pages.

Brinton's idea had worked.

CHAPTER [19]

The Davidson County courthouse, a large imposing rectangular structure dating from 1937 and built of granite and Indiana limestone, loomed over a wide-open square on a gentle knoll in downtown Nashville. On the sixth floor, Courtroom 611 was directly next door to the district attorney's office. Both opened onto a long hall, outfitted with benches against the walls and tall windows looking out onto the grassy plaza and office buildings across the street.

The courtroom walls and floor were painted a pale green. Walnut wainscoting matched the judge's bench and jury box. Waist-high paneled partitions separated the front of the courtroom from the spectators' gallery. Dark green drapes hung from the windows to the judge's right.

An illustration printed in *The Tennessean* showed the courtroom's layout, with Judge Cornelius's bench elevated in the middle of the far end and flanked by the American and Tennessee flags. To the judge's right, a level down and behind a three-foot-high walnut partition, was the court officer's seat. To his left was the witness box, also behind a partition, which then turned the corner to partially hide the jury box, outfitted with thirteen green leather padded chairs. The court stenographer, Reba McMahon, would sit at a narrow table facing the judge and witness box.

Two doors led out of the back of the courtroom, one of which was immediately adjacent to the jury box. The other, on the opposite side, led to the judge's chambers. At floor level, the defense would be seated to the judge's right at an L-shaped table facing the jury. On the other end of the same table, facing the judge and the witness stand, were the chairs for the prosecution. A single aisle divided sixteen benches, eight on each side, room enough to seat only sixty-four spectators.

District Attorney General Thomas Shriver (left) with Special Prosecutor John J. Hooker Sr.
Nashville Public Library, Special Collections, Banner Newspaper Collection

***

On Monday, July 14, 1969, another stiflingly hot day, thirteen months after a gun was held to Haynie Gourley's head and fired, John J. Hooker Sr., Attorney General Thomas Shriver, ADA Hal Hardin, Jack Norman Sr., and Cecil Branstetter met at 9:00 a.m. in Division III of the Criminal Court to begin the tedious process of picking a jury.

But there was a glitch on the first morning of the trial. The beginning of the *voir dire*, or vocal questioning of prospective jurors, was held up for about twenty minutes by a jammed lock. The pool of prospective jurors was temporarily stranded in a seventh-floor room. Court officers were finally able to open the door after about twenty minutes.

A second delay came when defense attorney Jack Norman Sr. made a stunning announcement. On the previous Saturday morning, July 12, a man had contacted Powell's lawyers and claimed that he, not Powell, had killed Haynie Gourley.

The confession was made by a painter's helper, thirty-year-old James Joe Noe, of 1214 Martin St. in Nashville. Noe said he killed Haynie Gourley because the Capitol Chevrolet president had "sent him to the pen and he wanted to get even with him."

Norman asked for a recess until 1:00 p.m. to check out the man's story. When court resumed, Norman revealed that, sure enough, Noe had served two terms in the penitentiary for burglaries at Capitol Chevrolet. Branstetter said Noe refused to talk, only saying, "I've said too much already."

Noe had been picked up at 4:00 a.m. on the previous Saturday and charged with burglarizing Preston Lincoln-Mercury. A police detective said the man was a former mental patient and was drunk when he made his confession.

Noe was taken to the Metro jail and was later brought to police

Josephine Gourley and son Billy Gourley arrive for jury selection. © *The Tennessean – USA TODAY NETWORK*

headquarters to be questioned. Thin and rawboned, with a long face and prominent Adam's apple, Noe repeated the claim that he killed Haynie Gourley "to get even with him."

Court records revealed that Noe was sentenced to a year and a day in the penitentiary after pleading guilty to stealing a car from Capitol Chevrolet four years earlier. On another occasion, he broke into the dealership and stole four spray-paint guns and the contents of a cigarette machine.

After holding up court for an entire morning, Noe's confession was dismissed due to the fact that he was white, and his story did not match Powell's claim that a Black man had killed Haynie Gourley.

In the jury selection process, the defense had fifteen peremptory challenges, or strikes, meaning it could remove a juror for any reason whatsoever. The State had six such challenges.

When questioning got underway, Assistant District Attorney Hal Hardin was concerned by Shriver's declaration that the prosecution intended to seek death in the electric chair if Powell were convicted of first-degree murder. Judge Cornelius ruled that anyone who opposed the death penalty could not be dismissed solely for that reason. Shriver made two more appeals to persuade Judge Cornelius to bar opponents of capital punishment from serving on the jury. Judge Cornelius refused.

Despite the ruling, Shriver persisted in asking every prospective juror to express an opinion on the death penalty. Hardin looked over at Bill Powell, with his aura of affability and his teenaged children sitting near him, and thought how this young family, just by their appearance, would garner sympathy from any jury. No one would convict him if the death penalty were a possibility.

The jury selection process was contentious from the beginning. One of the jurors selected the first day, Alto Lee Jacobs, a candy salesman, admitted that while he did not know Powell personally, the defendant had once befriended his son. Jacobs insisted that this fact would not influence his decision. Judge Cornelius refused to excuse Jacobs, even though the prospective juror admitted that he had an opinion about whether a third person had been in Haynie Gourley's car. Jacobs was accepted when Jack Norman asked if he could "go into the jury box as an honest man" and make up his mind based on the proof produced in court. Jacobs replied that he could. Hooker and Shriver were livid that the judge allowed Jacobs to remain.

As the days went by, jurors were seated, then dismissed. Sharp exchanges between the prosecution and the defense lawyers occurred at almost every turn. Taking into account the fact that Powell claimed a Black man had committed the crime, Branstetter and Norman used five of their peremptory challenges to dismiss every Black prospective juror.

Another potential juror, Mrs. W. P. Chastain, a housewife and mother of four children, said she was "real stubborn" and would hold the State to its burden of proof.

"I feel very strongly about that," she said, prompting Branstetter to say, "We think she'll make a good juror."

By day's end on Tuesday, a total of sixty-two persons had been interrogated. Only nine were excused because they had already formed an opinion in the case and thus could not give Powell a fair trial.

Finally, on Wednesday, Shriver stopped questioning the prospective jurors about capital punishment, although he still planned on seeking the death penalty if Powell were convicted. ADA Hardin was relieved, but he wondered if the damage had already been done.

By the end of the third day, only two jurors had been seated, and Judge Cornelius had to draw another 150 names out of a second jury pool.

The effort dragged on into Thursday. The day brought a ferocious clash between Shriver and the defense attorneys when Norman homed in on a particular prospective juror.

"They've been talking about the electric chair and 99 and 110 years and so on. You wouldn't hesitate a minute to turn him loose either, would you?" Norman asked, snapping his fingers.

The man said he would not hesitate "if I knew in my heart that he was innocent."

"That's right. We'll take that juror," Norman bellowed.

In the courtroom, Powell, at six-foot-four and weighing 230 pounds, appeared to be uncomfortable in a chair too small for his hefty frame. Out in the hall, however, he was at ease and courteous to everyone, calling newsmen by their first names, introducing friends to his attorneys, and answering questions posed by bystanders. If he was anything but confident that the trial would go in his favor, he did not show it.

Josephine Gourley sat stone-faced during the jury selection process but brushed away tears when the indictment against Powell was read, charging that William E. Powell "did commit the offense of murder upon the body of W. Haynie Gourley."

Each day, she was accompanied by her son Billy. The two would wait until the courtroom emptied before slipping out the back way to avoid the cameras. Her daughter, JoAnn, attended along with her husband, William Bainbridge III, and Haynie's younger brother, Everett Gourley, who lived in Nashville.

Helen and Bill Powell's teenage children—Mary Helen, seventeen, and Bill Jr., fourteen—were frequently seen in court sitting near their father. Since both teens had summer jobs at Capitol Chevrolet, they did not attend every day. Because Helen Powell was to be a witness, she was not allowed in the courtroom when the actual trial began but waited in the hallway, passing the time reading the newspaper or a book. When court recessed, she would accompany her husband to lunch.

Many young Nashville lawyers also attended, eager to see the two titans—Norman and Hooker—go against each other.

One young lawyer mused: "An hour of this is worth a month in the classroom at law school."

***

It had been a scorching week, with high humidity and temperatures hovering near 100 degrees, but on Saturday, July 19, the painstaking process of selecting a jury was over. An all-white panel of ten men and two women, plus an alternate male juror, was sworn in to hear evidence in the murder trial of William E. Powell. An astonishing total of 117 persons had been interviewed by the attorneys.

The state still insisted that it would seek the death penalty if Powell were convicted. After District Attorney Thomas Shriver read the indictment to the jury, Cecil Branstetter and Jack Norman Sr. stood up. Norman announced in a thundering voice, "The defendant pleads not guilty because he is not guilty."

When asked by reporters about the jury selection process, Branstetter said that the defense had looked for "intelligent jurors with analytical minds that can separate fact from fantasy."

Shriver said picking a juror was like playing "Russian roulette" and was more a matter of "hunches and intuition."

Hooker replied that he had sought jurors who were "positive, determined, and had the courage to do what is obviously unpleasant in assessing punishment." At the close of the *voir dire*, he admitted to Hal Hardin that by insisting on the death penalty "we lost a lot of good jurors."

Norman remained silent on the subject. He was not about to reveal the secret weapon he always employed when it came to jury selection, one that had worked for him over and over through the years. Given the make-up of this jury, he was certain it would work again this time.

The men and women of the jury were sequestered in a converted jail on the seventh floor of the courthouse, directly above the courtroom. The quarters, although a bit spartan, were comfortable enough. A cook prepared three meals a day. The jurors were only allowed outside the courthouse on Sundays. They were to talk to no one but could take walks on nearby streets. Any messages from their families had to be relayed through a representative from the Metro policeman on duty. The jurors were further ordered not to discuss court proceedings with each other.

Jack Norman was a master at schmoozing jurors. As a grand gesture made in front of the empaneled jury, he asked Judge Cornelius if the men and women could be permitted to watch the Apollo 11 moon landing, scheduled for Sunday, July 20. Ordinarily, jurors could not watch television or listen to a radio or read newspapers. Two of the jurors had been sequestered since Monday, July 14, and four more had missed the launch of Apollo 11 on Wednesday morning. Norman also asked if court could be delayed until 1:00 p.m. on Monday so the jurors could sleep in after a late night of watching the walk on the moon.

The judge agreed to his request.

On Sunday, July 20, a television was brought to the courtroom, and the jury was allowed to watch the landing that afternoon and the astronauts' walk on the moon that evening. Assistant District Attorney Hal Hardin was next door in Shriver's office, where he and several other members of the prosecution team watched the historical event.

The Powell case made NBC news when Chet Huntley and David Brinkley announced that sequestered jurors in an important Nashville trial would be allowed to watch the moon landing on television.

Spectators crowd the door of Courtroom 611 in hopes of finding a seat. *Nashville Public Library, Special Collections, Banner Newspaper Collection*

With testimony about to begin, a circus-like frenzy prevailed around Courthouse Square, with television crews and their oversized cameras moving in and out of the crowds. Curious spectators jostled for a glimpse of the two families

Monday morning at 6:00 a.m., when Assistant District Attorney Hal Hardin walked from his nearby apartment on James Robertson Parkway to the courthouse, he passed dozens of people already lined up for blocks, hoping for a chance to claim one of the sixty-four seats in Courtroom 611.

Front page stories and the transcript of the jury selection process and any other rulings about the case could now be had for the ten-cent price of a newspaper. Both the morning *The Tennessean* and the afternoon *Nashville Banner* had reporters and photographers camped out on sidewalks and in the smoke-filled hall on the sixth floor to capture the trial participants for a statement or a snapshot.

***

Testimony began at 1:00 p.m. on Monday, July 21, to a packed courtroom.

The contrast between the opposing sides couldn't have been more stark. In the right half of the room, the Gourley family, dressed in dark, somber expensive clothes, evoked a sense of wealth and privilege. On the left, members of the more youthful Powell contingent wore light-colored summer attire. One Nashville society type noted that the Gourley women looked as if they had just stepped out of Neiman-Marcus, while Powell's family and friends gave the appearance of having shopped at Casual Corner, a local store popular among high school and college students.

The atmosphere was thick with tension as the prosecution's first witness, Josephine Gourley, wearing a smartly-tailored black dress with white buttons and a collar piped in white, stepped up to be sworn in.

Questioned by special prosecutor John J. Hooker Sr., Josephine answered several procedural questions—that she had been married to Haynie Gourley for thirty-four years when he was killed, that she had two children, William Haynie Gourley Jr., age twenty-four, and Mrs. William Bainbridge III, twenty-nine.

For the next hour and ten minutes, she testified about the events leading up to her husband's death, beginning with the night of Wednesday, May 22, 1968, when Powell came to the Gourley home and agreed to leave the company. She described the morning of the murder and related the scene at her home as Haynie was about to leave for work.

"I was going to the beauty shop at Rich-Schwartz, and he handed me a hundred-dollar bill. I never charge anything. He always kept several one-hundred-dollar bills folded up in his wallet.

"He was so happy. I have never seen him so happy, and I walked to the car, and the last thing he said—"

Defense counsel Cecil Branstetter leapt to his feet, objecting to testimony about the mental state of Haynie Gourley the morning he left for work.

The defense was overruled, and Josephine Gourley was allowed to divulge the last words her husband said to her on the morning of his death.

"He said, 'I have my boy where I want him. This is the happiest day of my life.'"

"Then he got in the car and drove off, and that's the last time you saw him alive?" Hooker asked.

Josephine Gourley nodded.

Tall and handsome and soft-spoken, Billy Gourley took the stand next. Dressed in a dark gray business suit, he gave his age as twenty-four and said he had received a BA degree in business administration from Vanderbilt University, minoring in economics.

Hooker asked about his history of working at Capitol Chevrolet.

"I guess I started when I was about twelve or thirteen years old," Billy said. "Except for the time I attended summer school one year, I always worked at Capitol during summers. I became a full-time employee in November 1967."

Hooker next asked about his relationship with Bill Powell.

"I liked Mr. Powell. I didn't quite understand why he didn't really try and help teach me, but I liked Mr. Powell."

When asked about the night of Wednesday, May 22, 1968, when Powell agreed to leave Capitol Chevrolet, Billy gave much the same version as his mother.

Finally, Hooker asked about the morning of his father's death.

"I was sitting at my desk," Billy answered, choking slightly, "and he came to the opening in my office, and I got up and went over to him.

He said, 'Bill Powell wants to take a ride and talk. I'll let you know what he said when I get back.'"

"And those were the last words you ever had with him?"

"Those were the last words," Billy answered.

Hooker asked if Billy knew where his father carried his billfold.

"He carried it in his back pocket," Billy replied.

"Which pocket?" asked Hooker.

"He carried it in his back-left pocket because I carry mine in my right pocket, and he would say, 'No, you should put it in the left pocket where the button is.'"

Hooker then turned back to the subject of Bill Powell.

"Did Mr. Powell, at any time, any place after this occurrence where your father lost his life, ever talk to you about this occurrence?"

"No, sir, he never said anything," replied Billy.

"You mean all the time since May 24, 1968, to the present time he has never mentioned this incident to you in his life?"

"No, sir."

The defense did not cross-examine Billy, and he stepped down and joined his mother.

The prosecution then called Third National Bank president Sam Fleming, who had been Haynie's good friend and Capitol Chevrolet's banker for over two decades. Fleming described how Haynie had come to his office the morning before his death, seeking a loan to buy back Bill Powell's stock.

Fleming said there had not been enough time to draw up papers, so the loan had not gone through before Haynie was killed.

The next witness to take the stand was Thomas Jackson, manager of the Louisville zone for the Chevrolet Motor Company. Jackson told Hooker that he had known Haynie Gourley since 1937 and had often stayed with the Gourleys when he was in town for business.

Jackson was asked about the Thursday lunch meeting the day before Haynie was murdered.

He testified that he had emphasized to Haynie that should he buy Powell's interest in the dealership that no money was to change hands, and nothing should be signed until approval was received from the Chevrolet Division of the General Motors Corporation.

The next part of Hooker's questioning had to do with the contract Bill Powell and Haynie Gourley signed in 1966 when Powell bought a twenty-five percent interest in Capitol Chevrolet. Jackson explained that Paragraph Three of that document named both W. Haynie Gourley and William E. Powell as franchisees.

Hooker asked who owned the franchise after Haynie Gourley's death.

"William E. Powell," replied Jackson.

"So, then the only person who could operate the Chevrolet business after Mr. Gourley was killed was Mr. Powell?"

"Correct."

"Regardless of the fact that he owned only twenty-five percent and they owned seventy-five?" asked Hooker.

"That's right," answered Jackson.

"That's all," Hooker said, glancing at the jury.

When Jack Norman got up to cross-examine Jackson, the defense attorney showed why he was one of the top criminal lawyers anywhere.

He brought up what he called "wife trouble," suggesting that Josephine Gourley had caused the initial conflict between Haynie Gourley and Bill Powell because she wanted her son Billy to be promoted to an executive position.

Norman was able to get Thomas Jackson to testify that on Thursday, May 23, 1968, the four men—Haynie Gourley, Powell, Jackson, and Summers—were not able to have a private business discussion at Capitol Chevrolet and that they had to leave the premises to talk.

Billy Gourley sat there astounded, listening as Thomas

> Jackson agreed with Jack Norman, knowing full well Jackson was aware of all the meeting rooms and his father's own soundproof office where anyone could talk without being overheard.

Norman was clearly attempting to leave the jury with the impression that if any important business discussions were to take place, the parties would have to leave Capitol Chevrolet, thus the reason Bill Powell wanted to take a ride with Haynie.

Then, Norman, addressing Jackson, said something shockingly untrue: "When Haynie Gourley died on May 24, 1968, Bill Powell had no way in the world to know that he would become the dealer of Capitol Chevrolet."

> ADA Hal Hardin thought back to April, to Bill Powell's statements when he tried to have the indictment dismissed: "He, William E. Powell, alone had the legal right to operate Capitol Chevrolet." Of course, Powell knew full well he would get the dealership if Haynie Gourley died.

Thomas Jackson stepped down, but he had done harm to the State's case by falling into Norman's trap.

Next to testify for the State was John Glenn, Capitol Chevrolet's accountant and secretary of the company. He, too, turned out to be a disaster for the prosecution when Norman got his chance at him. However, it was learned that in 1967 Bill Powell made over three times the salary he earned at the previous dealership. Shriver was able to make the point that Powell had a lot to lose if he were forced out of Capitol Chevrolet.

Glenn said that on the day before the murder, Haynie had asked him to work out the specifics of Powell's departure and to draw up a new contract with General Motors. However, Glenn said, he did not have time to set anything in motion because Haynie was killed the next day.

On cross-examination, Norman asked about the training of Billy Gourley by Bill Powell. Glenn testified that Josephine Gourley had not been satisfied with Billy's training. This gave Norman an opportunity to hurl an insult at Josephine. "That's all right, my wife is that way, too."

Then, Norman came on full force, bellowing with crushing rhetoric that startled the courtroom.

"At the instant of Mr. Gourley's death, there was no way for Bill Powell or anyone else to know that Bill Powell could get this franchise unless General Motors thought enough of him to give it to him. Is that true?"

"That's true," answered Glenn.

> What? Billy was dumbfounded. Norman had set it up to make the jury think that Powell didn't know he would get the dealership if Haynie died. Norman had phrased the question brilliantly, de-emphasizing "unless General Motors wanted to give it to him." Of course, General Motors would never interrupt the operation of one of its most lucrative dealerships. But Billy also knew that if Powell had wanted to carry out Haynie's wishes for his son to inherit the business, he could have worked something out. But it all came too easy for Powell. In only three years, he was handed the huge, successful dealership that Haynie Gourley had spent thirty-six years building up.

Then Norman went off base, again saying something that wasn't true. He said the letter written to General Motors in early June 1968, not even two weeks after Haynie's death, was produced "in spite of Bill

Powell's being considered a suspect."

"The newspapers were full of that, weren't they?" asked Norman.

"Yes, sir," answered Glenn.

> "No, they were not," Billy wanted to shout. The newspapers said the police were looking for a Black man. In private, people had suspicions, but nothing was ever mentioned in the press about Bill Powell's being a suspect in the murder.

Norman prattled on, taking on a folksy tone. "After you wrote that letter to General Motors, notwithstanding this investigation was going on about Old Bill Powell, they decided to have him take over that franchise for a certain length of time, up until 1970, did they not?"

"Yes, sir."

"And that's the way it happened, didn't it, John?"

"Yes, sir."

"So, regardless of all this investigation, they entered into a new franchise agreement with him."

"Yes, sir."

Shriver's weak re-cross confirmed that one of the requirements and conditions of a survivor to become the dealer is the ownership of at least 25% of the stock in the company.

"Did Mr. Powell meet these conditions? And was he the designated franchise holder?" asked Shriver.

Glenn answered "yes" to both questions.

With that, Shriver said, "I believe that's all."

> Billy sat stunned by Norman's trickery. He thought about the timing of his father's death. In possibly another week or two, had his father lived, Bill Powell would no longer have owned twenty-five percent of

the stock, and his name would have been removed from Paragraph Three in a new contract. It had to be more than a matter of coincidence that his father was killed before the deal could go through. Did the jurors even realize this?

Capitol Chevrolet receptionist and switchboard operator, Billie Dee Boyer. *Nashville Public Library, Special Collections, Banner Newspaper Collection*

The next witnesses were employees at Capitol Chevrolet, who were questioned about the day of the murder. Billie Dee Boyer, the switchboard operator and receptionist, went first. She testified that a person could not hear conversations when doors were closed to Mr. Gourley and Mr. Powell's offices.

On cross-examination, Branstetter asked Boyer multiple times to estimate what time it was when Haynie and Bill Powell left the showroom floor on the morning of May 24, 1968. Over and over, she said she thought it was between five or ten minutes until eleven. She estimated that her call to the police and ambulance was made around 11:25.

Branstetter then got into the technicalities of the number of steps from the showroom floor up to the service department and how long it would have taken the two men to reach the area where Haynie's car was parked. Branstetter asked her repeatedly how many steps there were. Boyer kept answering that she was not good at judging distances and that she had no idea.

But Branstetter was not satisfied. He wanted to know how many minutes it would have taken someone to climb the steps and reach the area where Mr. Gourley's car was parked. She kept saying she didn't know. The best she could figure was one to two minutes.

Branstetter went on, stretching out his questioning by rephrasing the same question several times over, trying to get Billie Dee Boyer to shrink the time from the moment Mr. Gourley told her he was going on a ride with Bill Powell until she received the request to call an ambulance. Boyer would not budge. She thought a good fifteen minutes had gone by, not the five minutes Branstetter was trying to elicit from her.

The service writers and the shop foreman who were present when Powell and Haynie left and who witnessed the car coming in at a high rate of speed were questioned next. All said they did not know that Mr. Gourley was in the car until several minutes had elapsed. The men repeated Bill Powell's account of what happened, that a Black man had jumped into the car at a four-way stop and that Mr. Gourley had been shot as he reached in his coat pocket for his wallet.

Shop foreman George Crawford was asked about the dent in the steel frame of the front passenger seat of Haynie Gourley's car. Crawford said he could not explain why this was.

Service writer Chuck Williams, who had been the first to say out loud that Mr. Gourley was dead, took the stand. Having run countless errands for Mr. Gourley through the years, he told Shriver that Haynie always carried his wallet in his left hip pocket.

On cross examination, Branstetter had Williams go back over the details of Powell's story.

"So, when Mr. Shriver first had you say that Powell gestured toward his coat pocket—" Branstetter was saying.

Shriver jumped up. "I object to the 'had you say,' if your Honor please."

But it was too late. "Withdraw it," Branstetter said under his breath.

Patrolman David Allman from the Metro Police Department was next on the stand. Allman testified he had observed a hat, a pair of glasses, and a wallet on the back seat of Haynie's car. Allman said another patrolman arrived just as he was removing the wallet from the car. The second policeman pulled two $100 bills from an inner compartment. A photograph was entered into evidence showing a hat and a pair of glasses in the back seat. Neither appeared to have been crushed or damaged in any way.

> Hal Hardin thought Allman's testimony raised a serious question. Wouldn't the hat and glasses have been flattened if a man had sat in the back seat? But there was never any mention about this inconsistency by the prosecution. Hardin was beginning to worry.

Following Allman's testimony, court was adjourned at 4:37 p.m., to resume the following morning, Wednesday, July 23, 1969, at 9:00 a.m.

***

On Wednesday, July 23, the third day of witness testimony, Nashville awoke to another sweltering summer day. "95 degrees again" read the headline on the front-page weather report, predicting high humidity and a chance for early evening thundershowers.

Despite the heat, lines continued to form outside the courthouse, with more and more people vying for one of the coveted seats in Courtroom 611.

Once inside on the sixth-floor hall, the air was thick with acrid smoke from cigarettes and cigars and the sheer push of the crowds. There was a stampede to muscle through the door when it was opened at 8:30. Bailiffs were forced to expel the overflow once all seats were taken on the benches.

The trial was attracting more attention from courthouse employees than any in recent memory. Lawyers, clerks, and court officers would drop in whenever they had some spare time. Many stood by the door of the courtroom, waiting for a chance to slip inside when someone came out. They were all eager to watch sparks fly between Norman and Hooker.

The morning's testimony began with James Walter Hughes, the truck sales manager of Capitol Chevrolet, taking the stand. He estimated the time Powell was gone to be thirteen to fifteen minutes.

Branstetter attempted to get Hughes to say that only five minutes had elapsed between the time the car left and when it returned. Hughes refused to change his testimony.

> Hal Hardin's heart began to race when the next witness stepped up to the stand. He knew that what he had to say would be highly damaging to the defense and could blow a hole in Powell's story.

Charles Edward Donnelly, a large, thickset man dressed in a white, short-sleeved shirt and dark pants, raised his hand and took his oath.

Hooker came forward to do the questioning. A hush came over the courtroom.

What Donnelly testified to electrified the room.

Around eleven o'clock on May 24, 1968, as he waited in his delivery truck at the stop sign at Arlington Road and Elm Hill Pike, Donnelly saw a black car approaching.

"I've been trading at Capitol Chevrolet since 1945," he told Hooker. "I've known Mr. Gourley all these years. I didn't know Mr. Powell personally but I knew him by sight. I recognized Mr. Gourley's car. Mr. Powell was driving, and Mr. Gourley was sitting on the passenger side."

Donnelly said he went ahead and pulled out onto Elm Hill Pike.

The car was now directly behind him.

Approaching Spence Lane, Donnelly put on his signal to turn left. He testified that a flagman stood at the intersection where a paving crew was resurfacing the road. The man signaled for Donnelly to make his left turn without stopping.

As he turned onto Spence Lane, Donnelly said he glanced back and saw the flagman wave Mr. Gourley's automobile on through the intersection. The car did not stop, Donnelly said. He watched as it continued straight down Elm Hill Pike, with only the two men inside. There was no third man in the back seat, he said.

A loud rustling echoed through the courtroom.

Donnelly told how he waited to be unloaded at the ad agency. Someone came out and signed the waybill. Hooker entered the piece of paper, dated May 24, 1968, into evidence. There was no time stamp on the invoice.

A gasp rose from the packed courtroom at what Donnelly said next.

About ten minutes later, as he was still standing on the loading dock, he saw Mr. Gourley's car coming from the opposite direction.

According to Donnelly, Bill Powell was driving, and Mr. Gourley was visible in the passenger seat. The car crossed the intersection slowly, Donnelly said, because "wasn't anybody going too fast because there was construction people working the road there."

> Billy had not heard this testimony before. So, someone had seen Powell and his father go straight through the intersection without stopping. Billy's mind was racing trying to put the puzzle together when any euphoria he felt evaporated as Branstetter stepped up for cross-examination.

To divert attention from Donnelly's devastating testimony, Branstetter began grilling Donnelly on unrelated subjects. He asked Donnelly for long descriptions of every building and driveway on Elm Hill Pike near the intersection with Spence Lane and to designate the location and size of trees and hedges along the road.

The questions dragged on, with Branstetter asking Donnelly about the length and design of his truck and what gear he had used to slow down to make his turn. No objection came from the prosecution.

Branstetter wouldn't stop. He asked about a pavement roller parked at the intersection.

"That's one of those big contraptions that the man sits up on and has a big round drum?" asked Branstetter.

"Yeah," answered Donnelly.

Branstetter trudged on, asking how many dump trucks were parked near the intersection and to give yet another description of the asphalt roller. Branstetter again wanted to know the length of Donnelly's truck. He asked about the width of the building where he made his delivery. He had Donnelly go into the mechanics of how the back of his truck opened, whether it rolled up or if it was metal or wire construction. Branstetter also asked Donnelly to describe the jacks that lifted the heavy paper he'd delivered onto the loading dock and what the paper Donnelly delivered was used for. None of this had anything to do with what Donnelly claimed to see at the intersection.

> Hal Hardin saw that Branstetter's ploy was working. His own mind was clogged with useless details so that the shock of Donnelly's testimony had worn off. He was sure this was true for the jury, as well.

Only one of Branstetter's questions backfired.

"And then you come down to the residences and on down to a three-way stop at Spence Lane and Elm Hill Pike—"

Donnelly interrupted Branstetter.

"No, it's just one stop. It's just stopping on Spence Lane. There is no stop sign on Elm Hill Pike."

Branstetter realized his error and tossed out more questions about the asphalt roller.

It seemed preposterous to onlookers that the judge allowed Branstetter to continue this repetition of irrelevant details. Even more unbelievable, still no objection came from the prosecution.

On re-cross, Hooker seemed to wake up. "Mr. Donnelly, did you ever at any time that day see more than two people in this car?"

"No sir," Donnelly answered.

"Did you at any time see the black car stop? Or anybody get in it? Or the door ever open?"

"No, sir," Donnelly answered.

"That's all," Hooker said, a hint of satisfaction in his voice.

The next three witnesses to take the stand were members of the paving crew working at the intersection of Elm Hill Pike and Spence Lane.

Grady Wright, foreman for the Globe Construction Company, said he had not seen any Black people in the area at the time. He told Shriver that the only person on foot had been a white girl, perhaps a preteen. Neither Wright nor his crew of two—father and son, Hobart and Freddie Cook—had seen a black car stop and a Black man jump in.

The three construction workers said they saw nothing unusual and were at the site until 11:15. Then, they climbed into Wright's truck and went to a local convenience store for bologna and white bread to bring back for lunch.

Branstetter was unsuccessful in his attempt to have Wright say there was a four-way stop at the intersection. The foreman said there were three tripods covering manholes, and each had a yellow caution light, but there were no stop signs on Elm Hill Pike.

Most importantly for the prosecution, none of the three saw a black Chevrolet speed through the intersection going back toward town. The father and son said it would have been impossible for anyone to go through the intersection very fast since the road had been cut down to one lane.

But Branstetter did win a crucial point. The foreman said he stopped the flagman at 10:30, almost thirty minutes before Powell would have reached the intersection. This was in direct contradiction to Donnelly's testimony.

> Billy Gourley again tensed up. Surely Donnelly had not made up the story about a flagman. The foreman must be mistaken about the time. But it didn't matter. The contradiction had likely registered in the jurors' minds.

Next, a succession of Metro policemen took the stand. Sergeant Frank Galbaugh was the first to talk to Powell after he arrived by ambulance at Vanderbilt Hospital on May 24, 1968. Galbaugh testified that Powell told him the gunman began shooting the moment Mr. Gourley reached into his coat pocket for his wallet.

"Did that attract your attention, what he said about that?" asked Hooker.

"Yes, he said he reached into his coat pocket. I thought it was a little unusual. Most people don't carry them there."

Called to the stand next was Officer Ernest Castleman, who testified about a drawing made by Powell only an hour after he was admitted. The sketch showed the route Powell said he and Haynie took and where the alleged killer jumped into the car. Powell had also marked where he made a U-turn just past Spence Lane before driving back to Capitol Chevrolet.

A heated exchange took place between Norman and Shriver over the introduction of Powell's diagram.

"Pound on that desk all you want," Norman roared.

"There's no use hollering at me about that," Shriver shot back.

"I'm not hollering at you," Norman snapped. "I don't think enough of you to holler at you."

"I'm sorry, I formerly had a high opinion of you," said Shriver.

"I notice you said formerly," Norman snarled.

Judge Cornelius broke in, silencing the two. He ruled the drawing could be entered as evidence. These loud, boisterous outbursts between the opposing attorneys would continue throughout the trial. This was what the spectators had come to see.

Patrolman Joe Dodson testified next, recounting how he and another Metro officer had bagged shattered glass from underneath some trees on Elm Hill Pike just past Massman Drive. Dodson said he went back to the intersection of Elm Hill Pike and Spence Lane and knocked on the doors of several houses. Only one elderly Black woman was home, but she had not seen anything.

On cross-examination, Branstetter said something shocking.

"Do you have any records showing that the resident of that house was released from Central State some weeks or days before this incident?" he asked Dodson, referring to a Tennessee hospital for mental patients.

> Hal Hardin recognized Branstetter's tactic. Plant false information, then quickly withdraw it when the state objects. That way it was planted in the jurors' minds and couldn't be erased. But there was no objection from the prosecution. It didn't matter, thought Hardin. The jury would be left to think some crazed resident of Elm Hill Pike jumped into Haynie's car.

Before he adjourned court for the day, Judge Cornelius asked the lawyers for both the defense and the State to approach the bench, saying he had observed that there was too much repetition of the same evidence over and over.

However, neither the judge nor the prosecution had made an effort to stop Branstetter, and it was evident that his strategy was to defuse any damaging testimony by following up with his repetitive, mind-dulling questions.

***

Dr. T. E Simpkins, medical examiner for Davidson County, was the first witness to take the stand on Thursday morning, July 24, the fourth day of testimony.

Josephine Gourley cried softly as Simpkins described in grisly detail the path the three bullets took as they entered her husband's body, all from the left side. There were two contact entry wounds, Simpkins said, one to the upper shoulder area and one between the left ear and the jawbone, where the killer pressed the gun to Haynie's head and fired.

Simpson testified that the shot to the left side of the chest had been fired from possibly a foot away. A third bullet had fallen onto the examination table, Simpkins said. It had sliced through Haynie's coat and shirt about mid-back but had not broken the skin.

Simpkins had turned over the three bullets to police. A fourth bullet had passed through Haynie's head and exited the right side. This bullet was not found during the autopsy, the doctor said.

> Billy Gourley felt ill. He pictured his father looking on in disbelief as the cold muzzle of the gun was pressed to his neck. Did he not die right then, necessitating a second shot to his chest and a third to his head? It seemed obvious that the first bullet intended for his back had not reached its target. For all practical purposes, his father had been deliberately executed. This was no random, wild shooting spree as Powell had claimed.

Next, the state called William E. Coleman, a twenty-one-year veteran of the Tennessee Bureau of Criminal Investigation.

Coleman told how he examined the interior of the car, looking for any signs of dust on the back carpets. He said he found the black mats to be clean.

Hooker asked what Powell had said about the H.D. Lee Company.

"He said they were just riding along, talking about how the area had built up, and Mr. Gourley pointed to the H.D. Lee Company and said, 'I didn't even know that building was there.'"

"How far from Spence Lane and the intersection of Spence Lane and Elm Hill Pike would you estimate the H.D. Lee Company is?" asked Hooker.

"I would say it is approximately a mile."

Hooker paused to let this fact sink in.

The next witness for the prosecution was Courtland Cunningham, a fifteen-year veteran of the FBI in Washington, D.C.

Cunningham told Shriver he examined Bill Powell's pants and found no gun powder residue. He found no gunpowder residue around the other two holes in Haynie's coat, one on the left side at chest level and one on the back.

He did testify, however, that it was his opinion, after examining Haynie Gourley's coat, that the muzzle of a weapon had been held against Mr. Gourley's collarbone area, near the base of the neck.

Next on the stand was another FBI agent, Myron Scholberg, who testified that he found Caucasian hairs on both Powell's and Mr. Gourley's jackets as well as on the seat covers but no Negroid hairs on any of the items.

On cross-examination, Norman went on the attack.

"So there's nothing, no part of the fabric or anything else in the back seat of this car sent to you to make this examination with, is there?"

"I have nothing designated, no." The witness was excused.

> Billy Gourley sat there, deflated. Another screw-up by the police. How could they have failed to send the back seat covers and floor mats? The floor mats would have been especially crucial since they would have contained dust if there had been someone in the back seat.

The prosecution next put Officer Carl Harrison on the stand. He testified about the line-up on September 7, 1968.

"We put the hat on No. 3," said Harrison, "and Mr. Powell came back out and said that was him. And he marked it on the card and signed his name. He said he couldn't forget those eyes, 'stare-y' eyes."

Shriver continued. "And who else was put in the lineup?"

"There were four other male colored," replied Harrison.

"Who was No. 3?" asked Shriver.

"Gerald Wingard."

On cross-examination, Officer Harrison stated that in late August before the lineup had occurred, he received a mysterious phone call from an unidentified woman, claiming that Gerald James Wingard had told her he killed the Chevrolet man. The woman, who refused to give her name, said Wingard threatened to kill her, and she was pleading for him not to be let out of jail.

Branstetter did not pursue the subject and abruptly dismissed Harrison.

Robert Goodwin, a firearms expert from the Tennessee Bureau of Criminal Identification, identified the bullets that injured Powell and killed Haynie as typical of Winchester ammunition. Hooker entered four bullets into evidence and passed them to the jury in order and asked Goodwin to describe them.

The first bullet was mutilated, said Goodwin, and was in an envelope marked "left front door." It was presumably the bullet that wounded Powell and lodged in the kickplate on the driver's side. There was a second mutilated bullet that was flattened. Hooker asked Goodwin what could have caused this.

"Well, it's usually a very strong indication that the bullet had come into contact with some hard material."

> Hardin waited for Hooker to say where this bullet had been found. But he was disappointed. His own theory was that the killer first tried to shoot Haynie in the back, firing through the seat so that he would die never having known what happened to him. But the bullet hit a metal post in the seat, ricocheted, and pierced Haynie's coat and shirt without breaking the skin. This was the bullet that had fallen out of his clothes and onto the table in the emergency room at General Hospital.

Stepping up to the witness stand next was Detective Bill Larkin, who, along with Sherman Nickens, had been put in charge of the police investigation of the Gourley murder.

The paunchy middle-aged man with dark hair told Hooker that he left Capitol Chevrolet and went to General Hospital after a radio call came in. Hooker wanted to know if Larkin had recovered any of Haynie's personal belongings. Larkin said he received a tie clasp, cufflinks, watch, a pack of Doral cigarettes, and some coins. The items, Larkin said, were catalogued by a nurse and placed in an envelope which she handed to Billy Gourley, Haynie's son.

Hooker zeroed in on the cufflinks, which he held out for Larkin to examine. The detective verified that the fastener on one cufflink was broken off

"Is this the way it was delivered to you at the hospital?"

"Yes, sir."

The cufflinks were entered into evidence and passed to the jury.

> Hal Hardin had a theory about how the one cufflink had been broken. According to Powell's original story, Haynie was shot immediately and slumped over, so the cufflink could not have been touched by the man who allegedly jumped into the car. Hardin thought of Ernest Castleman's testimony about seeing a squarish-looking wound on Bill Powell's forearm. Hardin was pretty sure he knew how it got there.

Hooker next asked about Larkin's inspection of Haynie's car.

"Well, there was a hat and a pair of glasses on the rear seat," said Larkin.

Hooker failed to ask if the items appeared crushed in any way. This was the third mention of a hat and glasses in the back seat, but no explanation was given about how these items remained intact after a man possibly sat on top of them. The hat and glasses would not be brought up again.

Larkin's testimony continued until Judge Cornelius broke in to say the jury's dinner was almost ready.

CHAPTER [20]

The next morning, Friday, July 25, Larkin took the stand for cross-examination by Branstetter who asked Larkin if he had seen an American Airlines credit card in the wallet. Larkin said that he had not.

"Have you later received information or had the opportunity to check a lead where Mr. Gourley's personal airline credit card was used on a trip from someplace in California to someplace in Alaska?"

"No, sir."

> Billy Gourley waited. He knew his family had not been contacted by anyone from a credit card company. No one from the State objected to this question, and once more it seemed Branstetter got away with putting ink in the water by hinting that a credit card had been stolen from the wallet and had ended up being used in California and Alaska, proving there was a third person in the car.

Next, Branstetter asked Larkin about Mr. Gourley's cufflinks.

"When you left the General Hospital, I believe you also saw the two cufflinks?"

"Yes."

"And these were, like all of mine, part of the thing was broken off?"

Branstetter did not wait for an answer. No one challenged this sly intimation that Haynie's cufflink must have already been broken when he had gotten dressed that morning. Anyone who knew Haynie well would have known this couldn't be true. He would never have worn a broken cufflink.

Branstetter asked Larkin if he had investigated the fifteen Black men employed by Capitol Chevrolet. Larkin said he searched police files but found nothing.

"Did you receive information about a male Negro that had run into a restaurant at about twelve o'clock on May 24, 1968, and said, 'I was involved in an awful shooting. I wouldn't have gotten involved in it if I had known there was going to be a shooting.' Did you get that report?"

Larkin said yes, but after investigating the restaurant in the Trimble Bottom area of Nashville, he found that the incident had never occurred.

"Was there any other shooting or killing in Davidson County that you know of on this day between eleven and twelve o'clock?"

"Not to my knowledge. I don't recall it."

> Branstetter's stunt was not lost on two young lawyers who had come to watch the trial. He had repeatedly brought up the subject of other Black men. With no objection from the prosecution, he was once again able to plant false information that could not be undone in a juror's mind.

Next, Branstetter appeared to accuse Larkin of wrongdoing, saying he, Branstetter, knew policemen didn't make much money and had to supplement their incomes.

Larkin admitted that he had taken on several outside jobs for years.

"You had many conversations with Mrs. Gourley?"

"No, sir, not many."

"Have you, at this time, received any pay in connection with this case in addition to your regular salary?" Branstetter asked, intimating that Larkin may have made a financial arrangement with Mrs. Gourley.

"No, sir, I have not."

"Or expenses?"

"No, sir."

> Billy Gourley was furious. Branstetter was insinuating that his mother had made payments to Larkin. But he was not prepared for the bomb Branstetter dropped next, shocking the courtroom.

"Did you get a call from the bus company here in Nashville stating that on the morning of May the 24, 1968, that a Negro with an old hat, work pants, and a jacket, got off the bus with a gun at Fesslers Lane and Elm Hill Pike at 10:45 on May the 24, 1968?"

The courtroom exploded into loud whispers. Everyone waited for a defiant objection from the prosecution, but none came. Branstetter had struck again.

"No, sir. I didn't receive that call," answered Larkin.

With that answer, Branstetter thanked the witness, saying, "That's all."

Next, Ernest Lee Wasdon, who had arrived that morning from California, took the stand for the State.

Wasdon told Shriver that he had been employed during the months of April, May, and June of 1968 by the Parks Job Corps Center in Pleasanton, California.

Shriver handed Wasdon a photograph and asked if he could identify the man.

"Corpsman Wingard," replied Wasdon.

Wasdon described incidents that occurred on May 24 and May 29, 1968, saying Wingard had to be subdued. Wingard was sent back to

Nashville on June 1, 1968.

Here was final proof that Gerald James Wingard, positively identified by Powell as the man who jumped into the car on Elm Hill Pike, could not have killed Haynie Gourley.

With no cross-examination from the defense, Wasdon was excused to fly back to California.

***

After a recess for lunch, Hooker announced a new witness.

The spectator gallery began to whisper. Who was this slight Black man with dark skin, a narrow, angular face, and a pencil-thin mustache? He was dressed in dark pants and a clean starched white, long-sleeved shirt with an open collar. A black glasses case protruded from his shirt pocket.

There had been rumors of a surprise witness, but this unassuming little man did not look the part of someone who could destroy the defense's case.

As he had done when most of the State's witnesses were testifying, Jack Norman swiveled around in his chair so that his back was to the witness stand as Walter Lee Davis took his oath. With glasses perched on the end of his nose, Norman chewed on an unlit cigar and held a yellow legal pad in his lap, pen in hand.

It was clear that Norman's rude gesture was meant to intimidate the witness.

The courtroom grew quiet.

With Hooker questioning, Davis testified that he was fifty-four years old, was born in Maury County, Tennessee, and had lived in Tennessee all his life. He was the father of nine children, the youngest of whom was seven, the oldest twenty-seven.

Davis said that he had worked for Sheco Construction Company for two years. During May 1968, he was using his wife's car to ferry five workers from his home in Spring Hill, Tennessee, about forty miles south of Nashville, to a construction site on Elm Hill Pike.

Davis said that on May 24, 1968, Sheco Construction Company was preparing a site on Elm Hill Pike to build a Kroger warehouse and that he was a "powder man," which meant he did blasting to level the ground. That day, he said, he parked his car in a field on the site and headed to the Sheco construction trailer which was near the corner of Elm Hill Pike and Massman Drive. There, he got into one of the Sheco pick-up trucks to haul dynamite from the trailer to the blasting site.

Hooker handed Davis a set of pictures.

"I want you to state whether or not this is the truck that you were using on the morning of May 24, 1968."

Davis said it was.

Davis described how at "something to eleven," he left the blasting site and returned to the construction trailer. As he was sitting in the truck having lunch, he saw a car pull up under some trees on the side of Elm Hill Pike near Massman Drive.

"Were you able to see it plainly?" Hooker asked.

"Yes, sir," answered Davis.

"What kind of car and color was it?"

"It was a black Chevrolet."

Loud gasps sounded throughout the courtroom, followed by a low rumble of voices. Then, silence. One could hear a pin drop.

Davis said two men were in the car, about two-hundred feet from where he was sitting.

"Did you see anybody on the back seat?"

"No."

"Were these white men or colored men?"

"They were white."

"And were you looking right at them?" Hooker asked.

"Yes, sir."

"Well, tell what these two men that were in the black Chevrolet did then."

Davis began his answer, his voice soft, but deliberate.

"Well, after this car pulled off to the side and stopped, I would guess two-and-a-half to three minutes, they was sitting in the car. Then both of them got out, walked to the back end of the car. And I saw this driver motioning his hands at the passenger."

Davis made gestures with his hands as if he were scolding someone. The driver, he said, had his back to the road.

Hooker stood motionless for a minute. There was not a sound in the courtroom. All eyes were trained on the small figure in the witness box.

"What happened next?" asked Hooker.

"These two men go back to the car, gets in, driver gets in on his side, the passenger gets in on his side. This driver sits there, just a little short time. Then, he gets out, he walks to the rear of the car and opens the trunk. And he walked on around to the right-hand side and gets in the back seat. And about two-and-a-half minutes, not over three minutes, I heard a shot."

"How many shots did you hear?" asked Hooker.

Davis said he heard four shots and that the last one was loud.

The courtroom erupted into loud chatter. People were looking at one another. Billy Gourley sat stone still. The gallery grew quiet, the atmosphere tense and anticipatory.

Walter Lee Davis waits for his turn to testify for the State. © *The Tennessean – USA TODAY NETWORK*

"And then what did you see?"

Davis described how the driver, who he said was the taller of the two men, got out of the right side of the car and came around and closed the trunk. Then he climbed into the driver's seat, drove a few hundred feet up Elm Hill Pike, pulled into a driveway next to a rock wall, and backed out into the road. Then, he came speeding back toward town.

"What did you notice about the man who was riding in the seat on the right-hand side of the front seat?" asked Hooker.

"Well, I noticed this man, this passenger, leaned over like this." Davis hunched forward in the witness chair and dropped his head.

A rumble of voices rose from the gallery. Billy felt as if an arrow had pierced his heart. He looked at his mother. She was staring straight ahead.

Hooker waited until the courtroom was quiet again.

"What did you do then?"

"I started work doing the same thing, loading my holes, getting ready to make a shot at twelve-thirty."

Hooker purposefully looked at the jury, nodded his head in their direction, then sat down ceremoniously.

> So this is how it happened. Billy could hardly breathe. The terror and shock his father must have felt when a gun was held to his head and fired by a man he had trusted and put his faith in.

Branstetter got up and walked over to the witness stand. He paused for a moment.

"Walter, how old are you?" Branstetter asked.

"Fifty-four."

"Mr. Davis, what color suit do I have on?"

"Well, now, I can't tell from here. You mean—"

"Can you see very well?" snapped Branstetter.

"Yes, sir, I can see."

"Do you wear glasses?"

"No, sir, I just wear them in a close place."

"Where were you born?" Branstetter was firing questions in rapid succession, barely allowing Davis time to answer.

"I was born in Maury County."

"Do you remember what day or the year?" Branstetter asked, his voice dripping with condescension.

"May 15, 1915."

"1915. Are you the same Walter Lee Davis that was convicted of forgery and served time in the penitentiary here in Nashville?" Branstetter asked.

"Same one," Davis answered without hesitation.

"You served a year in the penitentiary here in Nashville, is that right?"

"Eight months and seventeen days," Davis corrected Branstetter.

Hearing this, spectators shifted noisily in their seats.

Then Branstetter let loose. For the next two hours, he slammed Davis, never once referring to his story about what he said he saw on May 24, 1968. Instead, he battered Davis with questions that had nothing to do with his testimony. Branstetter, instead, spent an entire hour berating Davis for not being able to estimate the size of a small storage trailer on the Kroger site.

"Would you say the small trailer was half as big as the large trailer, or less than half as big, or what size would you say it was?" Branstetter asked.

"I wouldn't say," said Davis.

"Well, how long was it, Walter, in feet?" Branstetter had moved in closer to Walter, almost shouting in his face.

"Well, I wouldn't state how long it was. I don't remember." Davis looked as if were thinking hard, trying to figure out how to answer.

Branstetter would not stop. He hammered Davis with another dozen questions about the trailer sizes, pressing over and over for an estimate.

Davis looked helpless, yet Hooker and Shriver never made an objection. Judge Cornelius said nothing. Branstetter continued his verbal onslaught, asking Davis to estimate how far he had parked his wife's car from the Sheco trailer on the morning of May 24, 1968. Davis tried to answer, but again Branstetter wasn't satisfied with his estimate. Branstetter mocked Davis if he said he didn't understand what Branstetter was asking, even though Branstetter had made his questions purposely vague.

"Are you hard of hearing?" Branstetter demanded to know every time Davis asked for a question to be repeated.

When he asked Davis to draw something on a map, and Davis said he couldn't, Branstetter became belligerent.

"I want you to draw it," Branstetter commanded sternly. "There's another trailer there. I want you to draw where it was located, because you were the one that pulled the truck down there. I wasn't out there."

When Davis finally tried and couldn't get the drawing right, Branstetter became impatient, lashing out at him when he hesitated. Yet the judge said nothing, and the prosecuting attorneys remained quiet.

Branstetter kept up his bullying, slinging rapid-fire questions at Davis, returning again and again to the size of the two trailers. When Davis would attempt an answer, Branstetter would cut him off, not allowing him to finish a sentence. With no one stopping him, Branstetter posed the same set of questions until Davis appeared completely cowed and confused.

As the repetitious questioning continued, people seated in the courtroom became restless. What did these measurements and trailer sizes have to do with what Davis witnessed? Why was Branstetter allowed to continue in this manner?

Just when it seemed Branstetter would move on to another subject, he once again brought up the location and size of the trailers.

Not once did he return to the subject of the men in the black car.

"Now, when you backed in between the trailers, to get to the door of the big trailer, where was the small trailer and the outhouse in relation to the cab of your truck?"

Davis hesitated, then tried to explain in a halting voice where these objects were.

"You're not sure, are you, Walter?" Davis admitted that he was not sure about the exact distances between an outhouse and the smaller trailer. By now, Davis was so rattled that if he knew the answer, he was unable to say.

But Branstetter kept up his assault. The uneasy rustling in the courtroom grew louder. Branstetter seemed not to notice. Neither did Judge Cornelius.

Branstetter accused Davis of lying about what type of truck he was driving on the day of the murder, contending that he had used a flatbed truck, not a pick-up. Branstetter further claimed that Davis picked up a load of dynamite at Sheco's property behind Capitol Chevrolet at the exact time he said he had seen the two men in the black car.

Davis tried to explain that he had only driven a pick-up truck and that he had not been to Sheco's storage facility that day.

"Just a moment," Branstetter said testily. "Let me finish. Don't be in a hurry."

At this point Judge Cornelius broke in. It appeared that he was about to bring Branstetter's barrage to a stop. Instead, he said sternly, "Any further laughing in the back and I'll clear it out, so you just decide yourselves whether or not you want to remain or whether or not you want to leave."

This interruption did not deter Branstetter. His questions came so fast that Davis was having more and more trouble getting a sentence out. At one point, Davis became so addled by one ambiguous question that he answered by saying, "I guess so."

"You guess so," Branstetter said with a sneer. "But you don't know, do you? You are not sure, are you? Let the record show the witness doesn't answer," Branstetter boomed, waving his arm in the direction of the court reporter.

At long last, Hooker stood up. "Well, the witness didn't answer if

Your Honor please, because he didn't understand the question. I didn't understand it either."

Another hour passed. Branstetter asked which policemen had come to Davis's home in Spring Hill. Davis was not able to give any names or descriptions, but this didn't stop Branstetter from asking the question time and time again.

Then, to the amazement of the spectators, Branstetter abruptly returned once again to the sizes of the trailers at the Sheco construction site.

> "Unbelievable," Hal Hardin muttered under his breath. He knew the initial impact of Davis's original testimony had long been lost in this cascade of useless details.

Branstetter next referred to an injury Davis sustained after falling off a tractor.

"Did you tell a policeman you were just about to lose your mind or memory?" asked Branstetter.

"No, I didn't tell anybody about losing my mind."

With this, Branstetter finally said the words, "That's all."

Hooker stood up on redirect. Norman was still sitting with his back to the witness stand, rocking slightly in his chair, staring down at his legal pad. As Hooker spoke, Norman began to rock harder. His chair was making a squeaking sound. Every eye in the courtroom was trained on Norman as the sound grew louder.

Hooker looked back at Norman, but neither Shriver nor Judge Cornelius made a move to stop the noise.

Norman continued to rock, now violently.

"Now, Walter," Hooker finally began, raising his voice against the din, "they asked you something about having been convicted for passing forged checks in Williamson County. Do you remember when that was?"

"About thirty-three or thirty-four years ago," replied Davis.

"Well, if it was 1936, that's thirty-three years ago. You must have been twenty-one years old, then, is that right?"

"Yes, sir."

"And how much was the check that was involved in that offense they have asked you about that you committed thirty-three years ago?"

Branstetter piped up. "May it please the Court, we are going to object to this—"

"I overrule the objection," Judge Cornelius said. "You brought it up on cross examination."

"How much was the check?" Hooker asked again.

"Close to my memory it was about twenty-two dollars."

Loud chatter emanated from the spectators' gallery. Norman stopped rocking, still with his back to the witness stand.

"Now, since that time, thirty-three years ago when you served nine months in the penitentiary for a twenty-two-dollar check, have you ever been in any other sort of trouble of any kind or character?" asked Hooker.

"No, sir, no more than got arrested for driving without a driver's license."

Hooker paused, then walked toward the prosecution table. It appeared the questioning of Walter Lee Davis was over, but Hooker said he had neglected to ask a question. He turned around to face Davis.

"Walter, I am sorry, you said the first officer that came to talk to you said Mr. Swann sent him?" Hooker was referring to Thomas Swann, the Sheco vice-president and Davis's boss.

"Yes."

"Then did Mr. Swann come down there?"

Davis answered that his employer had come twice.

"Did Mr. Swann tell you what his interest was in this case?" asked Hooker.

"Well, Mr. Swann, he told me he was for the other man."

"He was for the man that's living and not for the one that's dead?"

"Yes."

"Did Mr. Swann tell you when he came down there to see you that he did not want this man to go to the penitentiary?"

"Sure did."

"And somebody was going to be sorry if he did?"

"Yes, sir."

"That's all," Hooker said.

After more than two-and-a-half grueling hours on the stand, Walter Lee Davis was told he could step down.

> Hardin thought Davis's story fit exactly with the timeline and the discovery of the broken glass found under three trees along Elm Hill Pike. It explained why Powell slipped up by mentioning the H.D. Lee Company, which was right there on the other side of the trees. Davis's testimony fit with the number of shots fired at Haynie Gourley and explained why the fourth one was loud. But Davis had been so blindsided by Branstetter's confusing, harsh questions that he had begun to sound weak and unsure of himself. Hardin had to face the facts. Branstetter had likely succeeded in destroying Walter Lee Davis's credibility.

Dressed in a dark suit and narrow black tie, Sherman Nickens, the homicide detective who headed up the investigation of Haynie's murder, came to the stand.

With Shriver questioning, Nickens testified that he had picked up the suit pants Powell had been wearing at the time of the shooting from a dry cleaner the night after the murder. A receipt was entered into evidence, showing that the pants were dropped off at the cleaners on the afternoon of the killing.

Hearing this testimony, chatter broke out in the courtroom.

> One of the young lawyers seated in the courtroom was aghast. Why would anyone send a pair of pants with bullet holes to be cleaned the afternoon of the incident? He and his friends in the gallery thought the answer was obvious.

Next, Shriver went back over the notes taken by Nickens on the day of the reenactment ride when Powell gave a running commentary as Branstetter and an entourage of police and representatives from the DA's office drove down Elm Hill Pike on the Monday after the murder.

Shriver's reading of the notes revealed that Powell had once again referred to placing his hand on the trunk when he was being helped at Capitol Chevrolet after the shooting: "I came in through here pretty fast at Capitol Chevrolet and pulled up to the service manager's office," Powell had said on the ride. "I fell out of the car. I put my hand on the side and also on the rear of the trunk and I got around on the other side of the car and said, 'Help, Mr. Gourley has been hurt.'"

> "*...and also on the rear of the trunk.*" It hit Billy Gourley that this was at least the second or third time there was a reference to Bill Powell's placing his hand on the trunk of his father's car just after the murder. And what an awkward way of expressing it. One of the service workers at Capitol had already testified he'd found it odd that Powell had stopped and reached up and touched

> the trunk as the men were carrying him around the car. Now, after hearing Walter Lee Davis's testimony, Billy realized why. If anyone checked for fingerprints, Powell would have covered his tracks.

The hour was late. Judge Cornelius adjourned court, saying Nickens could resume his testimony the next day.

***

Court was called to order at 9:35 on Saturday morning, July 26. It was the sixth day of testimony. The weather was still oppressively hot, with high humidity and temperatures reaching the low 90s. Thunderstorms were predicted for late afternoon. The air in the hall outside the courtroom was stifling, already thick with cigarette smoke. A crush of would-be spectators crowded around the door to the courtroom. Reporters from both newspapers and camera crews from the television stations milled about.

Branstetter took up his cross-examination of Nickens, wasting no time bringing up the subject of the last-minute discovery of Walter Lee Davis and how Nickens had almost a year to learn about him. It had been another policeman working for the defense who had discovered Davis just three weeks before the trial began. The implication, once again, was that Nickens and Larkin had badly bungled the investigation.

Branstetter returned to the subject of the reenactment ride with Powell while he was still hospitalized, taking yet another opportunity to plant a falsehood in the jurors' minds.

"When the car that you and others were in pulled up to the intersection of Elm Hill Pike and Spence Lane, and I'll ask you if you didn't see a Negro man come out of a house with a shotgun over his shoulder, come out towards our car and turn back and walk back down behind some trees?"

"No, sir, I don't remember that," Nickens answered.

There was a loud reaction from the courtroom gallery, but Branstetter did not have to say, "I withdraw the question," because the prosecution raised no objection. Branstetter had struck again. The prosecution seemed asleep at the wheel.

Shriver told Nickens he could step down, then turned toward the judge and, to the great shock of the audience, said, "That's State's case in chief, if Your Honor please."

It was 10:30 a.m. on Saturday, July 26, 1969. The prosecution had rested its case. There was grumbling in the room from the spectators who expected a full day of drama after lining up early to get into the courtroom. They got up reluctantly and headed for the doors. Court would not resume until Monday.

***

Out in the hall, newspaper reporters rushed to surround Hooker and Shriver.

Hooker gave a statement: "Of course, we'd be delighted to have two or three more eyewitnesses, but this is like any homicide case. There just aren't witnesses to most murders."

"We'd love to have the murder weapon," Shriver told reporters, "But we don't make the evidence. We take the case as presented to us by the police."

"I certainly think we have made a case for the jury's consideration," Hooker added.

The Sunday edition of *The Tennessean* had one of the largest numbers of readers in the South. On July 27, editorial writer Frank Ritter blasted the prosecution, saying they had offered only circumstantial evidence and that the presentation of its case against Bill Powell was "not exciting." This was a blow to Gourley sympathizers. Hal Hardin could only hope that Hooker would pull out all the stops when Powell's attorneys launched their defense.

CHAPTER [21]

Helen and Bill Powell wait in the hallway during a break in the trial. *Nashville Public Library, Special Collections, Banner Newspaper Collection*

On Monday, July 28, the courtroom was filled by 8:30 a.m. for the second week of testimony and the beginning of the defense's case. Speculation was that Bill Powell would take the stand. The hall outside was packed with would-be spectators who had begun lining up on the street before 6:00 a.m. The huge overflow crowd was turned away, disappointed.

Still, no cameras were allowed in the courtroom, but *The Tennessean* reminded readers that their cartoonists would continue to sketch scenes from the trial and that the drawings would appear daily in the newspaper and on WSIX-TV's *Eyewitness News*. Reporters and photographers were camped out in the hallway, on alert to try for shots of trial participants.

With every word of the transcript available for all to read in both daily newspapers, anticipation was high. The entire city was spellbound.

Stenographers and reporters rush to send the trial transcript to waiting printing presses. *Nashville Public Library, Special Collections, Banner Newspaper Collection*

When Judge Cornelius took his seat, the courtroom grew quiet. The tension on the right side where the Gourleys sat was palpable. Josephine Gourley and her daughter JoAnn Bainbridge, as usual dressed in dark, somber colors, sat at the right front of the gallery, their faces taut and strained. On the opposite side, the Powell children and their friends signaled to each other animatedly.

At 9:15 the jury was called in. Branstetter announced his first witness for the defense, "Mr. William Powell."

The courtroom grew silent as Powell, wearing a dark gray suit and striped tie, stepped up to the witness stand. Several people commented on his size, that indeed he looked like a former football player.

Branstetter began his questioning in a mild, measured voice. There was no trace of the brutal fusillade he had hurled at Walter Lee Davis the week before. The court reporter had remarked that it was difficult to keep up with Branstetter, he talked so fast. But not now. Norman, the smug look on his bulldog face gone, had turned his chair to face the witness. No more of the disrespectful behavior he had flaunted during Davis's hours-long testimony.

Powell appeared calm and relaxed, not like a man who could be facing the electric chair. He stated that he was forty-one years old and that he was born in Little Rock, Arkansas, on March 20, 1928, and grew up in Mena, Arkansas, about thirteen miles from the Oklahoma border. His father, Powell said, had been an automobile mechanic in Mena.

Powell recounted how he came to Nashville in June 1946 after being recruited by the renowned Vanderbilt football coach, Red Sanders. Powell stated that he was at Vanderbilt for four years and graduated in June 1950.

Answering Branstetter's questions in a self-assured manner, Powell said he had been a member of the Vanderbilt varsity football team and had played the position of center. Powell was asked to name some of his teammates, to which he answered with a wide smile: Herb Rich, Bill Wade, Carl Copp, Pete Holt, Bucky Curtis, Bud Curtis, Smoky Stoger, and Red Clark.

He won a football scholarship to Vanderbilt, Powell said, but also worked while he was in college. He married Helen Suddoth, a Vanderbilt co-ed, during his junior year. Powell said that he and his wife had two children, a girl now seventeen and a boy fourteen. He indicated that both children were present in the courtroom.

Powell further testified that after graduation he had talked with several different companies, one being Mass Mutual Insurance Company and another the Third National Bank. He told how Sam Fleming, president of Third National Bank, had offered him a position.

Powell said he turned down the offer from Fleming and instead went to work for Palmer-Hooper Motor Company, which, at the time, was a Lincoln-Mercury dealership. He took the job in automobile sales because he had the opportunity to make more money than at the bank. He stayed at Palmer-Hooper for five years.

Following that, Powell said, he worked for Bob McAdams at Hippodrome Ford where he became the used-car manager. He stayed at the company for eleven years and was eventually promoted to general sales manager. In 1965, he was recruited by Haynie Gourley and left

Hippodrome to work for Capitol Chevrolet.

Branstetter asked how Powell usually referred to his personal relationship to Mr. Gourley.

"Well, I called him Mr. G. most of the time. It was always Mr. Gourley or Mr. G. or Boss."

> Billy Gourley sat still, but inside he felt a flash of anger at Powell's words. He had always believed Powell was a phony when it came to addressing his father. Powell was obsequious, always fawning over Haynie. Billy knew his father never realized what was happening, but for Billy, it had been all too obvious.

Powell testified that his agreement with Haynie Gourley was "if he liked me and we got along well, and we'd see how I operated," that he had "something better in store for me." Powell said he went to work for salary and bonus.

When asked to describe his relationship with Mr. Gourley, Powell sounded earnest.

"Mr. Branstetter, it was really very good. I knew quite a lot about Mr. G. when I went to work there. I had known that he came up with very meager means and started a dealership. He advanced himself quite far. He'd given me a good opportunity, really much more so than I'd ever had before."

Powell went on to describe how the two had gone on several trips together, that Mr. Gourley was beginning to play golf a little more often. "We just never had a cross word, no differences in policy, it was just a very nice relationship."

"Did you feel close to Mr. Gourley?" asked Branstetter.

"Very close, sir. He was just as much a father to me as my own father."

Again, Billy Gourley felt a stab of pain at Powell's words.

Still using a solicitous tone with Powell, Branstetter asked about the contract with Capitol Chevrolet that made it possible for Powell to buy into the business.

Powell said Mr. Gourley had wanted this opportunity for him, and that Capitol's accountant John Glenn and a Mr. Bass of the law firm Bass, Berry and Sims had participated in the drawing up of the contract.

Asked whether there had been discussion about Haynie's son Billy during the negotiations, Powell answered, "Yes, sir, Mr. G. and I talked about this at length, really, before Billy got out of school. When he came to work there, I guess it was sometime maybe around the first of December of 1967, we had established that he could work either two or three months in our service department and a like time in the parts department and then go into the accounting and the business end of it and at that time he would have known a great deal more about the dealership and then he would have attended the Dealers' Sons School in July."

"State whether or not you conscientiously entered into this program or the method and manner of entering into the program and training young Billy."

"Yes, sir, in fact, Billy and I talked about it."

"What was your personal relationship with Billy?"

"Well, it was really very good. I think Billy is one of the nicest, most conscientious young men I have ever had any dealings with. He was young; he was ambitious; he was eager; he had everything in his favor. I don't think there was anyone who ever disliked him."

"You still feel the same way about him you just expressed, you feel that way today about him?"

"I certainly do."

"Is it your present knowledge and opinion that with experience and training, that Billy Gourley still would and could make a good automobile man?"

"Yes, sir, he would."

"With your relationship as it was, and as it is now, would you still like to see him do that?"

"Yes, sir, for his daddy's sake."

> At this latest exchange, Billy Gourley wanted to jump up and tell everyone how Bill Powell had treated him, that he had ignored his obligation to teach him the business and had never once told him he would make a fine automobile man. In fact, he had done everything he could to hold him back from advancing. Billy looked at the jury. They seemed to be hanging on Powell's every word.

Asked about the trip to Memphis he and his wife had taken with Josephine and Haynie Gourley a few days before Haynie was killed, Powell explained the foursome had attended the annual Tennessee Automobile Dealers Association meeting at the Rivermont Hotel in Memphis.

Powell described how he had done the driving as the couples rode together in Mr. Gourley's '68 Cadillac. On Tuesday evening, the last night of the convention, Powell testified they all attended a banquet and that he danced with Mrs. Gourley. The couples left Memphis about ten o'clock on Wednesday morning to come back to Nashville, where Powell drove first to his home and took out their luggage, and the Gourleys went on to their house.

Powell then gave his version of what happened the Wednesday evening before the murder when he was asked to come to the Gourley home to talk about Billy. Powell said he arrived around 10:15 or 10:30, contradicting the much earlier time Billy Gourley had testified to. He described how Billy had met him at the door, and he joined the family at the dining room table. Powell said Josephine Gourley was very upset and that she was crying and claiming that Helen Powell didn't like her.

"Who talked first?" asked Branstetter.

"I think Mr. Gourley spoke up and said that we needed to discuss Billy, that he had some discussion with some of the dealers in Memphis at the convention, that their sons were making a little more progress possibly than young Bill was and we needed to discuss it, and effective June 1 that he wanted Billy to become a manager."

Branstetter asked what was said about Powell's training program for Billy Gourley.

"They felt like that I possibly mistreated Billy, maybe not taking as much time with him as I could have."

"At some point did you state that probably you should just leave the company?"

"I had a feeling they weren't satisfied with the way I was helping train Bill, and I made the statement that if they felt like this, that it would just be best that I get out."

"Is that about the way the conversation ended?

"Yes, sir."

"And you left?"

"Yes, sir."

"Who saw you to the door?"

"Bill Gourley."

"Was he very cordial?"

"Very nice. 'Good-night, Mr. Powell. See you tomorrow.'"

Then, Branstetter asked about something that had occurred around three weeks before the Wednesday night, May 22 meeting at the Gourley home.

"Calling your attention to an incident dealing with a demonstrator, did you at one time have some conversation with Billy Gourley about rules dealing with demonstrator automobiles?"

"Yes. We had cleaned up automobiles and asked everyone not to drive them, simply because they would get dirty again. He took one of the cars home, and this is what the discussion was about."

"Did you state that that rule applied to you and everybody else, and it should apply to him, in a nice way?" asked Branstetter.

"I told him that if we were to get the respect of other people at our dealership that we must do the same things that we asked them to do. And he should not have driven the car."

"And that was about the extent of the whole incident, wasn't it?" asked Branstetter, his tone signaling that the encounter had not been of much importance.

"That was it."

> Billy could only sit still and listen to how Powell glossed over the event, remembering how humiliating it had been as Powell scolded him in front of the two other managers.

Branstetter changed the subject and asked why it was necessary to build a new facility.

"Well, our business grew larger. We went into the leasing business. We began to sell more trucks, more cars. Our service business got bigger. We just simply couldn't take care of it in the facilities we had on Broadway."

Powell stated that the agreement with a local physician who owned the property and constructed the building was to lease the new facility for twenty years at $85,000 a year.

"Who signed that lease, Mr. Powell?"

"My wife and I signed the lease as guarantors for the lease individually."

Branstetter asked how many employees the dealership had when it was located on Broadway. Powell said that before the move, there were 142 or 143.

"At the present time, do you know how many people are depending upon Capitol Chevrolet for a livelihood, who are working there today?" asked Branstetter.

"Approximately 160."

As to the financial status of the business, Powell said the business brought in twice as much as it had in previous years. He also stated that

Mrs. Gourley was paid well over $100,000 for the year 1968.

"State whether or not, to your knowledge, that she was in or about the premises performing any work whatsoever?"

"No, sir."

Branstetter walked toward the jury, smiling slightly, as if he were savoring this information about Josephine Gourley.

Branstetter next asked about the morning of Haynie Gourley's death.

Powell said it started out like any other day. He arrived at work at his usual time of 7:30 a.m. and held a sales meeting at 8:15. Powell said Haynie had driven into the service department between 10:15 or 10:30.

"Then did you see him later on in his office that morning?"

"Well, I knew we needed to have a conversation. I stopped at his door sometime after ten o'clock. I believe Mr. John Sloan was in his office."

"Mr. John Sloan, is that from the Cain-Sloan Company here?" asked Branstetter. Powell answered yes.

"What did you say to Mr. Gourley?"

"Well, I apologized. I didn't know that he had anybody in his office. And I simply said, 'When you have an opportunity, let's get away from here and talk.' He said, 'I'll be with you in just a minute.'"

"Anything unusual?" asked Branstetter.

"Nothing unusual."

> Billy flinched at this answer. Of course, it was unusual to "get away" to talk when there were places all over the building where they could have had a private conversation. There was everything abnormal about taking a ride to discuss business. It had never happened before. Billy was certain of that.

Branstetter asked what time they left the building. Powell estimated they pulled out of the service bay at five minutes to eleven or at eleven o'clock.

Next, Branstetter asked Powell what Mr. Gourley had said on their ride.

"Was there a discussion about, particularly, a building or company being in this particular area?"

"We had seen the H.D. Lee Company from the Interstate as you come back from the airport, and he wanted to know what kind of company it was, and I told him I didn't know."

> Hal Hardin knew what this was about. Branstetter was giving Powell a chance to repair a crucial mistake he'd made in the hospital when he'd said that Haynie pointed to the H.D. Lee building on the fatal ride. That company was located across from where Walter Lee Davis sat in his truck, so it had to be explained away. It was obvious that Branstetter and Powell had planned this set-up since the question was completely out of sequence.

Powell then went into the story about being behind a bread-type delivery van turning left onto Spence Lane and how he had rolled slowly behind it, not coming to a complete stop "when the Negro got in the car."

"I don't know where he came from," Powell said, his voice vaguely reflective. "I had not noticed anybody standing there. All of a sudden someone said, 'All I want is your money.'"

"Did you know there was some third person in the car prior to this? Just prior to this?" asked Branstetter.

"Right then I knew it."

> Two lawyers from a prominent firm observing the trial had heard Branstetter's demolition of Walter Lee Davis. Was Powell's hearing any worse than Davis's? How did he not hear a car door open and shut, they wondered, whispering to each other. The doors on the '68 Caprice were long and heavy. There was no way opening and closing the door didn't make a noise.

"What was said following that?" asked Branstetter.

"Mr. Gourley raised up in the seat to either get a look or to turn sideways and he reached through his coat into his rear pocket and made the statement, 'James, you can have all we've got.'"

> So now Mr. Gourley is reaching *through* his coat to his rear pocket. How would one do that, Hal Hardin wondered. Hardin could only hope the jury would remember Powell's odd choice of words, an obvious effort to explain his initial story, that Mr. Gourley had reached into his coat pocket for his wallet.

Branstetter asked if Powell had come in contact with the man.

"Yes, sir, at the time I flew my arm up when the shot went off, or about that time I grabbed for Mr. Gourley, and he slumped down in the seat."

"What did Mr. Gourley say?" asked Branstetter.

"'Oh, Lord, what's going on?'"

Branstetter asked Powell if he knew how many shots had actually been fired. Powell said he had heard the testimony, but at the time he thought there had been only two shots.

Then, Powell volunteered without being prompted.

"We proceeded on down a way, and I have indicated that we turned around right before you get to Massman Drive."

> So now Powell was referencing Massman Drive, thought Hardin. Powell had heard Walter Lee Davis's testimony. In all the newspaper accounts and on the map he drew in the hospital, Powell had never mentioned Massman Drive, only Spence Lane, over a half mile away. This change would have meant the gunman was in the car for much longer than Powell had ever indicated.

Branstetter asked if Powell recalled seeing the assailant get out of the car.

"I don't know just exactly how he got out. I never did hear the door close. I made a U-turn in the middle of the street."

Branstetter did not question Powell's hearing, as he had with Walter Lee Davis. And he didn't ask if Powell felt a rush of wind as the car door opened. He let it stand that the mysterious assailant must have been quiet as a mouse as he entered the car and when he exited.

"What did you do when you made the turn?"

"I had ahold of Mr. Gourley."

"Did you say anything to him?"

"Yes, sir, he was still alive."

"What did you say to him?" Branstetter asked.

"I said, 'Hold on, Boss, we're going back as fast as we can go.' I had him in my right arm, and I was driving with my left arm. We came back through Spence Lane."

> Hal Hardin had seen Haynie Gourley's wounds. It was appalling for Powell to say Haynie was still alive. Both Simpkins and the TBI agent testified that a gun had been held to Haynie's head and neck, execution style, and that two of the shots that entered his body would have killed him instantly.

Powell next told how he drove 80 miles an hour and "almost had a wreck" when a car pulled out in front of him on Elm Hill Pike. He then drove into the Capitol Chevrolet service department, "hollering" for someone to call the police and an ambulance, saying, "Mr. Gourley's been hurt." He described how he opened the door and fell to the concrete floor, and how "all these people materialized" to help him.

"They took me to Mr. McCaffrey's office and at that time I was awfully concerned about Mr. Gourley. They sat me down in the office and the next thing I knew I was laying on the floor on some cushions. Somebody tied my necktie around my leg. Still didn't know where I had been shot, my stomach was burning—and that's about it."

"Mr. Powell," Branstetter said, "how long was it from the time you left Capitol Chevrolet, saw Mr. Hughes, until the time that you got back to Capitol Chevrolet?"

"It couldn't have been more than four or five minutes, if it was that long."

Branstetter turned to another subject, maintaining a deferential tone.

"Bill, I forgot to ask you, do you go to church?"

"Yes, sir."

"Do you and the members of your family belong to a particular church?"

"First Presbyterian Church."

"Who's the pastor?

"Dr. Walter Courtenay."

Branstetter, eyeing the jury with a self-congratulatory smile, paused to let this last statement sink in.

Hooker stood up for cross-examination and walked over to Bill Powell.

"What is your weight and height?" he asked Powell.

"I am six foot three-and-a-half, weigh 215 pounds.

"What was Mr. Gourley's weight and height?"

"Mr. Gourley was right at six feet, weighed about 180, 185."

"Now what was your age on May 24, 1968?"

"I was forty years old."

"And what was his age?"

"Seventy-two, I believe."

"In other words, he was thirty-two years your senior?"

"Yes, sir."

Hooker asked how much Powell made at the dealerships he worked for before coming to Capitol Chevrolet. In 1964, the year before he left Hippodrome Ford, Powell said he made $24,000 as general manager.

Hooker then had Powell quote his earnings beginning at Capitol Chevrolet in 1966. Powell was not certain, but he did say he earned in excess of $80,000 for the calendar year 1967.

Hooker changed the line of questioning, asking if Powell was familiar with the contents of Paragraph Three of the agreement with General Motors. Powell answered yes.

"And the franchise is now presently, as far as Paragraph Three is concerned, in the name of William E. Powell?"

"Yes, sir."

"And this is the first franchise, automobile franchise you have ever owned in your life?"

"Yes, sir."

Hooker turned to the morning of May 24, 1968, asking what subjects Powell wanted to talk to Mr. Gourley about. Powell said they had seven or eight matters they needed to discuss. Hooker asked if the two had talked about any of these topics before reaching Spence Lane where the gunman allegedly entered the car.

"We couldn't have talked two or three minutes before this colored man got in the car," Powell testified.

"When did this discussion come up about the H.D. Lee building?" asked Hooker.

"As we drove out the back entrance of Capitol."

Hooker paused for a moment, looking at Bill Powell as if waiting for a logical explanation as to why Haynie Gourley would bring up the subject. Powell said nothing.

"Now, the H.D. Lee building is way over beyond on Elm Hill Pike, beyond the point where you turned around, wasn't it?" asked Hooker.

"Yes, sir."

"How far beyond? How far would you say the H.D. Lee building is beyond Spence Lane?"

"About a mile," Powell replied.

Hooker asked Powell if he had seen the workmen at Spence Lane. Powell said that he had not. He also denied seeing a flagman at the intersection and said that on the way back, after he had turned around, he saw no one.

"Did you see this truck that was being driven by Mr. Donnelly, who testified here in the case, a Time delivery truck?"

Powell answered that the truck in front of them at the intersection was not the kind of truck Donnelly drove.

"I have seen his truck," Powell added. "It was not the truck that was in front of us."

Hooker then asked Powell if he had tried to fight the man off, or if he made an effort to stop the car. Powell said he remembered swinging his arm back at the same time the shots began. He said he thought the man had hit his arm with his chin or with the butt of the gun, that he had a bruise afterwards but had "no idea where it came from."

Asked how many shots were fired, Powell said he heard only two.

Hooker moved in closer to Powell, looking him straight in the eye.

"Mr. Gourley was sitting right by you. Did you see the man when he put the pistol right against his neck under his ear there and pulled the trigger, did you see that?" Hooker boomed.

"No, sir, I didn't."

"When he put the pistol up here in contact about the area of his collarbone and fired, did you see that?" Hooker formed the shape of a gun with his thumb and forefinger thrust against his left shoulder.

Powell said he only remembered smoke and thinking he had been hit in the stomach by the second shot.

"What did the man do, just keep shooting?"

"He came over the front seat I thought with both hands, but apparently he had a gun in one hand, and took something off the front seat of the car. Mr. Gourley had made an effort to bring his wallet out of his hip pocket, and that's pretty much what I remember."

> A choking noise slipped from Billy Gourley's throat. This was new, this explanation as to how his father's billfold got into the back seat.

Hooker turned to the subject of the shot Powell sustained to his leg.

"Do you mean you think the man stuck his hand with the pistol in it over the top of the seat and shot you in the leg?"

Hooker grabbed his chair from the prosecution table and dragged it over and placed it in front of the jury and sat down.

"Like this is the left-hand side of the car with the driver's seat," Hooker said, "and you were sitting in it there, you were shot in the left leg, were you not?"

"Yes, sir."

"When this man stuck his arm over there with the pistol in it did you make any effort to grab it?"

Powell said he felt like the shot came across his ear. He claimed he never saw the pistol.

Hooker then asked Powell to sit in the chair, mimicking the position he would have been in when he was shot in the leg. He also asked Powell to show where his wound was. Branstetter spoke up and offered to have the car seat brought in. Hooker declined and continued with the demonstration.

"Where did the bullet go in?"

"Right in the back," Powell said, pointing to his left calf.

"Did it enter the bone?"

"No, sir."

"Where did it come out?"

"The other side."

Hooker next asked Powell to describe the alleged shooter.

"He was a Negro. He had pock marks on his left cheek. He had a felt hat pulled down about here, I would say, oh, halfway on the forehead. The white part of his eyes had goldish-brown streaks in them. I don't recall if the man had a mustache. I don't think he did, but since then I have looked, and I would say the majority of colored people have mustaches, but I don't remember a mustache on this man."

And how did he speak, asked Hooker.

"Like the majority of colored people, I guess."

Hooker addressed something Powell told the policemen on the day he led a retracing of the route he took on May 24, 1968.

"What I am trying to get at," Hooker said, "so we will be sure and understand each other, you told these officers on this ride you got your hand on the trunk, and you told here this morning you got your hand on the trunk. What I am trying to find out, wasn't the reason you claimed you got your hand on the trunk was for fear somebody had seen you raise that trunk there that day like Walter Lee Davis testified to here last week?"

"No, sir."

Hooker asked why Powell had placed his hand on the trunk. Powell answered that he was trying to get around to the other door to help Mr. Gourley.

> Odd, thought George Crawford, who was sitting halfway back in the courtroom. The shop foreman had helped Powell into the service manager's office. A good three or four minutes elapsed before anyone realized Mr. Gourley was in the car.

"So you were trying to get around to help Mr. Gourley? Weren't some other people over there helping him at that time?"

"Not at that time. They couldn't see him. He was down on the floor."

"Did you know he was dead?"

"No, sir."

Hooker paused a moment, took a few steps, then turned back to the witness stand.

"Did you say in the hospital that Mr. Gourley reached for his inside pocket for his billfold?"

"No, sir, I don't think I said that. I said he went through his coat pocket and reached around into his hip pocket."

> There he goes again, thought Hal Hardin, reaching *through* his coat pocket to get to his wallet in his hip pocket. How exactly would one do that, Hardin wondered? How were the jurors picturing this?

Referring to Billy Gourley, Hooker asked Powell if he had ever explained to him exactly what happened on the ride.

"No, sir."

"Why didn't you?"

"I never did have the opportunity."

Hooker pointed out that Billy Gourley worked at Capitol for ten months after his father died in May of 1968 until Powell was indicted in March 1969.

"In all that time, did you ever undertake to explain to him after that how his father got shot all to pieces that day?"

"No, sir."

"Have you ever, from that day, from May 24, 1968, on down to the present, ever gone to see Mrs. Gourley and undertake to tell her and explain to her how it was that her husband got killed that day?"

"No, sir."

Hooker raised his voice and glared at Powell.

"How long did you travel along this road that day with Mr. Gourley, with these bullets being pumped into him, how long a distance did you travel while all of these shots were being fired?"

"I'd say a quarter of a mile."

"The shots started at the intersection of Spence Lane?"

"Not immediately at Spence Lane, a little further down, I believe."

"And then for a distance of a quarter of a mile kept shooting?"

"Yes."

Then Hooker lowered his voice almost to a whisper and clasped his hands behind his back and walked closer to face Powell.

"The man started shooting and you just kept driving?" he asked.

"Yes," answered Powell.

"That's all, said Hooker, sounding disgusted.

On re-direct examination by Branstetter, he kept repeating how cooperative Powell had been with the police until Hooker finally objected.

"Just a minute," Hooker said, "if Mr. Branstetter is going to testify, I wish he would take the witness stand and be sworn."

This exchange elicited some muffled laughter from the gallery, and Judge Cornelius ordered Branstetter to "stop testifying and leading the witness."

Branstetter told Powell he could step down.

Bill Powell had been on the stand for over four hours, but he had remained calm and deferential. Not once did he raise his voice, nor did he seem rattled by Hooker's questions. When Powell walked back to the defense table, he smiled broadly at his children in the first row. They waved back at him, grinning and nodding their heads.

Hal Hardin thought Powell had just put on the performance of a lifetime. He came across as humble, his voice deep and reassuringly innocent and sincere. Branstetter's pace with Powell had been unhurried, his tone respectful as he lobbed easy questions his way. With Walter Lee Davis, Branstetter had been accusatory and endlessly repetitive. He'd veered way off course with both Donnelly and Davis. But not with Powell.

CHAPTER [22]

While Bill Powell was testifying in Courtroom 611, something of great significance was unfolding across town, something that could change the entire trajectory of the trial.

The previous evening, Sunday, July 27, Metro Police Patrolman R.C. Jackson was sitting on John Spivey's patio in Donelson, twelve miles east of Nashville, at a fish fry. Something was said at the other end of the table that caught Jackson's attention. He moved closer to listen to a discussion about a gun that had been found the year before on Elm Hill Pike but had never been turned in.

Jackson, a four-year veteran of the Metro police force, began asking questions. When was the gun found, and who found it? Where was the gun now? A neighbor of Spivey's, Jackie Ballard, would only say that it had been found near Capitol Chevrolet, but Ballard refused to say anything more.

What he overheard bothered Jackson. The next morning, Monday, July 28, at the very moment Powell was on the stand testifying, Jackson was at his sister's house in Madison, Tennessee. He put in a call to Jackie Ballard at Jim Reed Chevrolet in Nashville where Ballard worked. Jackson again asked Ballard for the man's name who found the gun. Still, Ballard would not reveal anything about the gun or even who else knew about it. He said he didn't want to get involved. When Jackson asked again, Ballard said cryptically, "Hold the phone."

For fifteen minutes Jackson waited and was about to hang up when a man's voice came on the line.

"Who am I speaking to?" asked Jackson.

"I do not wish to give my name," the man said stiffly. Jackson did not recognize the voice.

The unidentified man initially refused to give Jackson any information. He would only say that the person in question was a hard-working man with a family and that he was in a position where he could not lose any work without his family going hungry.

Jackson told the man on the other end of the line that the matter was serious and that as a police officer, it was his duty to recover the gun.

Finally, the man blurted out the name Henry Arthur Lewis, and after much cajoling by Jackson, the man revealed that Lewis was an employee of Walton Construction Company.

Jackson hung up without ever knowing the informant's name or why he would not identify himself. Jackson then called Walton Construction's dispatcher who said Lewis was working in Nashville and gave an address on Vaulx Lane off Gale Lane, near Vanderbilt University.

Jackson drove to the site, arriving around 11:00 a.m. He spotted Henry Lewis operating a front-end loader. Lewis stopped the machine when he saw the patrol car and climbed down. After Jackson explained the urgency of the situation, Lewis reluctantly agreed to take Jackson to the gun.

Jackson drove Lewis in his patrol car to Lewis's brother's house in Old Hickory, sixteen miles northeast of Nashville. The brother answered the door, had a discussion out of earshot of Jackson, disappeared for a moment, then came back and handed Jackson a .38 Smith & Wesson pistol.

When Jackson and Lewis left Old Hickory, they drove directly to Metro Police headquarters and turned in the gun.

Next, Lewis led Jackson to Elm Hill Pike to a spot across the road from Mount Zeno Kindergarten where Lewis said he found the gun at the end of August 1968. The location was close to Capitol Chevrolet and a half mile from Spence Lane where Powell said the man jumped into Haynie Gourley's car. The site was well over a mile from Massman Drive where Walter Lee Davis claimed he saw two men stop in a black car. The hunt for clues had centered around the stretch of Elm Hill Pike starting at Spence Lane and extending east to Mill Creek. Lewis took Jackson on an entirely different stretch of Elm Hill Pike—one that had never been searched.

Lewis led Jackson to an embankment across the road about ten feet off the pavement, now grown up with dry weeds. They walked a few paces to the east, and Lewis pointed to a spot where he had seen the white handle of the gun sticking out of the ground. They crossed back over the road, and Lewis showed Jackson where the pile of fill dirt had been where he dropped the five empty shell casings from the gun's cylinder. The ground had long since been smoothed over so it was impossible to pinpoint the exact place, Lewis said, but he thought it was right in front of the kindergarten building.

Back at police headquarters, officers examined the pistol. The end of the barrel was rusted, but the serial number was still intact, meaning the gun could be traced.

The search was now on for the owner.

***

Back in Courtroom 611, the defense called to the stand Thomas C. Swann, a heavy-set white man in his late forties with dark hair and an air of self-importance. Swann was one of three owners of Sheco Corporation, the company that had installed pipeline for the 1968 construction of a Kroger warehouse at Elm Hill Pike and Massman Drive. He was also the employer of the State's star witness, Walter Lee Davis.

In answer to Branstetter's questions, Swann stated the company maintained a two-and-a-half-acre equipment yard at 612 P'Pool Avenue, directly behind Capitol Chevrolet. Swann said building equipment and materials were stored on the lot, along with a magazine for the storage of explosives.

Thomas C. Swann of Sheco Corporation arrives to testify for the defense. *Nashville Public Library, Special Collections, Banner Newspaper Collection*

"State whether or not Walter Lee Davis knew where that lot was on P'Pool Avenue and had been in and about it from time to time to your knowledge?"

"Yes, sir, he had been there many times. He slept there at night a lot of times," Swann said.

Branstetter asked Swann about the day of the shooting.

"Have you had occasion to go back and check your timecards to determine the names of employees working for you on May 24, 1968, and the locations of their work?"

"Yes, sir, sure have," answered Swann enthusiastically.

"On Friday, May 24, 1968, where do your records show Walter Lee Davis working?"

Swann answered that Davis had been working on an eight-inch pipe. He then began a complicated explanation of pipes and grades and laterals and main lines. A lengthy question and answer session followed, with Branstetter asking about equipment on the site that day, and Swann going into great detail about jack hammers and drills and air compressors.

Referring to one of the large air compressors operating a jack hammer, Branstetter asked Swann how much noise these particular machines made.

"You can hear them running for a mile," answered Swann.

Again, Branstetter repeated questions about sizes of pipes, equipment, and what machinery was working where. The point Branstetter seemed to be trying to establish was that Walter Lee Davis could not have been on the site the day of the slaying, because records show the size of pipe being laid that day did not match Davis's testimony about blasting on the back of the property.

Then, Swann asked if he could draw on a labyrinthine plat of the site. He walked down from the stand and launched into a long and confusing explanation of pipe sizes and penciled in the location of backhoes and ditches and talked about "air tracking" and "staving up."

> One of the two young lawyers watching the proceedings said in a loud whisper, "There's no way a jury is following this mishmash of construction jargon." Swann, he noted, seemed to be relishing his role of spouting off technical terms he obviously thought sounded impressive.

Swann proceeded to produce receipts for explosive powder signed by Walter Lee Davis during the week ending Saturday, May 25, 1968. One, Swann claimed, was signed on May 24, indicating that Davis had picked up supplies at the P'Pool Avenue location behind Capitol Chevrolet. The receipts were entered as exhibits and passed to the jury.

After being shown a photograph of Sheco equipment taken in the past few days, Swann launched into a description of the truck he said his company used to transport dynamite on May 24, 1968, which, he pointed out in the photograph, now held a water tank. Swann claimed that this same truck, which was larger than a pick-up, was the one used by Davis on the day of the murder.

"And is this the truck that was assigned to the Elm Hill job for carrying dynamite on May 24, 1968?" asked Branstetter.

"Yes, sir."

Branstetter then sent shock waves through the crowded courtroom.

"I will ask if on the morning of May 24, 1968, between ten minutes after eleven and eleven-thirty, in that neighborhood, if you were on the company's lot at P'Pool Avenue back of Capitol Chevrolet?"

"Yes, sir, I was."

"I will ask you to state whether or not that very same truck was on that lot at the time you were there sometime shortly after eleven o'clock on May 24, 1968?"

"This truck was on my equipment yard, yes, sir."

"Did you see anyone in or about the truck?"

"Yes, sir, a colored man was in the truck."

"And this is when you saw this truck that you have described on your lot back of Capitol Chevrolet?"

"Right. The truck was coming up to the lot from presumably the powder magazine."

"Yes. That's all," said Branstetter.

"Pulled up in front of the field office," added Swann.

"That's all. Thank you."

> Hal Hardin was confused. Was Swann implying the man in the truck was Walter Lee Davis? Had he not recognized his own employee?

Judge Cornelius asked the lawyers to approach the bench and discussed continuing the cross-examination of Swann the next day. He then announced that court would resume at 8:45 the following morning because of what he anticipated would be "a long, hard day tomorrow."

Court stood adjourned at 5:21 p.m.

***

With the transcript appearing in its entirety in both daily newspapers, fascination with the trial reached a fever pitch. Reports from the courtroom dominated the city's television news broadcasts, with each airing extensive coverage of the day's events and feature stories about the participants. WLAC-TV asked Judge Cornelius if the channel might be permitted to televise the closing arguments and the judge's instructions to the jury. Chris Clark, the station's director of news and public affairs, made the request in a letter to the judge with copies sent to the four lawyers. Clark never received an answer.

Jud Collins, the news director of WSM-TV, told reporters that at the trial's conclusion cameras would be set up in the corridor outside the courtroom for live interviews with lawyers and witnesses. The intensity of interest in the trial was such that Collins announced on air that regular programs, including network shows, would be interrupted "when anything of consequence develops."

Every night, Billy Gourley returned home to his mother's house. They spoke little. Both were too exhausted after the long days in court with emotions pulled in all directions to go over testimony or even discuss the proceedings of the day.

"The trial was everywhere," Billy would say later. "You couldn't turn on the television. You couldn't look at the newspapers. It surrounded us. There was no way to get away from it."

Court resumed at 8:50 a.m. on Tuesday, July 29, with all parties and counsel present, but with the jury absent.

Shriver spoke up, saying there was a matter of importance to be discussed. He announced that he had received information Monday afternoon that a gun, a .38 Smith & Wesson revolver, had been turned in. The weapon, Shriver said, had apparently been found on Elm Hill Pike the previous year.

A shuffling noise rose from the courtroom at this pronouncement as people strained to hear Shriver.

"It had been found by a man who lives in Wilson County approximately a year ago," Shriver said. "At present, it was also our information that five spent shells that were in the cylinder of the gun were emptied at the place where the gun was found, and we are now having people digging in that area to see if they can be found. Also, the police are checking on the serial number, which is intact on the gun, to see if they can trace ownership of it."

Judge Cornelius told the lawyers that the gun had no value in the trial as yet and called the jury back in.

Thomas Swann re-took the stand to continue his testimony for the defense.

Eyes rolled in the gallery when Branstetter again asked about the size of pipes on the Kroger construction site. Swann said there had been a change from a twenty-one-inch pipe to a twenty-four-inch pipe for one line, and a thirty-inch pipe substituted for the planned twenty-seven-inch pipe. No one from the prosecution objected when Branstetter revisited this subject, and he gave no reason for repeating the very same question he'd asked multiple times the previous day.

He then yielded to Hooker for cross-examination.

Hooker stood up, walked over and pounded his fist on the railing of the jury box.

"What's your real interest in this trial?" he bellowed, turning to face Swann.

"No, sir, none whatsoever, with the exception of one thing. My men became involved in this, and Mr. Davis tells one man one story and one another and one another, and they started calling me and worrying about the stories that were being told."

Hooker gave Swann a disapproving look. He then asked about a visit Swann made to Davis's home in Spring Hill on Wednesday, July 16, two days after the trial began.

"So the first trip you made down to see Walter Lee Davis you went with Mr. Kilgore, an associate of Mr. Branstetter's, and Mr. Moody, an associate of Mr. Branstetter's?" asked Hooker, referring to two lawyers in Branstetter's office.

"Whenever I talked with Walter Lee Davis, sir, Mr. Kilgore and Mr. Moody were over at the restaurant called Stan's Restaurant. I went and talked with Walter Lee Davis myself. I felt I should talk with Walter."

"You can't tell these ladies and gentlemen that Mr. Moody and Mr. Kilgore went down to Spring Hill and waited at Stan's Restaurant while you went and talked to the witness?" Hooker turned his back to Swann and faced the jury.

"Yes, sir, they did. I felt that Walter would not tell me his story if anyone else was in the presence."

"Did you later tell them what Walter said?"

"Yes, and I told Walter I was going to tell the attorneys."

Swann then backpedaled and said the real reason he went was because Davis had been injured in a tractor accident, and he wanted to check on him.

He admitted that he got in touch with Powell's lawyers about going to see Davis.

"Why did you do that?" asked Hooker.

"Sir, whenever I am in trouble about something I always try to call someone and get their advice," Swann answered officiously.

"But, Mr. Swann, you say that at the time you didn't even know Mr. Powell."

"I would say according to my diary it would be the day before that I met Mr. Bill Powell standing right here on the square. I shook hands with him."

There was a rustle in the courtroom.

"Where did you see Mr. Powell?" asked Hooker, sounding surprised.

"He was standing on the corner over here on Second Avenue. I just shook hands with him," Swann said proudly.

"And didn't you know at that time that he had been indicted for the murder of Haynie Gourley?" asked Hooker.

"Yes, sir, I knew it. Let me say something, sir. I'm not trying to protect Mr. Powell. I am not trying to protect the Gourleys. I am trying to protect my men that has got involved in this thing by several different stories being told, and my records will prove it, and that's what I'm trying to do. All I want to see in this case, sir, is justice."

A slight snicker sounded from the spectator gallery at hearing this. The two young lawyers elbowed each other.

Hooker asked for more details about the encounter with Powell.

"Anybody with you?"

"Mr. Bill Moody," Swann answered, referring to a lawyer from Branstetter's office. "Mr. Moody came over to my office that morning," said Swann self-importantly.

Hooker then asked if it was a coincidence that the two had run into Bill Powell.

"No, sir. Let me tell you just exactly the way it happened, will you?"

"Take all the time you want to tell it," Hooker said with a hint of mockery in his voice.

"We were coming across Woodland Street Bridge in a car and turned the corner there on Second Avenue," Swann explained. "I was sitting in the car and Mr. Moody said he had to speak to Mr. Powell a minute. And he said, 'I want you to meet Tommy Swann.' And I shook hands with the gentleman, and they went on to lunch and that was it."

"Did you and Mr. Moody and Mr. Kilgore go to Spring Hill together?" asked Hooker.

"Yes, we went to Spring Hill together."

"In whose car?"

"Just to be honest with you, I believe it was a Capitol Chevrolet car."

Shock at Swann's words echoed through the courtroom.

> Billy felt a flash of anger. The thought that Bill Powell furnished a Capitol Chevrolet car for this pompous man to ride in was appalling. And his pride at meeting Powell. It was obvious this man was anything but neutral, despite his claims.

Hooker moved closer to the witness stand and leaned in toward Swann.

"And didn't you tell Walter Lee Davis on the afternoon that you went down to Spring Hill with Mr. Powell's lawyers that you were for Mr. Powell in the case?" asked Hooker.

"No, sir, I did not."

"And didn't you say that Mr. Powell, being a young man, and if Mr. Powell went to the penitentiary, something would be taken away from his life?" asked Hooker.

"No, sir, I did not. I said, 'Walter, for God's sake, please tell the truth.' I said, 'The truth will stand up. The truth will survive.' And Walter said—he was shaking his head—and says, 'All I'm telling is what I know.'"

Hooker talked faster now.

"And didn't you tell him that Mr. Powell was a good friend of yours, and that you would hate to see an innocent man go to the penitentiary or get hung?"

"No, sir, I didn't tell him that."

"And didn't you tell him that if Mr. Powell was convicted that somebody was going to sweat?"

"No, sir. I did not. I told Walter, I said, 'Walter, please get your story straight.' I said, 'When someone gets on the stand and lies,' I said, 'I believe they call that perjury, I'm not for sure. I'm not familiar with the terms of law.' And I said, 'You have conflicting stories, and please tell the same story, or get your stories right.'"

Hooker asked Swann if Davis had told him what he saw on May 24, 1968. Swann said he had a diagram that he and Walter recently drew about that day. Hooker asked to see it, and Swann pulled out a piece of paper, which Hooker entered into evidence. On the paper were three squares and some rough lines.

"So," Hooker began. "You got this drawing here and you have Massman Drive and you have shown the trailer and then you show where he said the car stopped in front of these trees and you got—"

Branstetter spoke up, "Just a minute, he hasn't said anything about trees."

"Don't holler at me from behind that way," barked Hooker. "You scare me to death."

Hooker turned back to face Swann.

"And what did he tell you when that car stopped that these two men that were in the car did?"

"He said it looked like the two people were arguing in the car," Swann said. "They were using their hands and then one man got out of the car, went to the trunk of the car, raised the trunk lid, looked like he got something out; got back in the car and then came, proceeded on up Elm Hill Pike and turned around up there near the stone wall, turned around and went back toward town."

"What did he tell you he heard before the car went on east toward Elm Hill Pike?" asked Hooker.

"I asked him if he heard anything that sounded like shots. He said, 'No, sir, I didn't hear nothing.'"

"Why, Mr. Swann, didn't he tell you that he heard four shots and the car pulled off and came on back toward Elm Hill Pike?"

"No, sir, he did not. He kept—he said he just couldn't remember," Swann said, stumbling over his words.

Hooker doubled down. "Didn't he tell you when the car came on down west on Elm Hill Pike that the man in the passenger side of the car was all slumped over?"

"He said it looked like someone was leaning over, I believe that's the way he put it."

Swann admitted that he went back the next day to see Davis and took his foreman Bob Chowning with him. Swann again claimed he was only trying to "protect his men."

Hooker asked Swann what Davis had said at this second meeting.

"He said he was going to tell just what he saw. And Bob Chowning was standing there telling him, 'Now, Walter, you've told me one story, and you've told Tom another one.' He said, 'You told B. F. another one, you told another person another one.' Walter started saying, 'Maybe they just lost their memory.'"

"Didn't he tell you over again what he had seen that day?" asked Hooker.

"Yes, sir, like the diagram."

"And he told you and Chowning on the seventeenth the same thing that he had told you on the sixteenth, didn't he?"

"The same thing, yes, sir."

"All right. What were you intending, trying to scare this man?"

"No, sir, none whatsoever. We just want the truth to survive, sir."

At this juncture, Judge Cornelius called a recess. Out in the hall, there was discussion among the crowd about Thomas Swann. Several people wondered aloud if Swann would be charged with witness tampering, or even perjury.

When court resumed, Thomas Swann was called back to the stand, with Hooker continuing his cross-examination.

Hooker was pacing back and forth in front of Swann and glancing at the jury.

"Why, Mr. Swann, isn't it a fact that you are here this morning for the deliberate purpose of trying to destroy the integrity of Walter Lee Davis?" Hooker's voice boomed across the room.

Swann was indignant. "No, sir, I am not."

"But you were out there all Sunday afternoon, day before yesterday, making measurements out in the area where this tragedy occurred in order to get evidence to discredit and destroy Walter Lee Davis, weren't you?"

"No, sir, I was out there measuring for one reason, to protect myself and my men."

"Well, protect yourself? Nobody has jumped on you, have they?" asked Hooker.

"Walter had told me his story," replied Swann.

Hooker steered the questioning back to recent events.

"Well, you found it enough of your business to go with Mr. Powell's lawyers to Spring Hill to talk to a witness in that case, didn't you?"

"Whenever my records prove something, show something, sir, and my men are involved, I'm going to do everything I can to protect them."

Hooker shook his head and asked Swann if he had gone to Spring Hill for another reason.

"I had business in that area, sir," Swann replied self-importantly. "I looked at a piece of property, sir."

Swann admitted he had actually only copied a telephone number off a "for sale" sign.

"And you drove all the way to Spring Hill to look at a "for sale" sign on a piece of property?"

"Sir, my wife and I have been looking for property for about three months now in Williamson County. And we had heard about some property being for sale. And I checked it, it was a good location."

People seated on the benches chuckled at Swann's definition of "business" in the area.

Hooker asked if Swann had been in touch with District Attorney Shriver since May 1968.

"No, sir, I haven't. Let me say this, sir, if I may."

"You just volunteer anything you want to, Mr. Swann," Hooker said, sarcasm in his voice.

Swann said that he had met Shriver when he was running for the office of district attorney and that he had voted for him.

Branstetter spoke up and quipped, "Not going to ask if he's going to vote for him again or not?"

"I vote for the truth, sir," Swann said sanctimoniously.

There was more snickering in the courtroom at hearing this self-righteous proclamation.

Hooker paused a moment, then resumed questioning.

"Tell these ladies and gentlemen of the jury, Mr. Swann, what your real interest in this case is."

"Protecting my men that's involved. That's all I want. To see justice and like I have stated before, I am not for the Gourleys; I am not for the Powells, but I have four good men involved in this and I am in this for one thing, protecting them."

"You are trying to protect Walter Lee Davis by convincing the jury he has sworn a lie. Is that the way you are trying to protect him?" Hooker asked.

"I am basing what I have said on my records and that's all I have to go by."

"Well, Mr. Swann, when you were down there seeing him didn't you know that the defendant, Powell, had claimed and was claiming in this trial that a third person got in this car when it was running and shot shots for a distance of a quarter of a mile and then got out of the car without it ever stopping?"

"No, sir, I did not know it but I did read it in the papers, I will put it like that."

"And you are telling the jury you didn't ask Walter whether a third man was in the car or not?"

"No, sir, no, sir."

"But he did tell you the only people he saw were two men, didn't he?"

"He saw two people in the car."

"That's all," Hooker said finally.

Branstetter thanked Swann and told him he could step down.

The time was just before 12:13 p.m. The judge told the jury that the cook had their lunch ready.

Billy's friend and fraternity brother Jimbo Cook had attended every day of the trial from the beginning, even sitting through the lengthy jury selection process. Each morning, he was in line by 6:00 a.m. in order to secure a place in the gallery.

Cook watched Thomas Swann walk out. Then he got up and followed him into the elevator.

"His shirt was wringing wet, I guess from all the lying he did," Cook told his father James Cook that night. Jimbo Cook described Swann as "a puffed-up clown." "It was laughable that he said he was trying to protect his workers. He was up there for one reason. He was out to sabotage Walter Lee Davis's testimony to save Bill Powell's neck. I believed everything Walter Lee Davis said and nothing Swann said. I hope they charge him with perjury and witness tampering. He is a criminal."

At 1:35 p.m., court reconvened, with B. F. Hunter, the next witness for the defense, taking his oath after the jury filed in.

Hunter told Branstetter he was a supervisor for Sheco Construction Company on May 24, 1968, working at the Kroger warehouse site at the intersection of Elm Hill Pike and Massman Drive.

Branstetter read from a statement taken from Hunter describing his conversation with Walter Lee Davis a week and a half before Davis testified.

"That at the time he ate lunch he went to the trailer, looked up Elm Hill Pike, saw a car stop at the drive of the old white house, looked like they were arguing and went up there at the drive at the old white house, turned around, spun gravel, came down the road. It looked like they were going 60 miles an hour, and when they came back it looked like the man in the front was slumped, but you heard no shots or anything else."

"Is that substantially what Walter Lee Davis told you within the last three weeks?" asked Branstetter.

"Yes, sir. I don't believe he used 'the old white house,' but he did say they stopped at the drive and looked like they were arguing and went up to turn around there and spun gravel out as they came back down the road and it looked like they were going about 60 miles an hour."

Branstetter yielded to Shriver. Hunter broke down and confessed that, after all, Walter Davis hadn't told him anything, that what he heard was from another source, that it was all hearsay.

Hunter said that Davis was a man of good character and that he had never known Davis to tell a lie. He added that Davis was very polite and showed no resentment toward white people.

"And that was one reason why you liked Walter?" asked Shriver.

"That's right."

Next on the stand was yet another Sheco Construction employee, Wiley Conerly. Conerly said he had moved to Nashville after the murder occurred. Branstetter asked Conerly about previous statements he made to defense lawyers.

Conerly essentially stuck to Davis's account about the two white men stopping, that the driver got out and opened the trunk, got into the back seat and after that Davis heard some noise. Conerly added that Davis said a station wagon pulled up alongside the car, then came out of the driveway "real fast." The black car turned around and sped back toward town. He testified that Davis had observed that the man in the passenger seat was "leaned over." Conerly emphasized that Davis said there were only two white men in the black car.

"Did Walter Lee Davis—I will ask you, make substantially that statement to you?" asked Branstetter.

"Yes, sir," answered Conerly.

Branstetter went back to the table, sat down, and whispered something to Bill Powell.

On cross-examination by Hooker, Conerly admitted that he was not familiar with the Kroger job site, nor did he know anything about Massman Drive. He said he had been questioned by a Mr. Kilgore from Branstetter's firm, who had caught up with him at a doctor's office.

"Did Walter tell you that the trunk was raised up?"

"Yes, sir."

"Who did he say who raised it up?"

Conerly said Walter indicated that it was the driver who got out and raised the trunk and then got into the back seat.

"You knew he was telling you about this killing, didn't you?" asked Hooker.

"Yes, sir."

Next, there was confusion when the defense attorneys stated they wanted to call Davidson County sheriff's deputy Clarence Watson to the stand. It was Watson who had delivered the subpoena to Walter Lee Davis at his home in Spring Hill, Tennessee, three weeks before the trial began.

Shriver objected. The issue in question was that Watson was an officer of the court who had served subpoenas, in particular the subpoena handed to Walter Lee Davis, and then had taken rotations serving in the jury room, meaning the jurors were familiar with Watson.

Judge Cornelius ruled that since Watson had been "square in the middle of the jury" that it was not permissible for him to testify.

With no jury present, Clarence Watson, a court officer in Division III of Criminal Court and a deputy sheriff, was sworn in.

Branstetter, who had just said aloud that the defense was working to impeach Walter Lee Davis as a witness, questioned Watson.

"Did Walter Lee Davis state to you at the time or about the time or following the time when you were there serving him with a subpoena, that if they tried to lay this on A. B. Dansby, that he would come up and clear him?" Branstetter asked, referring to another Black employee of the Sheco company.

"Something to that effect," answered Watson.

Regarding the question of whether or not a station wagon had been mentioned in Watson's conversation with Davis, the deputy sheriff's answer differed from a previous Sheco witness.

"He stated to me he pulled up to this particular intersection, in this particular location, he turned around there and when Mr. Powell pulled into the particular location that a black station wagon was coming in a westerly direction and he had to wait until the black station wagon got by before he could turn around."

"Now, 'Mr. Powell,' you mean the black automobile," Branstetter corrected Watson.

"No, sir, he didn't say any names, he just said 'the black automobile.'"

"Did he mention the word 'shots'?"

"Yes, sir, he did mention the word 'shots.'"

"What did he say?"

"He said that he heard three shots, that they were not too loud and then one loud shot."

Loud whispers echoed through the gallery at hearing Watson's last words.

"That's all," said Branstetter.

The rapid clicking from the court recorder's table stopped, then resumed when Hooker stood up to cross-examine Deputy Watson, asking if Davis had told him anything else when he delivered the subpoena.

"Well, he told me the whole story as to what he saw and basically the whole thing was about what he testified to in court."

Again, noise from the spectators.

"The car stopped, and two men got out of the car?"

"That's correct."

"Said they raised—one of them raised the trunk, the big man, the driver?"

"He did make the statement that the driver raised the trunk," said Watson.

"And then did he say that they got back in the car and—that they got out and were discussing there and behind the car, and then they both got back in the car and then the driver got out, came around and raised the trunk, went around to the righthand side of the car and got in the back seat?"

"That's correct, sir."

"And while the driver was in the back seat that he heard these four shots?"

"After he told me two-and-a-half, three, three-and-a-half, about less than four minutes he heard the shots."

"Then after the shots that the man in the back seat, the driver—and he did describe him as being the bigger of the two?"

"Yes, sir, he did say he was the bigger."

"And he got out of the back seat and came around the car and got back in under the wheel and they drove off?"

"He closed the trunk lid," added Watson.

"Now, coupled with what you told in response to Mr. Branstetter's questions, that's all that he told you about this tragedy?"

"Yes, that connected with the fact that they drove up the street."

"That's all," said Mr. Hooker.

> Hal Hardin thought here in a nutshell was corroborating proof that Walter Lee Davis was telling the truth. Shriver had made a mistake by objecting to Watson's testifying in front of the jury. Hardin felt the jury must already believe that Davis could not have made up a story which precisely fit the timeline and coincided with where the glass from the car window was found and the number of shots fired. The Sheco men told different versions of the mysterious station wagon story. From their testimony, it seemed obvious they were influenced by Thomas Swann. The truth was, according to Watson, that the station wagon had only passed by, causing the man driving the black car to wait to pull out onto Elm Hill Pike. The jurors—the very people who would have trusted Watson—would never know that he corroborated Davis's testimony exactly, that Davis had in all likelihood witnessed the murder of Haynie Gourley.

Hardin would forever believe that Shriver's blocking Watson from testifying would be the biggest mistake of the trial.

***

Next, a surprise witness took the stand.

The defense called Charles M. Wilson of Madison, Wisconsin. Hooker, Shriver, and Hardin conferred with each other. They had no idea who this man was. Spectators looked at each other, shrugging their shoulders as they watched in anticipation.

Branstetter introduced Wilson as an expert witness. A slight, sixty-five-year-old man with a long face, receding hairline and dark, bushy eyebrows, Wilson recited a long list of credentials, including publications he had appeared in, various professorships, and membership in several professional organizations. He claimed he had done extensive work in the identification of fired bullets, fired shells, and firearms. Wilson also mentioned that early in his career, he held a teaching job at the prestigious Northwestern University School of Law, even though he himself was not a college graduate.

According to Wilson, he had only recently retired as superintendent of the State Crime Laboratory in Madison, Wisconsin, which he had established twenty years before.

"State whether or not you had occasion a few weeks ago to examine certain items of evidence in the case of State versus Powell," said Branstetter.

"Yes, sir, I did."

"Have you had occasion to extend x-ray techniques normally used by the medical profession to include crime identification?" asked Branstetter.

Wilson answered yes, that he had taken advantage of new developments with "soft x-rays" and had applied this technique to detect metal particles present in clothing worn by gunshot victims.

Branstetter then handed Wilson the coat Powell was wearing the day of the shooting and asked if he had examined it.

"Yes, sir, this is the coat which you, Mr. Branstetter, made available to me in your office here in Nashville on July 7. I returned to Madison with this coat and undertook to make some x-ray studies of certain areas on this jacket, represented to me as belonging to Mr. Powell, the defendant in this case."

Branstetter asked Wilson to explain exactly what he did with reference to the coat.

Wilson said he made a series of soft x-rays of the right front panel, the lapel, and the right shoulder area from the armhole down to the elbow on the right arm.

At this point Shriver spoke up.

"If Your Honor please, I don't know what this testimony is, but it sounds like something I have never heard of before. Perhaps we'd better excuse the jury and get into it a little bit, because I don't know whether it is admissible in this court of Tennessee or generally in courts."

"I think the jury would very much like to see it," retorted Branstetter testily.

Judge Cornelius sustained Shriver's objection and at 4:36 p.m. sent the jury up.

Wilson explained his method in a fifteen-minute recitation of abstruse technical terms like "Beryllium window," "Lindeman glass window," "kilovolts," "milliamperes of currency," and other jargon that would likely be unintelligible to a layman. With a slight smile, Wilson appeared to puff up in his chair, claiming that his method detects the presence of metal particles in fabric, a method he, Wilson, had originated.

After some discussion between the judge and Shriver, Shriver was allowed, still in the absence of the jury, to cross-examine Wilson on what he had just testified to, whether he had invented some sort of test that could be useful in this case.

"You said that the Wisconsin Supreme Court has accepted it as valid?"

"Right."

"Have any other courts accepted it?" asked Shriver.

"Not to my knowledge," answered Wilson.

"Have you used it in courts in any other state?" asked Shriver.

Wilson answered that he was not aware that the method had been employed elsewhere, but that he had promoted its use.

"What is the difference between a soft x-ray and a regular x-ray?"

asked Shriver.

Again, Wilson launched into an extended monologue which included a description of an experiment using worms that Wilson had applied to clothing.

When the spectators heard the part about worms crawling on fabric, laughter erupted in the courtroom. Judge Cornelius did not respond, and the noise died down.

After going on about metal particles sprayed from a gun, Wilson concluded by stating, "This would give you some idea as to the position of the gun at the time the revolver is discharged in close combat conditions."

"Where on Powell's coat did the soft x-rays indicate metal shavings?" asked Branstetter.

"They were all confined to the right sleeve, from the shoulder to about a little above the elbow. There were none on the right panel," replied Wilson, adding that none were found on the front of the jacket.

"With reference to the coat, in order to have deposited metal products of the type you have found, from what direction would the gun have been fired, and from what location?" asked Branstetter.

The courtroom grew quiet.

"It would have to be behind the wearer, and to the right of the wearer, and above the wearer."

Sounds of shock raced through the spectator gallery. Billy Gourley felt his heart sink.

"Do you have any further conclusions as to the location of the weapon that deposited these metal shearings on the coat?" asked Branstetter.

Wilson answered that if Powell was in the driver's seat behind the steering wheel at the time the metal shearings were "acquired by his coat," it would be impossible for him to have self-inflicted the wound in his left leg. Powell absolutely could not have held a gun in such a position to deposit these particles on his own shoulder, he said.

Branstetter gave a triumphant glance in the direction of Hooker and Shriver.

"That's all."

Hooker then rose and addressed Judge Cornelius, citing the late hour of 5:35 p.m., asking that court be adjourned without the State's cross-examination of Wilson. Hooker complained that neither he nor Shriver was familiar with the unusual techniques testified to by Wilson. Hooker argued that having never heard of any such experiments, the State needed to familiarize themselves with the validity of Wilson's tests.

Branstetter argued against adjournment, but was overruled by Judge Cornelius, who announced that court would resume the next morning at 9:00 a.m.

At 5:45 p.m., the court stood adjourned.

CHAPTER [23]

After court was over, an entourage from the prosecution drove out to Hooker Hill, Hooker's 350-acre farm near the historic town of Franklin, Tennessee, to discuss what to do about the testimony just given by Wilson. The prosecution had been blindsided by this purported expert witness who, in Hal Hardin's words, "seemed to come out of left field."

Wilson had maintained that he was an expert in gunpowder residue, but what he testified to on the witness stand was something else. He was claiming that his "soft x-rays" had shown that there were actual metal particles present from a gun having been fired over the right shoulder of Powell's coat, proving that the shooter fired from the back seat and from above Powell, just as Powell had claimed. If Wilson was correct, there was no other explanation for the presence of these metal particles on the right shoulder of the coat or for their absence on the other surfaces of the jacket.

The three men at the prosecution table had been relieved that Wilson's testimony had come at the end of the day, so now there was time to find out more about this character with his high-sounding oration on the witness stand. If the jury believed him, then they would believe that a gunman had indeed been in the car.

The challenge was how to discredit Wilson as an expert witness and debunk his theory.

Gathered in Hooker's handsome library were Homicide Detectives

Sherman Nickens and Bill Larkin, District Attorney Tom Shriver, ADA Hal Hardin, Tyree Harris Jr., a law clerk in the DA's office, Charlie Hunter, investigator for the district attorney's office, and TBI ballistics expert Robert Goodwin.

Passing drinks around, Hooker announced, "We have to find a way to disqualify this imposter."

Everyone agreed there had to be some way to discredit the pompous witness and his lofty jargon, knowing his pretentious discourse likely impressed the jury.

If Wilson's findings were allowed to stand, they would sink the prosecution's case.

Hooker wasted no time. He picked up the phone and went straight to the top, putting in a call to FBI director J. Edgar Hoover, whom Hooker had known through his friendship with Bobby Kennedy and his involvement in the Hoffa case. Hoover, although past his prime and growing ever more crotchety, came through. Soon, FBI agents from around the country were calling other agents to find out if anyone knew about this man Wilson and his soft x-rays. At one point, Hooker had an exchange with an agent in Iowa, but that eventually led nowhere.

The phone kept ringing, and Hooker kept calling. It was getting late, and court was due to begin at nine a.m. the next day. Those gathered around began to leave.

Around midnight, everyone had gone except for Hal Hardin, who, at twenty-seven, was barely a year out of Vanderbilt Law School. The exceedingly handsome assistant district attorney had continued to capture the attention of many young women who had seen him on TV or his photograph in the newspapers or watched him from the gallery of the courtroom.

Hardin and Hooker had been drinking Dewar's since early evening. Hardin, though, knew that on these types of occasions Hooker would think big. Hooker was sitting at the kitchen table when Hardin walked in from a cigarette break. Hooker hung the phone back on the wall.

"Hal, I want you to go to Wisconsin," Hooker said in his deep, resonant voice.

Hardin, feeling slightly tipsy, could see Hooker was serious.

"When?" asked Hardin.

"Now," answered Hooker.

Hardin was speechless. It took a moment for Hooker's words to sink in.

"Just how am I supposed to get there?"

Hooker leaned back in his chair and said pontifically, "I've got a jet on the runway warming up at Berry Field. Go get on that airplane."

Hardin laughed nervously. "It's midnight. What am I supposed to do when I get to Wisconsin?"

Hooker looked at Hardin like it hadn't occurred to him either.

"Bring me a witness. I'll see you in court tomorrow at nine," Hooker said, and that was the only instruction Hardin was to receive.

Hardin hesitated, but said, "Okay, I'm going."

There were thunderstorms in the area, and Hardin did not like to fly, even in good weather. As Hardin walked out the door, Hooker's wife Effie slipped a bottle of scotch into his coat pocket, whispering, "Here, this will help."

Hardin got into his car, which made a crunching sound on the gravel drive, and drove off into the night.

When he arrived at the Nashville airport, sure enough, there was a small jet on the tarmac with its engines running. Hardin climbed the steps, and the pilot took off into the night.

Hardin had been up since before dawn. As was his habit, he walked daily from his downtown apartment to the courthouse at 6:00 a.m. It was now well past one o'clock in the morning. He hadn't slept and had been in the same suit and shirt all day, now both rumpled. His tie was knotted loosely around his neck. Hardin could feel the stubble of a five o'clock shadow on his face. He had no idea what he would do when he arrived in Madison. He had no hotel room, no contacts, and no clue where to go.

The jet touched down after an hour-and-a-half flight. At the airport, Hardin waked the driver of the only taxi in sight. Hardin's instincts kicked in, saying to himself, "Well, I guess I'll go to the sheriff's office," and he asked to be taken to downtown Madison. Still smelling of scotch, unshaven and disheveled, Hardin walked into the Dane County Sheriff's Office a little before 5:00 a.m., startling the woman night clerk who eyed him suspiciously.

"She thinks I'm some drunk wandering in off the street," Hardin thought to himself. He straightened up and explained his mission. She seemed to soften and told him to have a seat.

As luck would have it, Dane County Sheriff Vernon Leslie came into work early. At first, he was skeptical, but when Hardin said the name Charles Wilson, Sheriff Leslie responded immediately. "I know this guy. He's a crook. He's no good. We don't even use him. His lab is really bad. I can tell you all kind of things."

Hardin's spirits soared. This is the man who can really attack this guy, he thought.

"I need you to come to Nashville with me and testify," Hardin said. "This is really big. You're a law enforcement man, and I'm begging you. I need you to come down and testify today."

"Today? How am I supposed to get there?"

Hardin sort of smiled to himself, leaned back in his chair as Hooker had dramatically done hours earlier, and said with a swagger, "I got a jet out at the airport warming up on the runway waiting for you."

Much to Hardin's amazement, the sheriff agreed and turned to his deputy and asked him to come with him. The three returned to the airport where Hardin faced a moment of embarrassment. The jet that was supposed to be "warming up" would not start. Apparently, the airplane had a dead battery. A crew was called in to jump start the engines, and given Hardin's fear of flying, this setback did not help his confidence.

But the plane landed safely at Berry Field in Nashville, and Hardin, still bleary-eyed, drove the sheriff and his deputy to the courthouse. When Hal's close friend Charlie Hunter, chief investigator for the district attorney, saw the beleaguered-looking Hardin, he advised him to "go home and shower." Hardin still reeked of whiskey and had not had a change of clothes or a shave in over twenty-four hours. He had been awake for the same amount of time, but he was buoyed by the fact that just a few hours before, he had been sitting in Hooker's house with no hope of finding anyone to discredit Wilson. Despite his fatigue, Hardin was proud; he felt like a cat who had just caught a mouse. He had succeeded in a mission that had seemed out of the realm of possibility just hours before.

Hooker's far-fetched gamble had paid off.

CHAPTER [24]

Spectators look on as Billy Gourley, middle, follows his mother Josephine Gourley out of the courtroom during a break in the trial. © *The Tennessean – USA TODAY NETWORK*

Court resumed at 9:13 on the morning of Wednesday, July 30. Cecil Branstetter once again called Wilson to the stand for the defense.

But Branstetter did not mention soft x-rays. Instead, he brought up another subject.

"Mr. Wilson, would you describe for the record the history and development of what has variously been referred to as a paraffin test?"

"The so-called paraffin test," answered Wilson, a note of authority in his voice, "or as it is sometimes called the dermal nitrate test, is reported to have been developed by a gentleman by the name of Gonzales from Mexico."

Hooker spoke up and addressed the court, stating that Judge Cornelius had already barred any reference to a paraffin test and overruled the defense several times.

Branstetter argued that his expert witness could have examined paraffin using a different method where it would not have mattered that Powell had washed his hands the moment he arrived at the hospital after the shooting. Branstetter said Wilson knew of a method of examining paraffin called an atomic neutron test. Wilson said he could have determined without question whether Powell had fired a gun in the preceding twenty-four hours, just by taking particles from the paraffin. Branstetter said the district attorney and Metro police should have known about this new testing procedure.

Referring to the paraffin used on Powell, Branstetter insisted, "Had it been preserved, we could have taken it and sent it by Mr. Wilson to the laboratory and had it analyzed under the new testing procedure and could have demonstrated that Mr. Powell did not fire a gun with or without washing his hands. We can do this in five minutes, Your Honor."

The judge responded by saying he had already ruled that any reference to a paraffin test was inadmissible. Judge Cornelius further stated that Wilson's claim about an alternative test "is purely speculative."

With that, the judge overruled Branstetter and declared that the trial proceedings should resume.

Branstetter continued to argue with the judge and finally asked permission to allow Wilson to at least describe the test. The judge acquiesced.

"What is the test?" Branstetter asked Wilson.

"The name of the test you are seeking is Nuclear Activation Analysis which is made on the paraffin. It has nothing to do with the Dermal Nitrate Test, but the paraffin itself would retain the detonation products of the primer."

"And it would be these detonation products that would be tested by the Neutron—"

"Activation Analysis Method, yes," answered Wilson.

There was snickering in the courtroom as Wilson repeated these words.

The discussion of the paraffin test controversy had taken place in the absence of the jury, which was called back in at 9:27 a.m.

When the defense called the next witness to the stand, Billy Gourley had yet another moment to consider how one little twist of fate might possibly have saved his father's life.

In an effort to establish a timeline for the fatal ride, Jack Norman called John Sloan to be sworn in. Sloan had been in Haynie's office just before he left with Bill Powell. It was revealed that Haynie had shown Sloan around the building and when he went to leave, Haynie asked him if he would like to be taken downtown to his office in Haynie's own car, given the fact that Sloan was leaving his brand-new car to have a glitch fixed.

Sloan testified that as he was about to accept Haynie's offer, it was learned that Capitol employee Albert Rich was headed to Third National Bank and could give Sloan a ride.

> Billy couldn't help but think that if Sloan had borrowed Haynie's car that maybe Bill Powell would have missed his opportunity to get his father alone. But he quickly thought better of it. Powell could have driven his own car, and the outcome would probably have been the same.

The defense then presented several character witnesses who all spoke of Powell's "peace and quietude" and "truth and veracity." Already, the lieutenant governor of Tennessee had testified on Powell's behalf as had Powell's brother-in-law John Witherspoon. Included on the newly revised witness list were two judges, three company presidents, a pediatrician, and James H. Reed III, president of Jim Reed Chevrolet in Nashville, a prominent rival of Capitol Chevrolet.

Perhaps the most powerful of the witnesses was Carlton "Pete" Holt who had played football alongside Powell at Vanderbilt. Holt was now president of Transit Ready Mix, a concrete business. When asked if he knew Powell's reputation for peacefulness and quietude and good order, Holt answered emphatically, "I would stake my life on his honesty and integrity."

Judge Benson Trimble, an across-the-street neighbor of Powell's, was equally enthusiastic about Powell's propensity for telling the truth.

"Without any doubt whatsoever," answered Trimble.

The final character witness, Dr. Randolph Batson, Dean of the School of Medicine at Vanderbilt University, was just as ardent about Powell's word under oath.

"Doctor, state whether or not in your opinion, in your knowledge, that he is entitled to full faith and credit on his oath in a Court of Justice."

"By all means, yes," Batson answered.

Since the very beginning of the trial, Powell's wife Helen had been barred from the courtroom, as were all witnesses until the time they were called, so she had not observed firsthand any of the proceedings.

Helen Powell took the stand, stating that on May 24, 1968, she was having her hair done at a beauty shop when she received word around noon that her husband had been shot. She had gone directly to Vanderbilt Hospital where she found Powell in the emergency room. She also stated that she had seen uniformed policemen there, questioning her husband.

Branstetter's last question of his final witness, was: "You have no personal knowledge of anything that happened that day with reference to your husband prior to the time you arrived at the hospital, other than the fact that he had left home to go to work?"

"That's all," she replied.

"Thank you, Mrs. Powell. The defense rests, Your Honor."

***

When the jury came back in at 1:38 p.m., the State began its rebuttal. The first witness called was William Coleman from the TBI.

Hooker asked Coleman if he had been back to the scene to conduct experiments at the location where Walter Lee Davis said he saw the black car stop.

Norman immediately objected to testimony about any test ordered by the prosecution. The jury was sent out.

Coleman explained that on July 14, 1969, the day the trial began, he and Robert Goodwin, also with the TBI, along with Charlie Hunter from the DA's office and Lt. Reasonover from the Metro police, took a car and a ballistics box and parked across from where the Sheco Construction Company's trailer had been the previous year. The idea was to test if Walter Lee Davis could have heard shots from where he sat next to the Sheco trailer.

During the test, shots were fired into the box with both car windows closed and the trunk open. Then, the gun was fired again with the right front window down.

Coleman told the judge that he, Lt. Reasonover, Charlie Hunter, and Officer Kirkland had stood where Walter Lee Davis had indicated the trailer had been. Agent Goodwin fired the shots inside the car.

Altogether, three test rounds were fired, always with the fourth shot fired when the right window was down.

"And at that point where you all were standing, did you have any difficulty hearing these shots?" Hooker asked.

"We did not," Coleman said.

Judge Cornelius then asked: "What says the defense?"

Norman came forward, positing the argument that because the experiment involved a hearing test and given that Davis's hearing and Coleman's hearing might not be the same, insinuating that Davis even had trouble hearing in court, that there was no way to know if Davis would have been capable of hearing any shots as he had claimed on the witness stand.

Norman argued further that weather conditions were not the same and could have affected the hearing of any shots that might have been fired.

Hooker insisted that the weather on the day of the shooting and the day of the experiment was not that different and that care had been taken to recreate the same measurements of the distance from the trailer to where Davis had indicated the car had pulled over.

Norman snapped at Hooker, insisting there was no previous reference made that would allow more testimony about Walter Lee Davis's story.

Hooker countered, saying the attack on Davis's credibility opened the question up and that "we have the right to corroborate that he heard four shots."

Judge Cornelius sustained the defense's objection but allowed Hooker to continue with his questioning of Coleman. The TBI agent testified that even at a distance of 381 feet, some 181 feet further away from where Walter Lee Davis watched, gunshots inside the car could be heard. In addition, Coleman said that on the day before the official test, without benefit of knowing where the trailer was located, shots were fired at 500 feet from where the men were standing, and even at that distance, gunshots could be heard.

But all the testing was for naught. Judge Cornelius ruled that the results would not be allowed. Had the group taken Walter Lee Davis to the site, he said, "it might have had some bearing." The jury would never hear this important information.

One more blow to the prosecution's case.

> When Billy Gourley heard this, he was crestfallen. Walter Lee Davis had witnessed the murder of his father, but at every turn, verification of his testimony was blocked. The jurors would never hear about this test. They had not heard the sheriff's deputy's exact account

> of Davis's testimony. Billy feared they would only remember Thomas Swann's lies.

There was a glimmer of hope when Detective Sherman Nickens was called back to the witness stand. On rebuttal, Shriver asked Nickens about interviews with B. F. Hunter, a Black employee of Sheco Construction Company. Nickens said he had spoken with him twice.

"All right, Mr. Nickens, on July 9, 1969, did you have an occasion to interview a Mr. B. F. Hunter at the Metropolitan Police department?"

"Yes, I did."

"All right. Now I want to ask you if Mr. B. F. Hunter didn't tell you that Walter Davis had not told him anything to do with the Gourley case, or words to that effect, that his information came from a Mr. Chowning, another foreman at Sheco Construction Company?"

"Yes, sir."

Nickens was told he could step down.

> Jimbo Cook just knew it. Here was more proof that Thomas Swann had lied on the witness stand. He had told his employees what to say. Swann was actually the one with different versions, not Walter Lee Davis. Surely the jury had seen through this man. Jimbo wondered if Swann had been paid by the defense. If not, those trips to Walter's house in a Capitol Chevrolet car should tell them that this man was only there to sabotage a humble man's truthful testimony.

After a brief recess, the prosecution resumed their rebuttal, calling Sheriff Vernon Leslie from Madison, Wisconsin, to the stand in the absence of the jury.

The sheriff had been waiting outside in the hall since nine that morning, after flying to Nashville with Hal Hardin. It was now four o'clock.

On the stand, Sheriff Leslie was questioned by Shriver. He stated that he was an elected official and that Madison, the capital of Wisconsin, was the county seat. Now in his fourth year as sheriff, Leslie said that altogether he had been with the sheriff's office for sixteen years.

Shriver asked Leslie if he was familiar with a man named Charles M. Wilson. Leslie answered yes, that he had known Wilson for at least fifteen years, during which time Wilson operated the State Crime Laboratory in Wisconsin.

"Have you ever had occasion to have either ballistics evidence sent to the State Crime Laboratory or clothing to be tested to determine if guns had been fired in the immediate proximity of the clothing?"

No, Sheriff Leslie replied, and said that their office had sent out clothing and ballistics evidence to be tested, but not to the State Crime Laboratory.

"Where do you send your evidence?"

"To the FBI lab."

"Do you consider Mr. Wilson competent in the field of ballistics and ballistics testimony?"

"I do not."

Whispers broke out in the spectator gallery at hearing the sheriff's curt answer.

"Do you have any reason for stating that?" Shriver asked.

"Just because I have never known him to appear as a ballistics expert in the state of Wisconsin."

"Have you ever had any acquaintance with a soft x-ray process for detecting metal fragments in clothing?"

"I never heard of it until this morning," replied the sheriff.

"Do you consider Mr. Wilson competent to testify about any scientific matters connected with crime detection or crime or crime laboratories?"

"I do not."

A murmur rose in the courtroom.

Norman stood up to question Sheriff Leslie.

In a condescending tone, Norman said, "You're a sheriff, just the sheriff?"

"Right," answered Leslie.

"That's all, Your Honor," said Norman, turning his back to Leslie.

Judge Cornelius asked about the State's next rebuttal witness.

"Our next witness," said Shriver, "won't be here until 8:47 in the morning so we would like to request a recess until then."

Judge Cornelius addressed the jury, saying that court would resume at 9:00 a.m. the next morning. Court was adjourned at 4:19 p.m.

Sheriff Vernon Leslie and Chief Deputy Reynold Abrams flew back to Wisconsin. The two lawmen had been in Nashville for less than 12 hours.

***

Thursday, July 31, was yet another steamy day in Nashville with temperatures headed to the low 90s. Court reconvened at 9:46 in the morning. Shriver called FBI agent Bill Heilman to the stand.

Norman spoke up, his powerful voice echoing throughout the courtroom, "May it please the Court, we understand that this is a witness that is sought to impeach Mr. Wilson, so we will want Mr. Wilson to sit in the courtroom." Judge Cornelius agreed, and the jury filed in.

With Shriver questioning, Heilman, a tall, balding man wearing a dark suit and narrow tie, revealed that he was a special agent for the Federal Bureau of Investigation, assigned to the laboratory in Washington, D.C. A member of the FBI for twenty-seven years, Heilman said he was chief of a section known as the Instrumental Analysis Section.

Asked if Heilman had ever heard of soft x-ray process, he answered that his unit used it "all the time." His explanation agreed with Wilson's definition of what soft x-rays could detect, saying "soft x-rays are used for locating small particles in materials that aren't very dense, like cloth and flesh."

But any agreement with Wilson ended there. Heilman said there was absolutely no way of determining the composition of foreign particles using this method. Heilman said he had brought along an example with him.

While an assistant plugged in a shadowbox, Shriver continued the questioning.

"Mr. Heilman, you state that you cannot tell what a particle is by means of soft x-ray?"

Heilman explained the only thing one can tell from the x-ray is the existence of foreign material. A soft x-ray would only locate a particle. You absolutely cannot tell what it is made up of, he said.

Heilman was next shown several soft x-rays made by Wilson of Powell's coat. Heilman said they were all over-exposed, making it impossible to make out anything definite.

"Mr. Heilman, are there tests which are routinely done to test if a gun has been fired in the immediate proximity, say of a coat?" asked Shriver.

Heilman explained that if it is suspected that someone has been hit by a bullet or a gun that has been fired in close proximity to the person, the piece of clothing would first be put under a microscope. When a cartridge fires, he said, it leaves by-products.

"A soft x-ray is used to determine if there are particles," said Heilman. "Then the pieces are removed to be examined with a spectrograph."

Before cross-examination of Heilman by the defense, the judge allowed the jury a five-minute recess for a smoking break.

After the jury returned, Norman made a surprise move, addressing the FBI agent.

"I want to ask you so that we'll remove any doubt, so that this jury can know the absolute truth, will it be satisfactory to you for Mr. Wilson to accompany you with this coat and his x-rays to your laboratories, the finest in the world, and there make these tests and tell this jury what they are. Could this be done?"

"If they're still there and can be located, they could be analyzed, yes," Heilman replied.

"We ask that be done immediately, Your Honor," said Norman, stepping before the judge.

"What says the State?" asked Judge Cornelius.

"We have no objection," answered Shriver.

There was loud grumbling from the spectator gallery. After they had gone to the trouble to procure a seat, the day's proceedings were now to be cut short.

It was decided that Wilson would accompany Heilman to Washington, D.C., so Wilson's soft x-rays could be examined that evening in the FBI's laboratory.

Wilson and Heilman left the courtroom immediately and boarded a plane provided by Tennessee Governor Buford Ellington.

The court was adjourned early, at 10:37 a.m., to be resumed on the morning of Friday, August 1, 1969.

CHAPTER [25]

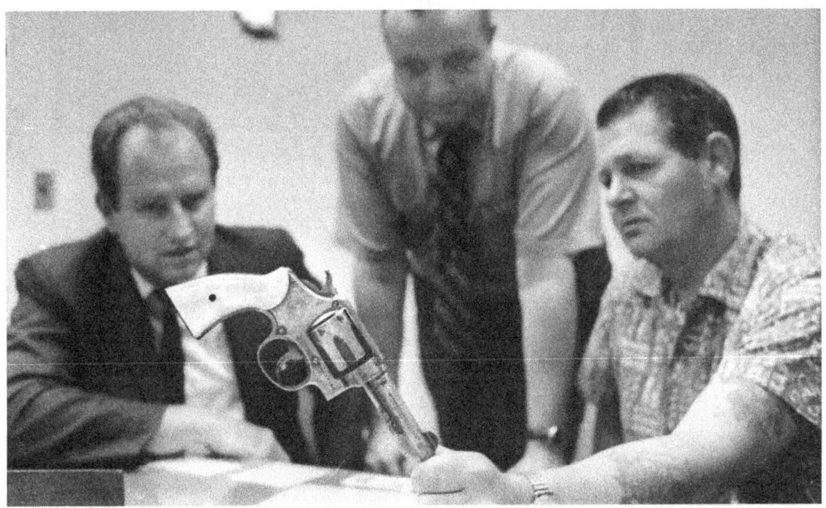

Metro police examine a .38-caliber Smith & Wesson revolver. *Nashville Public Library, Special Collections, Banner Newspaper Collection*

John Lentz was in his law office in downtown Nashville. It was 3:00 p.m. on Wednesday, July 30. He sat stock-still, staring at a larger-than-life photograph of a sinister-looking weapon on the front page of the *Nashville Banner.*

Like almost everyone in Nashville, Lentz was closely following the trial of Bill Powell. Lentz grew up in Belle Meade, not far from the Gourley residence, and knew the family well. After graduating from Vanderbilt Law School in 1967, Lentz joined the Tennessee Air National Guard and was assigned to basic training at Lackland Air Force Base in San Antonio, Texas. He wound up in the same training class as

Billy Gourley. He knew well the special relationship between Billy and his father and would watch as Billy opened letters from Haynie, who wrote to his son every day.

Lentz's own father was a prominent attorney and was appointed Chancellor of the Chancery Courts of Tennessee, an honor bestowed on him by the governor. After basic training, the younger Lentz joined the prestigious Nashville firm of Martin & Cochran and eventually specialized in entertainment law, representing country music stars, production companies, recording studios, and record labels.

As Lentz was reading the caption under the photograph of the weapon, his phone rang. It was Lentz's client Bob Frensley, calling from Louisville, Kentucky.

"John, I just got a call from a Lieutenant Bowers from Metro police," Frensley said. "He asked me if I had ever purchased any stolen guns. I told him no. They want me to come to Nashville and look at a pistol they found."

"I think I'm looking at it. There's a huge picture on the front page of the newspaper," Lentz said. "Some guy found it last year and never turned it in."

"Is it a snub-nosed pistol?" Frensley asked.

"No," Lentz said.

"Don't tell me what it looks like," said Frensley.

"Okay," said Lentz, baffled by Frensley's request.

"It has white handles, right?"

"Yes," answered Lentz warily. "How do you know that?"

Frensley was silent for a moment.

"John, that's the gun I gave to Bill Powell."

Lentz caught his breath. He sat frozen; a chill ran up and down his spine.

Frensley had worked at Capitol Chevrolet before moving to Louisville where he bought a Ford dealership in December 1968. He told Lentz that a friend from the National Guard had given him the gun in either late 1967 or early 1968.

Frensley said that when he received the gun, its original wooden handle was worn and rough, so he walked down the street to a pawn shop on Broadway and purchased two pearl pistol grips. He then went back to his office at the dealership and attached them to the pistol.

"Bill saw it and said he would like to have a gun for protection," explained Frensley. "I knew I could always get another one to keep for myself, so I gave it to him."

Lentz could hardly speak, he was so taken aback at this news.

"What should I do?" asked Frensley.

"You need to get down here. Let me talk to Mr. Cochran," Lentz said, referring to Carmack Cochran, a highly regarded attorney and one of the founders of Lentz's law firm. "I'll call you back."

Still shaken and trying to think, Lentz walked down to Cochran's office.

Cochran was adamant. He said Frensley should leave immediately for Nashville and let the police and the attorney general know what was going on. In addition, Cochran told Lentz, he should call Cecil Branstetter and tell him about Frensley and the gun. "They have a right to know," said Cochran, whom Lentz knew to be a stickler for the law.

Lentz called Frensley back. Frensley said he would leave immediately and come straight to Lentz's office.

Lentz then looked up Branstetter's number and left a message. When Branstetter returned his call, Cochran was on speakerphone. Lentz told Branstetter what Frensley said about giving Powell the gun pictured in the paper.

"He's on his way down here, and he's consented to testify," Lentz said. "I thought you should know what is going on."

Branstetter was silent for a moment.

"Tell him to go fishing," Branstetter said abruptly.

Lentz was caught off guard.

"I'm not following you," Lentz said.

Branstetter repeated, "Tell him to go fishing. The trial is over. Tell him to stay put. We're ready to go to the jury with the case. It's too late. Do not let him come down here."

Branstetter slammed down the phone.

***

Nashville awoke on Friday, August 1, to an outsized photograph of a gun with white pearl handles staring up from the front page of *The Tennessean*. Next to it, facing the photograph, was an equally large head shot of Bill Powell, appearing to be looking straight at the weapon.

The accompanying article said the gun was found in late August or early September 1968 on a stretch of Elm Hill Pike the police had never searched.

The weapon—a .38 caliber Smith & Wesson revolver—had been discovered close to Capitol Chevrolet and over a mile back toward town from the area where Powell said the alleged gunman had fled the car. The barrel of the weapon was rusted, but the serial number was still intact and legible.

The article went on to say that police investigators had been working frantically to determine ownership of the gun and learned on Tuesday night that the weapon had been traced to a naval station in Norfolk, Virginia, and was last inventoried there in the late 1940s. The prosecution, the article said, had subpoenaed more witnesses, including the owners of a pawn shop in downtown Nashville, two members of the Tennessee Air National Guard said to have at one time had possession of the revolver, and a former employee of Capitol Chevrolet.

Bob Frensley arrived in Nashville that evening and accompanied Lentz to Metro Police headquarters around 11:00 p.m. Frensley identified the gun as one he once owned. Around midnight, after meeting with the police, Lentz and Frensley walked across the street and met with District Attorney Thomas Shriver at his office where Frensley gave an account of how he had acquired the weapon and what he had subsequently done with it. Frensley agreed to testify for the prosecution.

Here was the key to the trial, Lentz thought. Motive, opportunity, and now means. Powell's fate was sealed.

***

Despite the drama playing out over the discovery of the possible murder weapon, there was unfinished business regarding Charles Wilson, the defense's expert witness. On Friday, August 1, court resumed at 10:15 a.m. after almost 24 hours in adjournment.

The jury filed in, and the state called FBI Agent William Heilman back to the stand. With Shriver questioning, Heilman said that he and Wilson had flown to Washington, D.C. to the FBI laboratory to examine Wilson's soft x-rays and the suit coat Bill Powell was wearing on May 24, 1968, the day of Haynie Gourley's slaying.

Heilman confirmed that Wilson had been with him the entire time at the laboratory where Wilson pointed out the place on the shoulder area of Powell's coat where he had found particles. The FBI technicians then took several soft x-rays of the same area.

On a shadowbox set up in the courtroom, Heilman pointed out an x-ray of the shoulder area of Powell's coat.

"That particular one was taken again as suggested by Mr. Wilson, with the film directly in contact with the outside of the coat which would duplicate the method that he took his."

Heilman said the x-rays Wilson had made, purportedly showing gun particles, were then taken to the FBI lab. But when soft x-rays were duplicated under Wilson's supervision, no particles of gun fragments were found.

"Under Mr. Wilson's supervision you took eight x-rays?" asked Shriver.

"Right."

"And found not a single particle Mr. Wilson found?"

"That's correct."

There was a loud stirring in the courtroom.

Norman rose for cross-examination, and Heilman repeated that he had found no traces of gun particles on the shoulder of Bill Powell's light gray coat.

Next to take the stand was Lindel Shaneyfelt, another FBI agent.

Shaneyfelt testified that Wilson's x-rays had not been properly processed and that what Wilson had called metal particles were actually air bubbles made when Wilson's film was developed.

The agent concluded that Wilson's soft x-rays revealed no particles on Powell's coat made by a gun having been fired over them.

Norman did not attempt a cross-examination, and the witness was excused.

Charles Wilson had flown back and forth to Nashville in a private plane, but that afternoon he was put on a Greyhound bus to travel back to Wisconsin.

CHAPTER [26]

Attorney John Lentz, left, accompanies his client, Robert O. Frensley, right, to Courtroom 611. Homicide Detective Sherman Nickens is in background. © *The Tennessean – USA TODAY NETWORK*

When court resumed after a short recess, Judge Cornelius asked if there were any further rebuttal witnesses for the state.

"Yes, Your Honor please, Bobby Frensley," Hooker replied.

The courtroom grew quiet. No one knew who this handsome, well-dressed man of thirty, with dark wavy hair was or what he had to do with the case.

With Hooker questioning, Frensley stated that he had been born and raised in Nashville. He had recently relocated to Louisville, Kentucky, where he purchased a Ford dealership in December 1968.

"Prior to December 1968, Mr. Frensley, where did you work?"

"Capitol Chevrolet Company."

Loud gasps sounded throughout the courtroom. People shifted in their seats. Then the room became eerily silent.

Frensley testified that before his move to Louisville he had worked at Capitol for six years, starting when the business was located on Broadway in downtown Nashville. He left the company in November 1968 to operate his new dealership. Frensley said he considered Powell a friend.

He testified that two days earlier, on the afternoon of Wednesday, July 30, he had received a call from Metro Police in Nashville about a gun found on Elm Hill Pike the previous year.

Frensley said he called his attorney John Lentz and told him that the police had requested he come to Nashville to look at a pistol that had been turned in and that might be involved in the Gourley murder. Frensley arrived that night. He was told by the police that the weapon had been traced to him.

Hooker spoke: "I hand you here a pistol," he said. "I ask you if this is the pistol you examined at the police station in Nashville at 11:00 p.m. on July 30?"

Frensley took the gun from Hooker.

"Yes, sir."

"Did you ever own this gun or have this gun?"

"Yes, sir, I did."

There was a rustling in the courtroom, and Hooker waited a long moment before speaking again.

Hooker asked Frensley how he acquired the pistol. Frensley explained that at the time he was a second lieutenant in the Tennessee Air National Guard and frequently had lunch with two other guard officers, Major Donald Hall and Col. Billy Huffine. On one of these occasions, Major Hall offered to bring Frensley a gun from the Civil Defense surplus stockpile. In late 1967, Hall brought the pistol to Capitol Chevrolet on Broadway and gave it to Frensley. The three men then went to lunch at the B & W Cafeteria on Sixth Avenue.

"And what did you do with the pistol after that?" asked Hooker.

Frensley said he walked to a pawn shop on Broadway and bought pearl handles, which he attached to the gun. He then took the .38 caliber Smith & Wesson weapon home and left it there.

A few weeks later, Frensley said, Bill Powell asked him if he could get one of the surplus guns for him. Powell said he wanted it for protection, that he didn't own a pistol, and if anybody broke into his home, he had no defense.

"I told him he could have that one," said Frensley.

"Go ahead," Hooker said.

"So I brought it in with the grips on it and gave it to Mr. Bill Powell."

With this, the gallery erupted. There was shock on the faces of the spectators. Hooker paused to let Frensley's testimony sink in. Finally, the room grew quiet.

"And is this the pistol?" asked Hooker, holding the gun in both hands.

"Yes, sir," answered Frensley, his voice barely audible.

Hooker passed the gun to the jury.

"From the time you gave the pistol to him in Capitol Chevrolet, did you see it anymore until after this tragedy?" Hooker asked Frensley.

"No, sir, I did not."

One could hear a pin drop as Hooker asked about the day of the murder. Frensley said he was at a barber shop and learned of the incident as he was leaving to go back to Capitol Chevrolet. By the time he returned, the ambulances had already left.

Frensley testified that at about four o'clock that afternoon he went to Vanderbilt Hospital to see Powell and was accompanied by Herman Keith, the secretary-treasurer of Capitol Chevrolet. Frensley said he asked Powell about the gun he had given him. Powell told him that he had loaned it to a friend.

The next day, Saturday, May 25, Frensley said he again went to see Powell in the hospital and once more asked about the pistol.

"This time he told me it had been stolen from his car," said Frensley.

Frensley testified that shortly after Powell was released from the hospital, he went to Powell's home. For a third time, Frensley asked about the gun. Powell told him the pistol had been stolen from his car, and he would rather not talk about it. Powell said he had already made a statement to the police that he never owned a pistol, and he would "just like to forget about it." Frensley said Powell then became angry and told him never to mention the gun again.

"Has he ever talked to you about the pistol since that time?"

"No, sir."

"That's all," said Hooker.

> John Lentz was dismayed. Hooker had failed to ask Frensley how the gun wound up on Elm Hill Pike, not far from Capitol Chevrolet. Lentz was also disappointed in the way Hooker revealed that Frensley had given the gun to Powell. There was none of the usual drama Hooker was capable of. Still, onlookers had seemed shocked at the revelation.

Court resumed after a recess for lunch. Norman carefully put down his cigar and walked over to the stand for cross-examination, his demeanor imperious and self-assured.

"Mr. Frensley," Norman began, his deep voice with its distinct Southern inflection echoing through the courtroom. "I didn't hear you. Did you say *when* you gave this gun to Bill Powell?"

Frensley said he didn't remember the exact date.

"Well, could you tell us within some reasonable time when it was?"

"It would have been the latter part of '67, or the first part of '68."

Norman pointed out that Capitol Chevrolet moved into its new building in February 1968.

"Well, it was before that, of course, wasn't it?" asked Norman.

Frensley hesitated a moment before answering.

"I don't remember."

Hearing this, Norman pounced, his voice suddenly icy with contempt.

"Why, didn't you swear here that you gave it to him while it was on Broad Street? Didn't you tell this court and jury just a few hours ago?"

"I told him I thought it was," Frensley answered.

Norman raised his voice. "Weren't you asked where it was that you gave him it, and didn't you tell him in the old place at 510 Broadway? Didn't you swear to that to the jury within the last two hours?"

"I told him that's when I received the pistol," answered Frensley, his voice so low he could barely be heard.

"No, sir. I am going to ask you again," Norman thundered. "Just before we went to lunch, did Mr. Hooker ask you where Capitol Chevrolet was when you gave it to him, and where you gave it to him, and did you tell him at 510 Broadway when Capitol Chevrolet was on Broadway? Do you deny that now?"

"I either gave it to him in '67 or the first part of '68."

Norman exploded. "I didn't ask you that. Did you or did you not—listen to me. If you don't understand, be sure you ask me so you will understand."

"I will, sir."

"Just before we went to lunch," Norman continued, "when Mr. Hooker was examining you, didn't you tell this court and jury on your oath that you gave Bill Powell that pistol at Capitol Chevrolet when Capitol Chevrolet was at 510 Broadway? Did you or did you not? Say yes or no and make any explanation you want to."

"Well, I gave it to him either the latter part of '67 or first part of '68."

There was a collective groan in the courtroom. What was going on? Frensley had been fine before the lunch recess. Now he seemed dazed and disoriented.

"I didn't ask you that," Norman roared. "Where was Capitol Chevrolet—you know where you took it and gave it to him. Did you take it to him out on Murfreesboro Pike, or did you take it to him down on Broadway?"

"That, sir, I don't remember."

"You say now you don't remember?"

"Whether it was in '67 or first part of '68," Frensley repeated.

"I didn't ask you whether it was in '67 or '68," Norman roared, his face contorted with anger.

Shriver stood up and protested.

"He doesn't remember. If Your Honor please. I object to repetition."

Judge Cornelius overruled Shriver's objection.

Norman resumed his blistering attack and continued to ask the exact same question another dozen times. Frensley kept answering he couldn't remember what year it was or where he was when he gave Powell the gun. At one point, he answered simply "at Capitol Chevrolet."

Norman walked away from the witness stand and stood in front of the jury box, shaking his head. Turning to Frensley again, he asked if he and Powell had ever talked about the gun from the time Frensley gave it to him until the day Mr. Gourley was shot. Frensley insisted it had never come up in conversation and that he only asked Powell about the gun after the shooting.

Next, Norman questioned Frensley about his Air National Guard service and how he acquired the gun, accusing him of having stolen it.

"I just asked Major Hall to get me a pistol if he could. He got himself one, he got me one," explained Frensley.

Norman's face turned a deep red.

"Well, let's see. How long have you been trafficking and dealing in pistols?" Norman bellowed.

"I've never dealt in trafficking with pistols," answered Frensley.

Norman kept bearing down, eliciting the fact that Frensley owned two other pistols which he bought "a year or two ago."

Whispers sounded throughout the courtroom. Spectators looked at each other and shrugged.

John Lentz was alarmed. Frensley was known to have

> a photographic memory. He would greet his former customers, citing details of the car he'd sold them, even down to the colors of the interior. He seemed to be in another world. There was no way he wouldn't know exactly where he was when he gave Powell the gun.

Then, totally out of the blue, Frensley told Norman that he had run the Tiki Club, a nightclub in Nashville.

"Did you ever run another one?" asked Norman mockingly.

"No, sir."

"How about the Starlight dinner place?'

"That's my mother-in-law."

"Well, you worked there some, didn't you?"

"Yes, sir."

"Both of them are two of the most notorious—" Norman began to say.

Shriver spoke up. "If Your Honor please—"

But Judge Cornelius allowed Norman to continue.

"I'll ask you if they're not two of the most disreputable night spots—"

"That might be your opinion," said Frensley.

"Well, that's the opinion of practically everybody," Norman said haughtily.

Judge Cornelius stopped Norman and ruled the statement objectionable, but not because of the irrelevant subject matter. "You can't speak for everybody, Mr. Norman." But the jury had heard the accusation.

Still completely off track, Norman again brought up the night clubs and posed the same questions about Frensley's two personal weapons, where they were purchased and when.

> Lentz saw that Norman was out to discredit Frensley, making him out to be a shady character. Why weren't

the prosecutors objecting? Lentz had thought from the beginning that Shriver was too new at the job and not experienced enough to lead a trial of this magnitude. And Hooker seemed sluggish, off his game. Norman was running roughshod over Frensley and getting away with it.

Norman again returned to the subject of the nightclubs and Frensley's recent purchase of two guns, repeating the same questions he had asked a half-hour earlier and demanding to know where he had purchased his weapons. Frensley said he had bought the guns at two different hardware stores.

"You say you don't collect pistols, no interest in them except when you were running the night club out there, you bought one then. You didn't think it would do the work and you bought a second one. You took that gun which was an army issue and changed the handles on it, didn't you?"

"Yes, sir, I did.

It was obvious to Hal Hardin that the defense's tactic of repeating questions having little to do with the case was once more successful in distracting the jury from testimony damaging to Powell. Branstetter had done it with Charles Donnelly and Walter Lee Davis, asking about minute details—pipe sizes, location of equipment. Norman was doing it now with Frensley, accusing him over and over of dealing in pistols and commenting on nightclubs where Frensley had once worked. Nothing was mentioned about the fact that the gun Frensley said he gave to Bill Powell ended up on the road where Haynie Gourley was murdered.

Norman circled back to the subject of Frensley's changing the handles on the gun.

"Why did you change the handle on the Army gun from its original wooden handle to its pearl handle?"

"Because those handles were all beat up," replied Frensley.

Norman bore down mercilessly, continuing to bombard Frensley with a torrent of irrelevant questions: Why did Frensley want new handles? Why did he buy two other pistols? When had he last worked at the Tiki Club? Did he collect pistols, and how had he known where to buy pearl handles? Had Frensley ever bought handles before? Where was the gun when he changed the handles, and why get them if they didn't fit properly?

There was still no objection from the prosecution or comment from the judge.

Next, Norman accused Frensley of changing the handles so the gun could not be traced to him.

"And you knew it wouldn't be easy to identify that gun from the beginning, didn't you, to trace it back to you because of the condition of those handles other than the serial number?" he bellowed.

"No, sir, not really," Frensley answered meekly.

> Hal Hardin thought Norman's questions were totally out of line, that the court would have sustained an objection by the prosecution had one been raised. As Norman raged on, Hardin again shifted in his chair, hoping to send a signal to prompt Hooker and Shriver to object to Norman's harassment. But they both sat silent.

Norman next did a re-hash of Frensley's trip to the barbershop and how he learned of the murder.

"Let me point out, I have my hair styled," said Frensley.

There was muffled laughter in the gallery at hearing this.

Norman whipped around to face Frensley, then walked over in front of the jury, swinging his glasses, looking at the jury but addressing Frensley. "I beg your pardon?" Norman boomed dramatically, flashing a sardonic smile at the jury.

"I excuse you," said Frensley. "I had an 11:00 appointment. That's the reason I know the time."

"Where did you have your hair styled?" Norman asked, mockingly, seizing on the word "styled."

"Wayne's Barber Shop on Gallatin Road."

Norman took advantage of Frensley's reply, demanding to know where exactly the barbershop was, how long the appointment lasted, and how long it took him to get back to Capitol Chevrolet, although none of these questions had anything to do with giving a gun to Bill Powell.

Then, Norman said something startling. He accused Frensley of stealing $25,000 from the government by not reporting for National Guard duty but claiming he had worked the hours so he would be paid.

Shriver jumped up at hearing this, saying the jury should be sent out. Judge Cornelius agreed. But it was too late. The jurors had already heard Norman's allegation. Shriver spoke up, insisting that no charges had been filed against Frensley. Judge Cornelius ruled against Norman, saying the information was inadmissible. But once heard, regardless of the judge's ruling, the jury couldn't unhear Norman's accusations and biting comments.

When the jury returned, Norman asked Frensley if he had been keeping up with the trial. Frensley said he hadn't really paid that much attention, as he was not living in Nashville and that he had a business to operate in Louisville, Kentucky.

"And you say you weren't interested in the trial?"

"I didn't feel like he did it," Frensley said, lowering his head.

The courtroom broke into loud whispers at hearing this. Billy Gourley's heart sank.

"You knew you'd given him the pistol, didn't you?" asked Norman.

"Yes, sir, but when the newspaper first came out, they said it was a snub-nose," Frensley said, referring to a type of pistol with a sawed-off or short barrel.

"You mean you just wasn't keeping up with it at all?" barked Norman.

"No, sir."

"But he was denying ever having a pistol at all. You read that in the papers, and you knew about that, didn't you?" Norman snapped.

"Yes, sir. He was my friend, and I thought he was innocent."

> Billy's stomach was in knots. Norman had successfully turned Frensley into a hostile witness, scoring points for the defense now instead of bolstering the prosecution's case. When Frensley had first taken the stand and revealed he had given a gun to Bill Powell, Billy had thought the prosecution's case was airtight. Now, it seemed to be slipping away the longer Frensley was on the stand.

Then, a bombshell.

"Now who did you ever tell you gave Bill Powell a gun?"

"Mr. Herman Keith," replied Frensley.

"When, where, and what did you tell him?" demanded Norman.

"The afternoon, as I told you that I went to the hospital, I asked Mr. Keith to ride with me."

"What did you tell Mr. Keith?"

"That I let Mr. Powell have a pistol."

"Where were you when you told Mr. Keith you let Mr. Powell have a pistol?"

"I don't remember whether we were riding out there or whether it was on the way back."

"Anyway, it was on that trip that you told Mr. Keith?"

"Yes, sir."

> Billy was heartened. So someone else knew that Bill Powell had this pistol. All Hooker had to do now was call Herman Keith to the stand to verify that Frensley told him about giving the gun to Powell. That would surely strike the final blow to Powell's denial and seal the case.

But Billy would be disappointed.

Then, another incendiary question by Norman.

"I am going to ask you if you didn't, night before last, come down here and put the gun in Bill Powell's hands?"

Frensley looked at Norman as if he didn't understand the question, then answered, "No, sir."

> The Gourley supporters broke out into loud whispers. What basis could there have been for Norman to ask such a question?" Norman had pulled the same stunt, proposing something that did not happen, that could not have happened. However, no objection came from Hooker or Shriver. Norman had gotten away with it yet again.

Norman kept up the harangue, accusing Frensley of getting rid of the gun so he wouldn't get into trouble for stealing it from the National Guard.

"Didn't you know that an investigation had started from the Navy on down and you knew it was coming into your hands and just as soon as you heard about it you got it out of your hands and into Bill Powell's hands?"

"No, sir."

"That's what you did, isn't it?" Norman thundered, his bulldog face flushed with righteous indignation.

"I never felt like this was the gun used to slay Mr. Gourley either," Frensley said quietly, again lowering his head.

Norman paced around in front of the jury box, giving time for Frensley's words to sink in, then turned to face the witness stand.

"Why didn't you say something about this to somebody in the year and two months after this thing happened?" Norman demanded.

"Because I didn't feel Mr. Powell had anything to do with this, with Mr. Gourley's murder and still—"

"You didn't feel this gun had anything to do with it?" Norman asked.

"No, sir, because the paper said it was a snub-nose. I didn't feel the gun had anything to do with it," said Frensley.

"All right then, you then saw the picture in the paper, and you thought that was your gun?"

"Yes, sir, I did."

Norman stormed back and forth, then stopped abruptly in front of Frensley.

"And that's when you decided to get it out of your hands and into Bill Powell's?" he pointed his finger at Frensley.

"No, sir."

"You knew they would be tracing that, didn't you?"

"No, sir."

"After you had stolen one gun and bought two—"

Hooker finally spoke up. "We object—"

But Norman continued.

"I'll bet you are going to say you didn't think they could trace it, right?" Norman asked.

"I didn't say that."

Then, Norman switched back to the days just after the murder, asking if

Chief Barton had talked to him about a gun.

"He called me up to his office and asked me if I knew anything about the case. I told him no, sir, at this time I didn't feel like I knew anything that would help him."

"All right. Well, there are 172 employees out there," said Norman, referring to Capitol Chevrolet. "Do you know why he just called you up and asked you if you knew anything about it?"

"No, sir."

Finally, after trying without success to pry information out of Frensley as to why Chief Barton had singled him out, Norman at last said, "That's all."

> The two young lawyers in the courtroom sat in awe. Norman had put on a masterful performance.

Hooker stood up for re-direct. He held up a copy of the *Nashville Banner* for Frensley to read.

"The gun we're looking for is a new snub-nose .38," Frensley read aloud.

"At that time, did you have any idea that the pistol that you had given or lent to Mr. Powell was involved in this tragedy?" asked Hooker.

"No, sir, I did not."

Hooker held up the gun in front of Frensley.

"On the morning of May 24, 1968, did you have this pistol?"

"No, sir, I did not."

"Had you at any other time been in the neighborhood of Elm Hill Road and Spence Lane with this pistol?" asked Hooker.

"No, sir."

"Are you absolutely certain that this is the pistol that you let Mr. Powell have?"

"Yes, sir."

"That's all."

After a grueling four-hour interrogation, Frensley left the stand, appearing dazed by Norman's withering attacks. But now the murder weapon had surfaced, and the prosecution no longer had a circumstantial case.

> Hal Hardin sat, relieved that the ordeal with Frensley was over. He had been a disastrous witness. Listening to him had been like riding a runaway roller coaster. It had been exhausting to hear someone who could have stood firm and been straightforward, instead oscillate wildly, then end up pilloried by Norman's bullying. If only Frensley had told the police about giving Powell his gun in May 1968, this trial would have been long over, or more likely, would have never taken place.

Frensley walked out of the courtroom, his head down. He did not look at either Bill Powell or the Gourleys. As Jimbo Cook had done with Thomas Swann, he got up and followed Frensley out into the hall. Cook could see he was soaked through, even to the shirt under his suitcoat.

But Jimbo was heartened. The weapon had been placed in Powell's possession, given to him by an employee of Capitol Chevrolet. The same gun had been found on Elm Hill Pike where police had never searched. There could be no doubt who killed Haynie Gourley.

***

Next on the stand was Metro patrol officer R. C. Jackson. People in the packed courtroom sat wondering about this surprise witness. Jackson recounted how he learned about the gun at a fish fry, then discovered Henry Lewis.

Jackson testified that the district attorney's office sent workers to

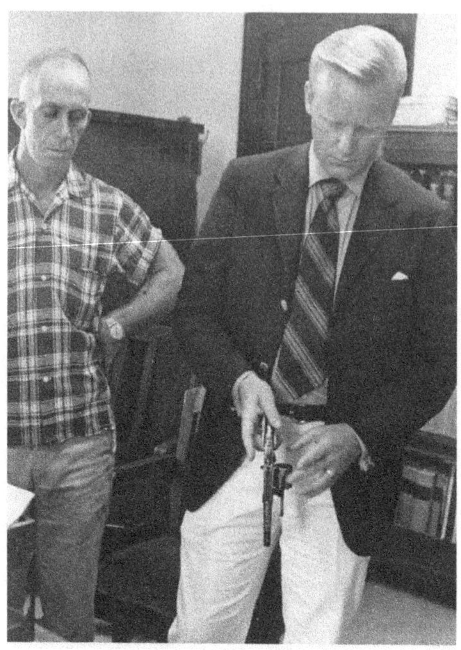

Officer R. C. Jackson of the Metro Police, right, holds the gun found on Elm Hill Pike in August 1968 by construction worker Henry Lewis, left. © *The Tennessean – USA TODAY NETWORK*

the site on Elm Hill Pike to dig trenches in an effort to find the long-discarded shell casings. But the workers had found nothing.

Henry Lewis was called to testify next. As he was sworn in, quiet came over the courtroom.

The soft-spoken construction worker described how in the late summer of 1968, he was on Elm Hill Pike at a site between Interstate 40 and the railroad crossing near Arlington Road. His company was laying a gas line, Lewis said, and after he had caught up with his work, he got down from his tractor and was looking for bottles for his son to turn in for cash. That's when something glistened and caught his eye.

As he got closer to the object, Lewis said, he could see it was a gun.

Lewis explained how he took the weapon home and was trying to clean it when his wife asked him where it had come from. When he told her, she said she didn't want the gun in the house, that it could be the one that killed that "Chevrolet man."

To placate his wife, Lewis took the gun to his brother's house in Old Hickory where he and Jackson retrieved it on Monday.

"All right," said Shriver. "I'll hand you State's exhibit 120 and ask you if you can identify that gun."

"That's it," Lewis said.

There was a rumbling among the spectators, then the courtroom

During the last week of the trial, police use a metal detector to hunt for five shell casings discarded by Henry Lewis (standing, second from right) in August 1968. Trenches were subsequently dug to no avail. The site, in front of Mt. Zeno Kindergarten on Elm Hill Pike, was close to Capitol Chevrolet. *Nashville Public Library, Special Collections, Banner Newspaper Collection*

went quiet.

"When you found the gun, did it have any bullets in it?" asked Shriver.

"Yes, sir, it had five empties."

"Now, this is a six-shot revolver. You state there were only five empty shells in it?"

"That's right."

"What did you do with the shells when you found them?"

Lewis replied that he had flipped the empty cartridges onto a pile of dirt, ready to be pushed back into a ditch the next day.

Jimbo Cook looked at his friend Billy. The two had been close all their lives. Their fathers had been best friends. Billy was three years older, but had always treated Jimbo like a brother. This man who "didn't want to become involved," had caused his friend so much misery.

The prosecution then recalled TBI ballistics expert Robert Goodwin to the stand. Goodwin stated that he had flown to FBI headquarters in Washington, D.C., with the gun and the four bullets retrieved from the car and Mr. Gourley's body.

Shriver brought out the gun and bullets.

"Are they the same four bullets that you previously testified to in this case?"

"Yes, sir, they are."

Shriver asked Goodwin to describe the gun.

"This is a caliber .38 special. It's a Smith & Wesson revolver, referred to as a Victory model, has a four-inch barrel, is a double-action type of weapon."

"Is it capable of shooting a 200-grain Western Winchester Lubaloy bullet that you talked about?" asked Shriver.

Goodwin answered yes and said his examination at the FBI lab revealed that the first inch of the barrel from the muzzle back showed a "heavy area of erosion or pitting."

Shriver asked what this meant.

"Well, so far as the rusting is concerned, and especially to this degree, it would be impossible to identify that bullet as having come through the barrel."

Billy Gourley's heart sank. He knew what was coming.

"So, you cannot say with any degree of accuracy, or cannot say at all positively that these bullets were fired out of that gun?" asked Shriver.

"No, we cannot."

> Hearing this, Jimbo felt a pain in his chest. So close. If only Lewis had not discarded the shells. If only he had turned in the gun and the spent shells last summer when he found them. The casings would have matched the bullets, the weapon would have been traced, and this case would have been solved. He looked at his friend Billy Gourley, sitting there so stoically. Billy had confided in Jimbo that the loss of his father was unbearable. Jimbo thought if Lewis had done the right thing, it would have at least spared Billy a year of uncertainty and having to live through this ordeal. It would be Billy Gourley sitting in an executive office at Capitol Chevrolet instead of Bill Powell.

As expected, on cross-examination Norman walked up to Agent Goodwin.

"As an expert," Norman said, his deep voice building up to a crescendo, "with all of your training and experience, I want to ask you this question, knowing this man's liberty is lying here on this line, can you swear to the jury or tell this jury that they can know without any doubt that any four of these bullets came out of a Smith & Wesson pistol, can you tell them that that is absolutely true?"

"No, I cannot do it," replied Coleman.

"Can't be done, no way in the world to do it, is there?"

"No, sir."

"That's all," said Norman, looking over at the jury, a slight smile of satisfaction crossing his face as he walked back to the defense table.

It was Friday afternoon. The time was getting late, and Shriver asked for an adjournment for the day, saying the State had two more witnesses to call, but only one was on the premises. The judge refused the request, saying he wanted to continue but did allow a recess at 5:34 p.m. for the State to discuss what to do. Meanwhile, Branstetter and Norman said they needed the overnight hours to answer the witnesses brought by the prosecution concerning the gun.

After the recess, Shriver made a surprise announcement: "The State closes its rebuttal, Your Honor."

The judge then informed the jury that court would adjourn until 9:00 a.m. the next morning.

The State's rebuttal case ended with no mention of how the pistol with the white handles ended up on a scrubby embankment next to Elm Hill Pike, miles from where Powell said the killer had disappeared and where the police had never thought to search.

CHAPTER [27]

Saturday morning, August 2, the line to get a seat in Courtroom 611 wrapped around the plaza surrounding the courthouse. Inside the sixth-floor corridor, a crush of people tried to get through the door; all but sixty-four were disappointed.

The tension in the courtroom was palpable. Those who supported Powell were fearful because a gun had turned up and had been traced to a former Capitol Chevrolet employee who testified he had given Powell the weapon.

There was chatter among bystanders that Jack Norman and Cecil Branstetter had outshone District Attorney Thomas Shriver and Special Prosecutor John J. Hooker Sr. The trial had been billed as a clash of the titans, pitting the two most renowned criminal attorneys in Tennessee against each other. Many were greatly disappointed by Hooker's spiritless performance so far. All were expecting to see Hooker, the great orator, make mincemeat of the defense, just as Norman and Branstetter had done with witnesses for the prosecution.

Still, the discovery of the gun appeared to seal the case in the court of public opinion. The coincidence was too obvious to overlook. Even though bullets taken from Haynie Gourley's body could not definitively be said to have been fired from the recovered weapon, people in the crowd gathered in the sixth-floor hall had formed a consensus: Bill Powell was guilty of murder.

***

Court resumed at 9:00 a.m., making this the twelfth day of testimony. The judge ordered the defense to proceed with surrebuttal, meaning the opportunity to answer evidence given in rebuttal.

The defense called several Capitol Chevrolet employees, including Herman Keith.

> Jimbo Cook couldn't wait for this part. Keith would corroborate Frensley's story, that on the afternoon of the killing Frensley had told Keith about giving the gun to Powell.

But Keith never had the chance to say anything about his conversation with Frensley when they visited Powell in the hospital on the afternoon of May 24. The defense objected, and Judge Cornelius agreed, saying that any questions pertaining to the gun should have been asked on rebuttal and now exceeded the limits of surrebuttal. Hooker argued that the State should have the right to ask Keith what Frensley did or did not tell him about the gun.

Judge Cornelius sustained the defense's objection, and Herman Keith was told to step down.

> Hal Hardin realized the prosecution team's case was greatly damaged by Judge Cornelius's decision not to allow Keith to testify about the gun. Norman and Branstetter seemed to have the momentum. Frensley had been a catastrophe on the witness stand, and now here was a major setback. The jury would never know that Frensley told Keith about giving Powell the gun.
>
> Hardin was buoyed, however, by the thought of Hooker's upcoming performance. Hardin was confi-

dent in Hooker's ability to sway a jury, something he had done countless times in his career when all seemed lost. Hardin had watched a rehearsal for Hooker's final argument where he began by dropping, one by one, five empty shell casings to the floor, representing the five bullets fired by Powell. His well-practiced closing argument, Hardin knew, would make the hair stand up on one's head, it was so powerful. No one could be as engaging and persuasive as Hooker when he was at his best.

Branstetter called Sherman Nickens back to the stand in an effort to establish if the area where the gun was found had been thoroughly searched after the murder.

But Nickens would not say specifically.

On cross-examination, Shriver asked Nickens where the central area of the search had taken place.

"Close to Spence Lane and back down the hill toward—going east, in other words," said Nickens.

"Was the principal search in the area of Mill Creek and Massman Drive?" asked Shriver, referring to the part of Elm Hill Pike past Spence Lane and well over a mile away from where Frensley's gun was found.

"Yes, sir."

Shriver sat back down, and Branstetter approached the witness stand.

"What is the nature of the buildings, structures, from P'Pool Avenue to Mount Zeno Kindergarten?" he asked.

Nickens said there were warehouses up and down the street on that part of Elm Hill Pike.

"There are at least two or three blocks of houses immediately west of Mount Zeno Kindergarten, are there not?"

"Houses, yes, sir," Nickens replied.

"It's a Negro residential area, isn't it?" Branstetter asked.

"Yes, sir, right across the track it starts residential, right and left, and then it goes into warehouses."

"Yes. Thank you," said Branstetter, looking over at the jury and nodding as Nickens stepped down.

Detective Bill Larkin took the stand again.

Larkin insisted to Branstetter that he had not searched the area around P'Pool Avenue and Mt. Zeno Kindergarten where the gun had been found. Instead, following Powell's description of where the crime occurred and where he turned around, the police had concentrated on an entirely different stretch of Elm Hill Pike, much further east.

Branstetter pressed Larkin to admit the search went on for weeks.

"About three days is all I was there and can testify to truthfully," said Larkin.

The defense called its next witness in surrebuttal.

The courtroom grew quiet as Bill Powell, dressed in a plaid sports coat and yellow shirt, took a seat.

Branstetter began the questioning.

"You were present in court on yesterday when one Bob Frensley stated that in the latter part of 1966 or '67 that he delivered to you a .38 Smith & Wesson pistol with pearl handles. State to this jury whether or not that is true."

"Mr. Branstetter, Bob Frensley knows that he did not give me a pistol in '66, '67 or '68," Powell answered with a hint of exasperation in his voice.

Hooker objected to Powell testifying about what Frensley knew. Judge Cornelius instructed Branstetter to rephrase the question.

"Did Bob Frensley, in 1966, '67 or '68, or '69, for that matter, ever deliver to you a .38 Smith & Wesson pistol?"

"He certainly did not," Powell replied emphatically.

Branstetter then ceded the questioning to Hooker.

"Did you ever have any conversation with Bob Frensley about a pistol?" Hooker asked Powell.

"No, sir. Bob Frensley had talked of pistols, not in my presence, but I knew that there was talk of pistols."

"Did you ever see him with a pistol at Capitol Chevrolet?" asked Hooker.

"I don't believe I did," Powell answered, his voice calm and reflective.

"Now, on the afternoon of Friday, May 24, 1968, after Mr. Gourley had been shot and killed, did Bob Frensley come to Vanderbilt Hospital to see you?"

"Yes, he did."

"Did he ask you at that time what had become of this pistol?"

"Yes, he did."

At hearing this, people shifted in their seats, then quieted down.

"In other words," Hooker said, "you are telling these ladies and gentlemen of the jury that on the day of this murder Bob Frensley asked you what had become of a pistol, a .38 special pistol that he had given to you?"

"He asked me and I also replied—"

Hooker cut off Powell's answer. "Do you know of any reason why on the very day of this murder and you were in the hospital, that he would be asking you what you did with this pistol if he hadn't given it to you?"

"He didn't ask me what I did with the pistol," said Powell emphatically.

"He asked you where it was?"

"He asked me had I seen the pistol, I believe that's the right nomenclature. I am not certain, but I feel certain that is the statement he made to me."

"Didn't you tell him you had given it to a friend?" asked Hooker.

"No, sir, I did not."

"What did you tell him?"

"I said, 'Bob, what pistol?' I never knew of a pistol, and to my knowledge, that's truly the reply I gave him."

Hooker then asked if Frensley had returned to the hospital one or two days later. Powell answered that he thought he had come to see him again.

"What did he ask you on this second occasion about a pistol?"

"Nothing," replied Powell.

"Didn't he ask you on the second occasion where his pistol was, and didn't you tell him that the pistol had been stolen?"

"No, sir, I did not."

"Then you went home, and after you had been home didn't Bob Frensley come to your house then?"

"Yes, sir."

"And didn't he ask you about this pistol at that time?"

"No, sir, he did not."

Hooker's voice quickened. "And didn't you tell him you had already told the officers you didn't have any pistol and you didn't want to hear any more about it?"

"I told him that I had told the officers that I hadn't had a pistol, and I didn't know anything about a pistol. This was in the papers, that I had made the statement and I did not do that," answered Powell defiantly.

"You've seen where this pistol was found, have you, Mr. Powell?" asked Hooker.

"Yes, sir."

"And this pistol was found on the route that you traversed after you claimed that this man got in the car, was moving, fired all these shots? You came right by the place, didn't you?"

"If I understand correctly where the pistol was found, yes, sir."

"Mr. Powell, I want to ask you, from May 24, 1968, when you asked Mr. Gourley to take this ride with you—you did ask him to, didn't you?"

"Yes, sir."

"You told him as soon as he got time, or the opportunity, that you wanted to take a ride?"

"Yes, sir."

Hooker began walking back and forth in front of Powell, pausing before he spoke again.

"I want to ask you if you didn't have this pistol with you at the time, and if you didn't fire it first into the back seat of this car with the idea that it would kill Mr. Gourley, and he would never know what happened to him?" Hooker's deep voice shook the room.

"No, siree."

"And thereafter firing it into the back seat of the car, didn't you then fire a shot into the side of his face that busted out the right-hand window of the car?"

"Mr. Hooker, you know I didn't do that."

"No, I am asking you," Hooker said.

"I tell you I didn't do it," Powell said.

"Didn't you fire a shot in the neighborhood of the collarbone?"

"No, sir."

"And then the brain?" Hooker's questions came loud and fast.

"No, sir."

"And then didn't you turn around and in order to hide and conceal the fact that you had killed this man, didn't you fire the pistol into your own leg on the way back to Capitol Chevrolet?" Hooker was roaring now.

"No, sir."

"And then didn't you take this very pistol that Bob Frensley said you had and throw it out there?" Hooker asked, making a tossing gesture with his left arm over his head.

"No, sir," Powell said again.

Hooker lowered his voice.

"As I understand your testimony now is that you never saw this gun?"

"That is true."

"That you never had any conversation with Frensley about it?"

"No, sir."

"And that when you took Mr. Gourley for this ride that morning that you did not have this gun with you? That's what you say?"

"That's exactly right."

"Well, in any event, I just wanted you to carefully look at the pistol," Hooker said, picking up the gun and holding it close to Powell's face, "and you say that you have never until this was introduced in this trial ever seen this pistol before in your life?"

"That's true."

Hooker said, "That's all."

> Hal Hardin had sent a note to Hooker to place the gun in Powell's hands, but for whatever reason, Hooker held onto the weapon himself. Hardin was disappointed. There would be no more questioning of Powell.

"Thank you, Mr. Powell, come down," Branstetter said to his client.

Powell walked down from the witness stand, this time without looking at his children in the front row.

Branstetter turned to the judge and said, "That's the case, Your Honor.

"No rebuttal from the State?" asked Judge Cornelius.

Hooker and Shriver conferred for a moment.

"No, no rebuttal," Shriver said.

All the examinations and cross-examinations and rebuttals and surrebuttals had ended. Only the closing arguments were left. After that, it would be up to the jury to decide the fate of the two families seated on either side of the courtroom.

After Powell stepped down, there was a heated argument over whether Hooker could present the final argument for the state. It had been planned that his would be the last word. Branstetter and Norman protested, saying that Shriver was obligated by law to close out the State's case. Hooker, they said, should give the opening statement, since he was a special prosecutor hired by the Gourley family. Following Hooker, the defense would have their final argument, with Shriver giving the rebuttal and the last word.

The judge overruled the defense. The die was cast. Shriver would give the opening statement, and Hooker, with his capacity for swaying a jury would be the last one standing.

But Shriver's insistence and Judge Cornelius's ruling would prove ruinous for one of the two families.

The judge announced a recess until 1:30.

At 1:40 p.m. when court reconvened, the atmosphere in the courtroom was fraught with tension. On the left side of the room, the Powell contingent, even given their brightly colored summer clothes, seemed more solemn now. There was the general feeling among spectators, and had been throughout the trial, that the Gourleys, in their dark hues, were the haughty rich people, and the Powells just middle class. The jury had never been told that both families lived in the exclusive Belle Meade community, and both were members of the city's most elite country club.

Josephine Gourley did not move a muscle as District Attorney Shriver, wiping his black-rimmed glasses with a handkerchief, walked over to face the jury.

CHAPTER [28]

Shriver began his summation of the case by apologizing to the jury for having been totally sequestered for three weeks and thanking them profusely. Then he said something that made Billy Gourley's heart sink.

"In many ways this case has not been a pleasant one for me," Shriver began, "because I personally know this defendant, know his family. But I was elected by the people of this community to do a job."

Shriver next apologized for having to do a summation. He was speaking in a monotone, but he did brighten when he told the jurors that they were going to hear some great legal oratory. "Mr. Hooker and Mr. Norman are lawyers of eminent reputation, great ability and great orators."

Shriver went on to say that he would be stating only the facts, that he would lay out the closing argument in three parts.

"The first part is why a man like William Powell would kill another man. The second part is what's wrong with what he says happened on that day. And the third part is what really did happen."

Stepping closer to the jury, he paced awkwardly back and forth, his hands clasped behind his back, his tall ungainly frame almost stork-like.

"It's probably outside of your and my experience to conceive of a man like William Powell killing another man. Hard to think of a man, a college graduate, a businessman, respected in his community—you heard his character witnesses—taking a human life deliberately and maliciously, intentionally, and with premeditation. I can't conceive of that."

This doesn't sound like a prosecutor, thought Billy Gourley.

"Now as to the why," Shriver continued, sounding professorial and not like a hard-nosed prosecutor. "We have in this case a man seventy-two years old, now deceased, Mr. Haynie Gourley. I'm half that age. I don't know what a man of seventy-two thinks about, but I can imagine that his thoughts would be: 'What can I do for my family before I die? What can I do for my son?'

"So, in this case, he wants to give his son a business and let him take it over and run it—his life's ambition."

What Shriver said next sent Hal Hardin reeling.

"Haynie Gourley had brought Bill Powell into the business for two purposes. One, he needed someone in Paragraph Three of the General Motors contract, someone with experience in the selling of automobiles to run the company in the event of his death, someone who could hold the Chevrolet franchise."

Billy Gourley was astounded. Where on earth did Shriver get this idea? This was not why his father had let Powell buy into the business. In fact, just the opposite was true. Haynie had never intended for Powell to be his successor to the franchise. It was always his father's intention that Billy would inherit the dealership and run it for the family.

Shriver fumbled on, seemingly oblivious to the harm he was doing.

"So, he sells Bill Powell twenty-five percent of his business so this man can take and run the business.

"The second thing Bill Powell was to do, and the other purpose of bringing him in this business, was to train Bill Gourley to run this business."

Then Shriver said something that made Billy want to jump out of his seat and shout him down.

"I don't know whether he trained him or not. You know, what he was doing about the training of Billy Gourley is really not of any significance in this lawsuit. The point is that Mr. Gourley, Mr. Haynie Gourley, seventy-two years old, now dead, and Mrs. Gourley, didn't think Bill Gourley was being trained."

> Hardin cringed at Shriver's use of the word "lawsuit." Hooker was a private attorney hired by the Gourleys as a special prosecutor. Shriver should pound it into the jury's heads that this is a criminal case, not a lawsuit pursued by the family. Already, Hardin feared the jury had associated the Gourleys with wealth, with enough money to influence the outcome of the trial.

Referring to Haynie and Josephine Gourley, Shriver said, "They didn't feel justifiably, or not justifiably, and it really doesn't matter, they didn't think that Bill Gourley Jr. was being taught the business."

> Across the room, Sherman Nickens was aghast at Shriver's words. It was Nickens's theory all along that Powell was never going to let Billy Gourley be his superior. That, to Nickens, was the whole motive for the murder in a nutshell.

Shriver continued, reciting what Bill Powell had to lose if he were to resign from Capitol Chevrolet and sell back his stock.

The first item Shriver listed, he gave the wrong date, saying Bill

Powell had earned $83,000 in the calendar year 1968. The amount was right, but the year was 1967. Shriver did point out that this sum was over three times, nearly four times, as much as Powell had ever made in his life.

"So he was going to lose a substantial salary. That's motive by itself," Shriver intoned.

"In addition to this, Bill Powell was a good automobile man, a good manager of that company and contributed substantially to the growth of the company. Here is a man who is proud of what he accomplished with the company. He built it up, helped Mr. Gourley build it up. It moved to a new building and brought on the second motive. He's going to lose all this."

> Billy Gourley was stung when Shriver intimated that it was mostly Bill Powell who had built up the business. What about the thirty-six years his father had worked hard, in the beginning starting with nothing, to make Capitol Chevrolet the best-known dealership in Nashville and one of the most successful in the Southeast?

Shriver plodded on, his voice a steady drone, showing little emotion.

The third motive, he said, was rooted in the fact that Capitol Chevrolet did not own its new building, but rented the premises from a local physician, Dr. Bruce P'Pool.

"The payment was $85,000 a year, and the lease was to run for twenty years. Haynie Gourley had just turned seventy-two when the building was completed in early 1968, and on the advice of his attorney and accountant who both cited estate concerns, did not sign the lease. Instead, Bill and Helen Powell stepped up and agreed to sign, personally guaranteeing the monthly payments for twenty years.

"Here he is personally responsible for that rent for that long period of time and no interest whatever in the business. One more motive."

Shriver then posed the question, "So, what does Powell accomplish if Mr. Gourley is dead?"

First, Shriver said, William Powell becomes the owner of the franchise. This leaves the Gourleys with stock, a new building, but no way to sell anything but used cars, because Powell is the franchisee. By the death of Haynie Gourley, Powell got the right to sell Chevrolet automobiles, which was a tremendously valuable asset, with Chevrolet being the number one seller in the country, outselling Fords.

"Motive," Shriver said, his voice so deadpan that Hal Hardin winced.

> "Was this Shriver's attempt at swaying the jury?" Hardin wondered.

Shriver went on, his delivery still passionless.

"Powell had agreed to quit the business, had said so in front of Haynie, Josephine, and Billy. But not even ten days after Powell was released from the hospital, he accompanied Tom Jackson and other General Motors executives to Josephine Gourley's home where the men from the company tried to persuade her to sell her stock to Bill Powell."

Shriver then posed the question. "What if Powell had lived up to his word that he would get out of the company as Mr. Gourley wished? How else could he have handled the situation?

"He could have said, 'Mrs. Gourley, I will go through with what I agreed to with you and your husband. If you want me to or if you want to get somebody else to run the business I will stay on until we find somebody, or if you want me to buy you out, take it over, I will do that. What do you want me to do, Mrs. Gourley?'

"Instead," Shriver said, finally with a little rise in his voice, "he goes out there with those men and sits dead silent in another room while they tell her that she ought to sell the business to him."

Shriver stated again that he thought what drove Bill Powell to take a life was the lease payment obligation. "It is the most convincing, overwhelming motive I have ever seen in a murder case, and I don't think you will likely find more anywhere in this world," he said, but his deadpan delivery did not match his inflammatory assertion.

> This seemed to Hardin the very weakest argument of all. The lease could be re-negotiated. Shriver had already made the point, and it fell flat again.

Then, Shriver made yet another mistake. He mentioned the shortcomings of the defense's case, namely what Powell said happened and their efforts to discredit "James Walter Hughes."

> Hardin shuddered. Shriver had obviously meant Walter Lee Davis, who testified that he witnessed the murder. Instead, he called the name of the manager of the truck sales department at Capitol Chevrolet.

Next, Shriver tackled the subject of why it was necessary to go for a ride to discuss business.

"There were private offices, carpeted, acoustic ceilings, closed doors," Shriver pointed out. "Had a conference room at the other end of the hall. Both of them had private offices. What are they going to go out and talk about in an automobile at 10:30 or 11:00 in the morning? For that matter, what was there to talk about? The details, the substantial details of this transaction, purchase by Mr. Gourley of Bill Powell's interest in that business, are all subject to the contract itself and not anything to discuss. Certainly, there is nothing to discuss that couldn't have been discussed much more easily in a private, air-conditioned office, with carpets and acoustical ceilings.

"Why did they go out in the first place? Where were they going?

"All right, they leave. Now the time we are not real sure about. Walter Hughes is the man that said he saw them leave."

At this point Shriver realized he had confused Walter Lee Davis with Walter Hughes.

Shriver made the correction and resumed.

"Hughes went and got a license plate, his keys, got in a truck and drove across the street."

> Billy Gourley winced again. He knew where Capitol Chevrolet cars and trucks were taken to be filled with gas. But the service station was not across the street. It was further down near the I-40 exit. It seemed to Billy that Shriver didn't know the facts as well as a prosecutor should.

Shriver continued: "He got gasoline, signed a ticket, came back across the street and as he was coming back, he saw Powell coming back. His estimate of the time that elapsed was fifteen minutes. There is not anybody out there that places the time less than twelve or thirteen minutes that they were gone. It couldn't have possibly taken him but seven minutes, seven-and-a-half minutes, at the most, to do what William Powell said he did, that is, drive out Elm Hill Pike, turn around at Massman Drive—"

> Here again Shriver got the facts wrong, Hardin thought. Powell's original story had been that he turned around just past Spence Lane. Massman Drive was brought up later by Powell when he learned broken glass from an automobile window had been found there.

"He comes back at 80 miles an hour," Shriver continued, "five to seven minutes at the most. So we have got somewhere between eight and ten minutes to account for somehow or other that Mr. Powell has not accounted for. That's the first question."

Shriver then came to the story Bill Powell told immediately after he reached Vanderbilt Hospital, mentioning Bill Larkin's name as the first there.

> Hardin knew that testimony had shown that this was not correct. Bill Larkin was far from the first to question Powell in the hospital, but Shriver continued, apparently not realizing his mistake.

"He told them that they were riding along, talking about how it was built up out there on Elm Hill Pike, and how lucky they were to be out there. And when they passed the H.D. Lee Company, Mr. Gourley remarked, 'I didn't even know that was there.' And when Mr. Gourley said that, Bill Powell says, 'I didn't either.' According to Bill Powell's testimony, they never got that far. They never got anywhere near where they could see the H.D. Lee Company. Where did Bill Powell, lying in the hospital, get the impression H.D. Lee Company in his mind? Why didn't he tell the police officers, 'We were talking about the H.D. Lee Company?'"

> Shriver should have said, "Why *did* Powell tell the police officers," Hardin thought, as he reflected on how Powell had changed his testimony on the witness stand. Powell had said that Mr. Gourley mentioned the H.D. Lee Company as they were going out the gate of Capitol Chevrolet, "because he had seen it from the

> expressway." How naïve is this jury, Hardin wondered. What Shriver said next gave Hardin some hope.

"The only reasonable answer to that question is: Bill Powell did what Walter Lee Davis said Bill Powell did. He drove down there by those three trees, shot Mr. Gourley, drove on past the H.D. Lee Company, saw it then, got the mental impression H.D. Lee Company again, going back, more impression, H.D. Lee Company, and went back to Capitol Chevrolet. Only way he could have gotten that."

Shriver finally began to point out discrepancies in Powell's story.

"All right, next thing. One of Capitol's employees, Charles Williams, said that when Powell was telling about what happened there in the office on the floor after he got back from the ride, he says that a Negro man got in the car, said, give me your money, and Mr. Gourley reached into his inside coat pocket. Charles Williams thought that was funny at the time, because he had run errands for Mr. Gourley and knew that Mr. Gourley carried his billfold in his hip pocket, just like most of us do, inside the coat pocket.

> It was obvious that Shriver meant to say *not* inside the coat pocket. Hardin again thought the man either lacked enough experience or that he was never going to be a forceful litigator.

"Now Bill Powell told the same thing to Officer Galbaugh, and the same thing to Coleman and Larkin. No, I mean to Officer Castleman and Dodson at the hospital."

This time, Shriver did correct himself.

"Now Coleman and Larkin get there later, and Mr. Powell has had time to reflect on that. Let's see, inside coat pocket. Now his hip pocket. And from then on it's been his hip pocket that he reached into."

Shriver continued. "All right. What else? Oh, one more thing about the billfold I think we need to mention. The purpose of this shooting, this alleged shooting, Negro man jumping in the car is, give me all your money, a robbery. Who was robbed? Nobody.

"They find Mr. Gourley's billfold in the back seat, still has $200 in it. Bill Powell's billfold isn't taken, because Ham Wallace, his own employee, testified he gave it to him before they went to the hospital. No robbery at all. Do you think a man's going to jump into a moving automobile, shoot everybody in the car for the purpose of robbing them, and then not take anything?

"The billfold's still there in the car. And the fact is, Mr. Powell says the shooting started as Mr. Gourley reached for his hip pocket. The man says, 'You don't go for your gun,' and he starts shooting. How did the billfold even get in the back seat? Mr. Gourley, according to Mr. Powell's statement, is already being shot when he's pulling out the billfold. No robbery. And I submit to you, that Mr. Gourley never pulled the billfold out. Bill Powell pulled it out later to substantiate his story."

Shriver paused for a moment, then continued, his voice studious.

"One interesting little thing I noticed. Mr. Crawford testified that Bill Powell got around and put his hand, when they got back, put his hand on the trunk of the car. Mr. Powell testified that he, in struggling around the car, put his hands on the trunk. Walter Lee Davis says that he saw Mr. Powell—he saw a man, a white man, in a black Chevrolet, go to the trunk of the car and raise it. Could it be Mr. Powell is thinking, 'I've got fingerprints on the trunk of that car, and I've got to justify them?'

"Now, then, was there a Negro man? What is the evidence about that? The only person that says there is, is Bill Powell. Charles Donnelly, driver of the truck, saw him coming. He knows Bill Powell, and he knows Haynie Gourley, and he knows Mr. Gourley's automobile. And he pulled out in front of them and saw them behind him, two men in the car, as he approached the intersection of Spence Lane and Elm Hill Pike. He did not stop, he says. He was flagged on through by a flagman.

"Now Mr. Cook, Hobart Cook, later said that he was a flagman, but that he quit. There may be some discrepancy there about what time he quit. I doubt Mr. Cook knows exactly what time he quit. Mr. Donnelly says the flagman flagged him on through, and that he did not stop, nor did the car behind him stop, nor did he observe any Negro men there, nor did he observe anybody get into the black Chevrolet behind him.

"Freddie Cook was there, sitting on the truck, Hobart Cook was there, sitting on the truck. Grady Wright was there, the foreman. He didn't see anybody. The only pedestrian they saw all day long, the only person walking all day long was a little girl, a white girl at that. They never observed any Negro man walk along there. There were no Negro men in that work gang. Surely one of them would have observed a man of dark skin come by there, if he'd come by."

> Shriver had made another misstatement. He had just said Hobart Cook was the flagman, then turned around and had him sitting on a truck at the time the crime allegedly happened. Jimbo Cook hoped the jury didn't catch it.

"Now maybe it's not so unusual," Shriver continued, "but I believe if I saw somebody get into a moving car, I'd remember it if it happened. And I don't see how at least some of these people that were there could have failed to observe it if it did happen. But it just—we're talking about building a pile of evidence, piece by piece, against this man. Why else do we say there was not a Negro man in the car? Well, the testimony of Walter Lee Davis, and I'll come to that in a minute.

"Agents Coleman and Larkin verified the fact, testified to by these construction workers, that they are laying the pavement there at Spence Lane and Elm Hill Pike, that they put down what these men call chips. Very dusty gravel. If any of you have ever put down a new driveway, and put gravel down, you probably had your wife fuss at you for tracking in the house. That stuff is very dusty. It picks up on your feet. No tracks of any kind in this black Chevrolet automobile with black carpets. If a man got in at that intersection, he would have tracked some of that dust on that carpet in such a way that it would be visible. Larkin and Coleman said it was not visible, it was not there.

"Now add to that what Mr. Powell says he did. What are the probabilities that a man would jump into a car while it's moving in the first place? Secondly, if he's going to jump in for the purpose of robbery, that he'll start shooting before he gets the money. Third, what are the probabilities that having done the shooting that he would get out of the car without getting the money that he went in there to get in the first place? Fourth, what are the probabilities that a man in a car, in the back seat, can get out while the car is moving, in the process of a U-turn, which would tend to sling you to the outside and not fall down, be able to get the door closed, and disappear from view, and never be found again, and nobody ever hear from him again?

"Remote possibilities," Shriver said, his voice trailing off. He stopped a moment and looked up at the ceiling.

"Now then Powell said he saw some workmen down there at the railroad track and thought sure they would do something about it as he sped away. What in the world did he think they were going to do if he didn't stop and tell them something had happened?"

> No, now he's done it again, Hardin thought. His recollection was that Powell never said anything about seeing men at a railroad track.

"And while he's speeding away, why does he speed to Capitol Chevrolet Company? General Hospital was just about as close. He passes numerous business houses where he could have stopped and gotten help more quickly, could have gotten the police on the scene to catch this supposed Negro man that got in the car. Instead, he goes back to the Capitol Chevrolet Company.

"Now, then, he gets to the hospital, and immediately starts identifying Negro men. He identifies Lorenza Perry from a picture. Then he goes and participates in the drawing of a composite picture of somebody he says looks like the man. And then he goes to the police department and picks Gerald James Wingard out of a lineup, and Gerald James Wingard was in California at the time this happened. He's identified three different people, the composite drawing that he did, Gerald James Wingard, and if you can show me any resemblance between the pictures of any of those people, be a great surprise. They are three very, very different looking people. You saw the pictures.

"One more thing that he has done to convince you, the people of this city, he's not the murderer.

"Now, then, their defense, as I said, consisted of his statements, and then it consisted of an attempt to show that Walter Lee Davis was not where Walter Lee Davis said he was.

"Then Mr. Swann. I don't really know what to think about Mr. Swann. The thing I couldn't help observe about him, and I don't pretend to be a mind reader or human lie detector, but I was just not convinced that man was telling me the truth or you the truth.

"Now, this business of what he told you that he had some business in Spring Hill and thought he would stop in on Walter, see how he was getting along. When he gets that diary out it develops that he went down there with Moody and Kilgore, associates of Mr. Branstetter, in a Capitol Chevrolet automobile for the purpose of seeing Walter about his testimony in court.

"Now, I assume Mr. Swann is a busy man, running a company, got time to go down there and see his employees about their testimony in court on the grounds that he doesn't want to see him get in trouble by telling a different story, and then he comes in this court and says I don't want to get him in trouble and calls him a liar on the witness stand. What does he think he's doing? If he's telling the truth, says he doesn't want to get his employee in trouble, but he is getting his employee in trouble with perjury charges. But he went down there with Mr. Moody and Mr. Kilgore, and he didn't tell you that at first, did he?

"Why was Mr. Swann so interested in Walter Lee Davis that he would make two trips to Spring Hill, Tennessee, when he was up here supposed to be running his company?

"I don't believe that I can accept the fact that just out of interest in Walter Lee Davis, Tommy Swann went twice to Spring Hill, Tennessee, to talk to this man about his testimony. You know Walter said he told him, said this Powell is my friend and if he gets convicted somebody is going to sweat. That comes awfully close to being a criminal threat to Walter Lee Davis.

"Now, why would he do that? Now, he says one other thing I thought was interesting, Swann did. He says that Walter was at his yard across from the Capitol Chevrolet Company and he's not sure when, 11:00 to 11:30, the police cars are already there because of the killing. This is on May 24. He said a Negro man was in a truck. He didn't recognize who it was. Don't you think he knew who he was and if he's so concerned, knows all his employees so well he goes to see them when they are sick to ask about their testimony, makes two trips, that whoever this employee was behind Capitol Chevrolet Company would be so well known to him he could tell this court and jury who it was?

"He knows who it was. It was Walter Lee Davis, or it didn't happen at all. I am inclined to think the latter. I think Mr. Swann knows it wasn't and I don't think he's telling the truth about it.

"Mr. Swann says, 'I just want justice. I just want to protect my employee.' Strange way to protect his employees, call them liars on the witness stand in a case of this importance.

"You saw Walter. Walter is a good man, nine children, hard worker. Everybody said he was. Everybody said he was truthful who testified about him. Walter is a simple man, and I really don't think capable of making up, creating, or fabricating the story he told in this courtroom. I don't think it is within the ability of Walter Lee Davis to make this story up. The only way he could come up with this information is he saw it, just like he said he saw it.

"What reason would he have to lie? No reason. Walter didn't want to get into it. Kept it quiet for a long time and finally somebody found out he knew about it, got him up here and made him testify. He is just not capable of lying about it.

"Well, the other part of their defense, this man Charles M. Wilson,

Madison, Wisconsin, Wisconsin Crime Laboratory, a laboratory the police officers right there in Madison don't even use, send their stuff to the FBI. He tried, and frankly, members of the jury, I don't know what to say about him. I don't know whether he's a fraud, a crook, or just incompetent. One of the three.

"He sat on the witness stand and tried to convince you he saw particles of bullets on the back of this shoulder and convince you they couldn't have gotten there except by a man in the back seat of the car firing over the shoulder of Bill Powell, convince you there were no particles on this part of the coat." Shriver ran his hand down the other side of his suit jacket. "And therefore, Bill Powell could not have shot himself in the leg.

"And what do we find out about that? We find out first that the process he used is useful only to locate particles; don't tell you what they are. The particles could be anything. It doesn't tell you anything except the fact they are there, but Mr. Norman ceremoniously takes a day of your time to send that coat off to Washington, and I am glad he did now. The truth is out. It tells you what the truth is in this lawsuit."

> Why, thought Hal Hardin, is Shriver saying yet again the word, "lawsuit" when this is a purely criminal case?

"We send that coat to Washington, D.C., and there wasn't a particle there at all of anything, bullets, plaster, anything else, and the things Mr. Wilson said were particles weren't particles at all but incomplete developing of that film, deliberately or just incompetence. I don't know which, but he sat here and told you these were particles and you heard them say they weren't particles at all but bubbles. The FBI examination didn't find any particles, and all the rest of them are bubbles from developing fluid. They ought to have been ashamed to have put that man on this witness stand.

"Now how did it happen? How did Mr. W. Haynie Gourley really get shot?

"I think what happened is pretty evident to us all now. William Powell goes to Mr. Gourley's office and says, 'We have got some things to talk about, Boss. Let's go riding.' I am sure Mr. Gourley thought that was strange. So they go riding, and they get out on Elm Hill Pike. Bill Powell says, 'I ain't going through with it, I'm keeping my interest in this business.'

"This is our theory. We don't know, nobody knows but Bill Powell what really happened that day. We don't know what was said. Probably said, 'I am not going through with it.' Mr. Gourley says, 'You agreed. I am going to throw you out if you don't.'"

> Billy Gourley was struck by these words. He knew his father would never have talked that way. Hal Hardin, meanwhile, was stunned by Shriver's admitting that the prosecution didn't know "what really happened that day." This is unforgivable. How could he have just made a case for reasonable doubt?

Shriver prattled on, seemingly unaware of the damage he had just done.

"Now, Walter Lee Davis says he saw a black Chevrolet automobile pull over on Elm Hill Pike and stop by three trees. You saw the pictures that we passed to you, clearly evidence that you can see that trailer from those trees and the trees from the trailer, see it either way, clear view, and Walter was there, and he saw it just like he said he did.

"Now he saw two men get out of the car and saw them go to the back of the car. He saw them gesturing. He couldn't hear what was said. They get back in the car. Then the man in the driver's seat, William Powell, is driving the car. The man in the driver's seat gets out, and he goes to the rear of the car, he opens the trunk. Now I am sure Mr. Gourley wondered, 'What is Bill Powell doing in the trunk of the car?'

"But it's his business partner. Did he expect to get shot? Of course not. They had been close associates, two-and-a-half, three years. He goes to the trunk of the car. I am sure Mr. Gourley was curious about it. Gets in the back seat. Walter says he heard three rackets and then a loud racket, sounded like shots. The man gets up to the end, passes the H.D. Lee Company, turns around, comes back, and Walter is down there beside Elm Hill Pike and sees them going back, and the man in the right front is slumped over.

"The glass is found right exactly—the glass out of the window of that car—there is no question, the window was broken out somehow or other. Our theory is by a bullet. Glass from that window is found exactly where Walter Lee Davis says the shooting occurred.

"How can there be any doubt that it happened just the way Walter said it did? Bill Powell gets in the back seat, fires through the seat into Mr. Gourley's back. He didn't even have the guts to shoot him in the face, face to face, shoots him in the back. The bullet hits the brace. They brought it in here and showed it to you, and the velocity of the bullet is spent. It goes through the seat. You saw Mr. Gourley's coat and his shirt, torn in the back, but it didn't go into Mr. Gourley's back.

"Mr. Gourley turns around, and Mr. Powell testified his arm was hurting. Did you see that cuff link that Mr. Larkin brought in, bent? I think that probably at this point there was a struggle and I bet Mr. Gourley did say just what Powell said, 'Oh, my Lord, what's happened?' I bet he said that, and I bet he struggled at that point, and Mr. Gourley's cufflink got bent, and Mr. Powell got a bruise on his arm. Mr. Gourley is facing the back seat, and he was shot in the chest, no powder marks on this lapel, must have been some distance in excess of two feet, according to the FBI testimony.

"Mr. Gourley slumps over. Powell leans forward and puts the gun to his—well I believe the gun powder marks on the coat right here, puts the gun right here, right against him."

Shriver made a gesture with his hands of a gun pointed down into his own shoulder.

"And the bullet goes down there, and he puts the gun right here." Shriver held his forefinger against his jawbone. "And shoots again, and the bullet goes out and breaks the window, and Walter Lee Davis hears the fourth shot. That's louder than the other three because the window is broken out. Bill Powell then gets out, goes around the car, gets in the front seat, drives down to Dabbs Avenue.

"Now we don't know when he got shot. We know of four shots fired then. We know Mr. Powell got shot in the leg, but there is plenty of opportunity because he still has got some time left, some time, two or three minutes that he has left. He—maybe down there at Dabbs Avenue, or maybe in the area back towards town. Drives on back on Elm Hill Pike, tosses the gun over the roof of the car, and it hits the muzzle into the dirt."

"Now ballistics people tell us that Mr. Gourley and Mr. Powell were shot by bullets fired from maybe, and we don't know beyond all doubt, but probably from a .38 Special, Smith & Wesson pistol. Lo and behold what's found on the very route that Mr. Powell took back towards town? A .38 Smith & Wesson pistol. The ballistics testimony is that the bullets were fired from a gun that had a good barrel in it, not rust, in good condition. Two circumstances alone to corroborate that this is the pistol. But the third one is probably the most telling of all.

"We know that five shots were fired. There was a shot into the back of the seat, one shot that went through Mr. Gourley's neck, and it came out and broke the window out, and that slug was never found. Two bullets in Mr. Gourley's body. One bullet found in the car, the one that went through Mr. Powell's leg. Five shots fired. When Mr. Lewis found this gun, it had five spent shell casings in the revolver cylinder and one cylinder with no casing at all.

"Five shells, .38 Smith & Wesson pistol. Barrel in good condition. Five shells in it on Elm Hill Pike between Spence Lane and P'Pool Avenue.

"Now can you top this? Bobby Frensley comes forward and says, 'I gave him the gun. It's the gun that I got from Major Hall. Major Hall got it from the National Guard, or the Civil Defense.' We checked the records, the serial number, and the very gun that's found on Elm Hill Pike is the one that Frensley gave Bill Powell. And Bill Powell's in here denying he ever had a gun.

"Bill Powell killed this man. You and I know he did. Premeditated.

We're talking about the elements now of first-degree murder. Essential element, premeditation.

"Now here's how you know he premeditated. He took him out there—they could have talked in the office—took him out there and he took a gun along, a loaded gun. He thought about it ahead of time. He shot him, and of course what I tell you about the law is not binding. The judge will give you instructions about what the law is. But premeditation can occur in an instant. It doesn't have to be of long duration and plan.

"If Mr. Gourley was going to put him out of business, he was going to get the business, whatever it took to get it, and he killed Haynie Gourley to get the business. Premeditation. Mere use of a deadly weapon presumes malice, but he shot this man four times, three times fatally, through the neck, through the shoulder, through the chest. I can't imagine anything more malicious than that, pumping four bullets into him, three of them actually wind up in him, and it's obviously deliberate intention. So that's first-degree murder.

"Ladies and gentlemen, it now comes your duty, after you hear the rest of these arguments, to decide this case. It's your job. It's a serious duty. We've done our duty. We've presented you the facts. I think the facts are conclusive absolutely. I see no way that this jury can do anything but find this man guilty of first-degree murder.

"I appreciate your attention during this trial, and especially during my final argument. And it now comes time for the defense to argue, and I will sit down and let them do just that."

Shriver walked over and took his seat at the prosecution table. The opening statement had lasted one hour.

> Billy's friend Jimbo Cook had changed his mind. Shriver was deadpan and apologetic at first, but during the second half of his summary, at least his delivery was more forceful. Jimbo didn't see how the jury could see

it any other way. He now looked forward to watching John J. Hooker Sr. work his storied magic.

CHAPTER [29]

All eyes turned toward Jack Norman. His demeanor was imperious enough to make the rafters tremble.

Jimbo's heart gave a flip. The man had been masterful at utterly destroying Bob Frensley. Plus, Norman had treated every witness for the State with contempt, turning his chair around so that his back was toward the witness box. Twice, he had rocked back and forth until his chair squeaked, and the jury watched him when they needed to be concentrating on testimony.

Branstetter, though, had done the greatest damage, bringing down witnesses with his uninterrupted verbal onslaughts that lasted as long as two hours, wearing down every important witness with endless repetition. He had masterfully anesthetized the jury and everyone else by going into minutiae well outside the purview of the case, so much so that no one remembered the initial damaging testimony.

But it was Norman to be feared now, as he was about to take the stage and go on the attack. He was known as a wily and vicious bulldog for good reason. He looked menacing just sitting at the table, black half-glasses perched on his blunt nose and all the while scribbling on a yellow legal pad.

Judge Cornelius then turned to the defense table to present their closing arguments.

"All right. What says the defendant?"

Norman stood up, walked up to face the judge, puffed out his chest and bellowed, "Charge the Jury, Your Honor."

Everyone sat stunned. Hal Hardin turned around to look at the spectators, who all seemed to be confused, questioning each other and shrugging their shoulders. For weeks, Hooker had practiced his closing argument. Dropping five empty shell casings to the wooden floor of the courtroom would be dramatic enough. That move alone could sway the jury.

Josephine Gourley did not move. Billy Gourley looked anxiously at Hooker for some sign, but Hooker was staring straight ahead. Shriver shifted in his chair, glanced at Hooker, then turned back and faced the front of the courtroom.

Without a hint of surprise at the bomb Norman had just dropped, Judge Cornelius began: "Any person in the courtroom who wishes to leave at this time may do so. While the court is in process of charging the jury there will be no one allowed in or out."

> Jimbo Cook froze. What was going on? Was this the end? The courtroom grew quiet at the judge's words. No one made a move to leave.

Judge Cornelius, his voice calm and even, proceeded to define first- and second-degree murder. with phrases like "malice aforethought" and "depraved or malignant spirit." He moved on to a definition of voluntary and involuntary manslaughter, followed by an explanation of what constitutes assault and battery.

"When you retire to consider your verdict, you will first inquire: Is the defendant guilty of murder in the first degree?

"If you find from the evidence beyond a reasonable doubt that the defendant unlawfully, willfully, maliciously, deliberately, and premeditatively killed W. Haynie Gourley as charged in the indictment, your verdict should be, 'We the jury, find the defendant guilty of murder in the first degree and fix his punishment at death by electrocution,' unless you are of the opinion there were mitigating circumstances, in which event, you may commute the punishment to life in the penitentiary or for some period of time over twenty years."

Judge Cornelius went on to say if there was reasonable doubt, the jury should acquit the defendant.

As he was explaining what it meant when a witness is impeached, Judge Cornelius said something startling.

"While on the witness stand," Judge Cornelius was saying, "Walter Lee Davis admitted that he had heretofore been convicted and sentenced to imprisonment." The judge told the jury they would have to decide if Davis was credible or not, considering that he had served time in the penitentiary.

Jimbo Cook waited for Judge Cornelius to mention other witnesses, but he didn't. Jimbo had heard Walter Lee Davis say that he was twenty-one years old and wrote a bad check for $22.00 and spent over eight months in the penitentiary for the crime. He was now fifty-six years old, and his only other run-in with the law had been when he was caught driving without a license. This is beyond prejudicial, Jimbo thought angrily. No one else has been singled out. Someone should declare a mistrial. This, after Thomas Swann so obviously lied on the stand. Jimbo glanced at Billy. He was staring straight ahead. Jimbo felt panic rise as he looked over at Norman rocking slowly back and forth in his chair, a smirk on his face and an unlit cigar clenched in his teeth.

The case was going straight to the jury without so much as a word of closing argument from either the defense or the prosecution. There would be no fiery oratory, no chance for Hooker to try and outdo his old foe.

After receiving more instructions to consider all the evidence and the testimonies of laboratory technicians, firearms experts, and medical doctors, the jury filed out of the courtroom at 4:03 p.m. to begin deliberation.

It was Saturday afternoon, August 2, the twentieth day of the trial. The jury had been sequestered for three long weeks. Nashville's most famous trial ever was at an end, and the fate of the two families was now in the hands of ten men and two women.

CHAPTER [30]

Bill and Helen Powell, along with Hamilton Wallace and his wife Lally, left the courthouse and had dinner at the nearby Gerst Haus, a popular German restaurant on Second Avenue. Then, they took a walk around the courthouse plaza.

Members of the Gourley family gathered in the district attorney's office next to the courtroom. Sandwiches were brought in, but no one ate. Hooker was uncharacteristically quiet. Shriver seemed relaxed. JoAnn Bainbridge and Josephine Gourley smiled nervously as they talked with family and the DA's team.

Billy walked out into the hall with Jimbo Cook and two other friends, wondering aloud how long it would take to reach a verdict. His future now lay in the hands of the jury.

"It could take them several days," said one of his friends.

Jimbo reassured him: "Billy, they found the gun. There's no way he's getting away with this."

Several members of the press, including WLAC-TV's Chris Clark, had gathered in a circle, placing verbal bets on what they thought the verdict would be. Billy walked up to Clark whom he had come to know during the trial and asked what their best guess was.

"Guilty. They'll give him forty years," answered Clark.

In his office, Tom Shriver stood and talked to family members who were all asking if it made a difference that Hooker was denied his closing argument.

Assistant District Attorney Hal Hardin may have been one of the most confident people in the room. As the jury was being charged, he had glanced over at the Powell children. He had grown rather fond of them, seeing Mary Helen and Bill Jr., sitting there day after day, smiling assuredly at their father. But as the judge spoke, Hardin felt sadness for the teenagers, thinking it was likely that they would soon see their father led away in handcuffs.

At 8:48 p.m., Billy Gourley was still in the hall when Shriver came out of his office door and announced that the jury had reached a verdict.

"They didn't take very long. What does this mean?" Billy asked Hooker as he came out of Shriver's office.

Hooker kept walking and didn't answer.

Powell and his family and friends had congregated at one end of the hall. Everyone headed to Courtroom 611.

Judge Cornelius came out his chamber and stepped up and took his place. The room grew quiet. All eyes were fixed on the closed door next to the jury box. Both families were unsmiling and tense.

After a few short minutes, the door opened and a male juror walked out, expressionless, looking straight ahead.

Then, the second juror, Mrs. W. P. Chastain, who worked as a bookkeeper for a local pharmacy, appeared. She was carrying a large beige pocketbook which she clasped in front of her. She was only a few steps into the courtroom when she looked over at Bill Powell. A large smile crossed her face.

> "Holy hell," Hal Hardin whispered aloud when he saw her. Billy Gourley crumbled inside. Jimbo Cook felt as if he had been punched in the stomach. Sherman Nickens muttered in disbelief, "Oh, no way possible." Nickens had already told several people that he had

> seen Mrs. Chastain wink at Bill Powell on one of the previous days. They had been skeptical. Now he was sure of it.

The rest of the jurors filed in, their eyes avoiding contact with either side of the courtroom. They sat down and looked up at the judge.

"All right," Judge Cornelius began. "Members of the jury, have you reached a verdict?"

"We have, Your Honor," the foreman E. F. Carroll Jr., an employee of South Central Bell Telephone Company, stood up. He held a piece of paper in both hands.

"What is the verdict of the jury?" asked Cornelius.

"We the jury find the defendant not guilty."

The courtroom erupted. On the left side, Powell's contingent leapt to their feet and began jumping up and down and screaming as if their team had just scored the winning touchdown. Helen Powell burst into tears and hugged her children who were on either side of her. Bill Powell reached over the wooden railing and embraced his family. For at least five minutes, pandemonium reigned. Judge Cornelius banged his gavel repeatedly, saying over and over, "Order in the court," but he was drowned out, and the celebration continued unabated. Court officers tried without success to get control of the crowd.

The righthand side of the courtroom, packed with Gourley supporters, sat in stunned silence; no one moved. Finally, Josephine Gourley stood up. Billy took his mother by the arm, and they began making their way through the cheering crowd blocking the doors to the courtroom. Out in the hallway, several friends of Powell's children were dancing around in circles and hugging each other. Friends crowded around Bill and Helen Powell. Powell gave both his attorneys a giant bear hug.

The Gourley family slipped quietly past them and walked into the district attorney's office next door. They soon left the building without comment.

As microphones were thrust in Hooker's face, he praised Josephine Gourley pontifically: "When the verdict was returned, she maintained the same brave composure she has had all the way through this trial. She expressed herself as feeling that the court had presided with ability and fairness in this case."

Norman was not so gracious when confronted by the press.

"This prosecution of Powell was conceived in meanness and executed with cruelty. Thank God for an honest jury that has rescued Bill Powell from a grossly unfair trial and a televised execution."

The jury had deliberated for four hours and forty-five minutes. Their verdict was unanimous.

Reporters sought statements from the jurors as they filed out into the hall. Some kept walking and refused to comment.

Gene Paul Ray, an employee of McQuiddy Printing Company said, "The state showed me nothing to prove its case."

Granville Underwood, who worked for the Metro Sanitation Department, said he felt Powell was innocent all along. Paul Jones, a worker for the U.S. Post Office, told a reporter that it was "ridiculous to think the State could build a case" on such testimony.

Billy Gourley escorts his mother Josephine Gourley from the courtroom after the verdict is handed down at 8:48 p.m., August 2, 1969. © *The Tennessean – USA TODAY NETWORK*

"The fact was that these things didn't even come to light until after Mr. Powell was indicted on March 27," said Jones. "The gun didn't come up until the trial was already under way."

Another juror, Willie Jones, a mechanic for the Nashville Housing Authority, said the jury did not believe Walter Lee Davis because his foreman testified that he had made four or five different statements even before he took the stand. Jones added that the jury did not believe Robert Frensley either.

But later, juror Robert Weaver, a driver for Industrial Towel and Uniform Service, admitted he had doubts, wondering if the jury had made the right decision.

"My own business partner asked me how we could be so stupid. I told him he wasn't there. We had to weigh the evidence. We could have sentenced this man to death, and I thought—and still think—that was an awesome responsibility."

Powell was asked by reporters what he thought when Mrs. W. P. Chastain flashed a smile at him as she returned to the jury box.

"That woman was just like my wife. She can't keep a secret for fifteen minutes."

When asked what he intended to do now, Powell told reporters, "I thought I'd go fishing and take a few days' vacation. But I've changed my mind. I decided instead that I'd better go to church. Then, I guess I'll get back to work and peddle a few cars."

Sherman Nickens, who had been the lead homicide detective in the case, rode down in the elevator with Jack Norman.

Lit cigar clutched between his fingers, Norman put his hand on Nickens's shoulder and said in his deep voice, "Don't take this personally, Sherman. The jury has spoken."

Nickens said nothing, and they walked out of the elevator in silence.

Only minutes after the verdict came down, word spread that Metro police had received a bomb threat. The woman caller told a police dispatcher: "I'm from out of town and there is a bomb at Capitol Chevrolet."

Police rushed to the dealership and searched the premises. Nothing was found.

Bill Powell, his arm around daughter Mary Helen and son Bill Jr., emerges from the courtroom after his acquittal. Helen Powell is at far right. Defense attorney Cecil Branstetter is next to Powell. *Nashville Public Library, Special Collections, Banner Newspaper Collection*

The Gourley family was in shock. About a week after the trial ended, Josephine and Billy met with Hooker at his farm. He expressed his disappointment in the verdict and performed the dramatic speech he had prepared to close out the trial. Hooker was convinced that his well-rehearsed argument would have swayed the jury to vote for a conviction.

However, during the trial, Billy had become more and more alarmed that Hooker seemed to have lost his golden touch, that his glory days might lie behind him. In retrospect, Billy found himself wishing his family had hired forty-year-old Nashville lawyer James Neal, who was in his prime and had gained a reputation as a fierce prosecutor. Along with Hooker, Neal had tried the Hoffa case that led to the teamster leader's conviction. Hoffa called Neal "the most vicious prosecutor who ever lived." Neal would eventually serve as prosecutor in the Watergate trial, convicting U.S. Attorney General John Mitchell and Nixon aides John Erlichman and H.R. Haldeman.

***

In a matter of days after the verdict, representatives from the Chevrolet Motor Division appeared at Josephine Gourley's door. She sent them away, saying she was in no condition to talk business.

Three weeks later, the men returned, informing her that she had no choice; she had to sell her stock in Capitol Chevrolet to Bill Powell. Unable to pass her late husband's business on to her son, as had been Haynie's lifetime wish, she sold her shares to Powell and his backers for $600,000. The figure had presumably been arrived at by basing the number on the fact that Powell had paid $200,000 for his 25%, thus her part would be worth three times that amount. Apparently, no one had bothered to advise her that the business was generating millions each year and that perhaps the price was not a fair one, especially taking into consideration the ease with which Powell had received an established, highly lucrative dealership, and the Gourleys had lost their entire future.

In his final interview with *The Tennessean*, Bill Powell told reporters the police should not give up searching for the Black man who killed Mr. Gourley.

"I think they should continue the investigation," he said. "The man is still out there, and he might do the same terrible thing again."

CHAPTER [31]

On a sunny day in the summer of 1982, eleven-year-old Ken Whitehouse, who would grow up to be a well-regarded journalist, stood in the living room of Helen Suddoth's house. Ken's mother Nancy was sitting where she could look out onto Helen's front lawn and driveway. Mrs. Suddoth, a widow who was almost eighty, was seated with her back to the window. The two women were close friends, even though Nancy Whitehouse was half Mrs. Suddoth's age.

The Whitehouse family lived across the street from Helen Suddoth on the corner of Lealand Lane and Draughon Avenue, a block off Woodmont Boulevard in Nashville. Young Ken often did chores for Helen. He cut her grass each week, and she paid him five dollars, which he secretly thought was not enough, considering her lawn was almost an acre. But Mrs. Suddoth was kind to the Whitehouse family and a wonderful neighbor. Often when Ken and his mother would visit, Mrs. Suddoth would share stories about her life. She was known for speaking her mind.

As he stood behind his mother's chair, Ken looked out the window. His face lit up. A shiny new silver DeLorean was turning into Mrs. Suddoth's driveway. In the driver's seat of the strange-looking car was Bill Powell, Helen Suddoth's son-in-law who had been married to Mrs. Suddoth's daughter, also named Helen. Powell had always been fond of his mother-in-law, and she was likewise extremely fond of him. After Mr. Suddoth died, Powell made sure Mrs. Suddoth was well taken care of and would stop by regularly to check on her.

Ken loved it when Powell came over. For an eleven-year-old boy, it was a thrill to see one of these rare DeLoreans up close.

Ken watched as the sun glinted off the stainless-steel car as it pulled on into the driveway and stopped. Then, the gull-wing doors began to rise, looking like some giant mechanical bird in a science fiction movie. Mrs. Suddoth, who was in the middle of telling a story, heard the noise and looked back over her shoulder, just in time to see Powell emerge from the car.

Without so much as a trace of emotion in her voice, she said, "Oh, Bill's here. He's such a good boy. I know he killed that man, but he's such a good boy."

She then went back to telling her story.

EPILOGUE

On a hillside in Forest Lawn Memorial Park in Glendale, California, a weathered bronze plaque is anchored to the ground in the Eventide section, Lot 2443, Space 2. It features a frieze of Jesus with outstretched hands and a figure kneeling in the background. Along the bottom is the inscription: "Lo, I Am With You Always..." In this same cemetery lie the great actors Clark Gable, Elizabeth Taylor, Humphrey Bogart, Spencer Tracy, and Jimmy Stewart, along with countless other world-famous movie stars and the legendary singers Sam Cooke, Nat King Cole, and Michael Jackson.

But this particular plaque marks the grave, not of a celebrity, but of a small-town woman who, in the summer of 1904, stepped off a train somewhere in Tennessee and disappeared into the night.

ANNECE BUCHER
BELOVED MOTHER AND WIFE
1958

After the trial ended, District Attorney **Thomas Shriver** announced that he anticipated no further prosecutions in the Powell case, despite reports of possible perjury actions against a witness who testified for the defense. Shriver served as DA until 1987 when he was appointed criminal court judge in Davidson County. On the evening of October 25, 1997, he failed to come home from a day trip out of town. The next morning, he was found dead of an apparent heart attack in his judge's chambers. Thomas Shriver was sixty-five.

John J. Hooker Sr. had a famous saying. "I am never going to retire. I want to die after one of my Christmas parties or while I'm in the middle of trying a case." On December 23, 1970, Hooker hosted his annual Christmas extravaganza for members of the Nashville Bar Association and prominent civic and business leaders at his elegant downtown office, where crystal and silver sparkled, and whiskey flowed freely. When he arrived at his farm late that night, he asked his wife to bring him a pen and a photograph of himself.

"I've been promising Hal Hardin I would sign one of these for him."

When his wife went to wake him the next morning, Christmas Eve, she found him dead. The photograph he'd signed rested on a bedside table. The inscription read: "To my friend Hal Hardin with highest esteem and affection, Regards, John Hooker, Dec. 1970." It still hangs on a prominent place on the wall of Hardin's law office.

At the time of his death at age sixty-seven, Hooker was preparing for the defense of novelist Jesse Hill Ford, author of the critically acclaimed novel, *The Liberation of Lord Byron Jones*, which was made into a movie, the last ever directed by William Wyler. Ford was charged with the murder of a soldier he claimed was trespassing on his estate outside Humboldt, Tennessee.

There was a massive funeral held at the First Presbyterian Church on Franklin Road. The two daily newspapers devoted several pages to his accomplishments. Jack Norman Sr. told a reporter, "A giant oak has fallen." U.S. Supreme Court Justice William O. Douglas was an honorary pallbearer at the service, attended by luminaries from all over the country.

In recorded interviews with his grandson about his life's work, **Jack Norman Sr.** said the prosecution in the Powell case "never had a chance." For decades before the Powell trial, Norman kept an index card on every person who had ever served on a jury in Davidson County.

He often referred to the compilation as his "secret weapon." He would use the information to establish a connection with the jurors he chose. Norman said it was a mistake for District Attorney Thomas Shriver to ask for the death penalty and that he knew from the outset the jury in the Gourley case would not convict Bill Powell. At Norman's death in 1995 at age ninety, a write-up in *The Tennessean* quoted him as saying: "The best closing argument I ever gave is the one I chose not to give," referring to the strategic decision he made in the Powell murder trial that blocked John J. Hooker Sr. from delivering one of his dramatic, and so often persuasive, closing arguments, which could have resulted in a different outcome to the trial.

Cecil Branstetter continued to enjoy a distinguished legal career and over the years received many honors from his peers. He served as the first chairman of the Metropolitan Charter Revision Commission and was often referred to as the "Father of Metropolitan Government." He spent the years after the trial dedicating time to public service and was well-known for giving back to the community. He became a founder and president of the Tennessee Environmental Council and also served as president of the Tennessee Conservation League. Cecil Dewey Branstetter passed away on May 7, 2014, at the age of ninety-three.

Assistant District Attorney **Hal Hardin** always believed Bill Powell murdered Haynie Gourley. Hardin's theory was that Powell first shot through the back of the passenger seat, hoping to kill his boss without his knowing what happened. "Why would a robber shoot through the seat?" he kept asking himself. Hardin theorized that when the shot was deflected off a metal brace in the seat and missed its target, Powell shot Haynie in the chest, then held the gun to his face and shoulder and fired twice more.

In an ironic twist, Hardin married the granddaughter of Jack Norman Sr., his rival in the Powell case. Five of Hardin's grandchildren attend the Ensworth School in Nashville, part of which is housed in Red

Gables, once the home of Jack Norman Sr.

Hardin went on to have a distinguished career, becoming the presiding judge of the trial courts of Nashville/Davidson County. He later received a Presidential appointment as United States Attorney in the Middle District of Tennessee.

Hardin still speaks with admiration about Jack Norman Sr., Cecil Branstetter, and John J. Hooker Sr. All remained friends and colleagues.

Most of the evidence collected in the Gourley murder case was burned by the police, but Hardin still has in his possession the .38-caliber Smith & Wesson pistol John Barros claimed was mysteriously left in his mailbox.

Hardin, who has racked up numerous prestigious awards given by the Nashville legal community, continues to practice law in a historic building directly across from the Davidson County courthouse where Bill Powell was acquitted on August 2, 1969.

Chief detective in charge of the Gourley case **Sherman Nickens** went on to investigate dozens of murders as head of the Metro police homicide division. He became a familiar figure on local television, giving press conferences on much-publicized crimes in Nashville. Nickens led the investigation into the murder of country music star David "Stringbean" Akeman, a regular cast member on the TV series *Hee Haw*. After performing at the Grand Ole Opry on Saturday night, November 10, 1973, Stringbean and his wife returned to their ransacked home and were ambushed and killed. Two of his cousins, who failed to find a stash of money rumored to be hidden in the house, were arrested and sent to prison.

Nickens believed Bill Powell was guilty from the moment he first heard Powell's account of the murder. "The police knew it. The district attorney's office knew it. The FBI agent who examined Bob Frensley's gun knew it. We just couldn't prove it."

Through his wheeling and dealing, which started even before the Gourley case, Nickens became a multi-millionaire and moved to Florida where he collects vintage Corvettes and enjoys boating.

Nickens had been fast friends with **Larry Brinton**, the crime reporter for the *Nashville Banner* who had the idea to publish the Powell trial transcript in its entirety and who later provided the lead that allowed Nickens to arrest the guilty parties in the Stringbean case. Brinton went on to have a second career in television news analysis. He and Sherman Nickens talked every day for decades until Brinton's death in July 2019 at the age of eighty-eight.

Robert O. Frensley, who had been a champion drag racer in his youth, returned to Nashville in 1970 and became a success in the automobile business, owning and operating a number of major brand dealerships in the middle Tennessee area. He was also a real estate developer and served on several charitable boards and commissions. A devout Catholic, he was a generous and reliable donor to the church and to his high school, Father Ryan, making regular gifts of real estate, cash, and automobiles. After the trial, Bob Frensley never again saw the gun he gave Bill Powell. He passed away in 2015 at the age of seventy-six.

Bill Powell never spoke to **Josephine Gourley** again after he and his wife Helen visited her upon his release from Vanderbilt Hospital. A few months after the trial, she sold her home on Belle Meade Boulevard to Dr. Tommy Frist, the son of the Gourleys' personal physician who founded Hospital Corporation of America and whose brother, also a doctor, would become majority leader in the United States Senate. The house has since changed hands. Jo Gourley was fifty-six years old when her husband was killed; she never remarried and died in 2000 at age eighty-eight.

Billy Gourley never again entered the Capitol Chevrolet building that had been his father's pride and joy. The bright future he anticipated—

attending the Dealers' Sons School in Detroit and eventually taking over his father's business—was snatched from him by the unintentional terms of a contract and the timing of Haynie's death. But he grieved much more for the loss of his father and for the horrible way he died than for his own hopes and dreams.

"I lost my best friend," he said. "That I lost my future at Capitol Chevrolet was secondary."

For a year following the trial, he worked in Nashville as a stockbroker, but the automobile business was in his blood. In 1974, he purchased a Chevrolet dealership in nearby Ashland City, Tennessee, naming it Bill Gourley Chevrolet. In 1981, he sold it and eventually made his way to Asheville, North Carolina, where he became an executive with a large Ford dealership. He retired in 2017, and two years later, he and his wife Sherry returned to Nashville where they now reside.

Bill Powell's obituary in the August 24, 2010, edition of *The Tennessean* told of his many honors and accomplishments and his "love of life." After his acquittal, he continued to own and operate Capitol Chevrolet Company and became the first Honda dealer in Tennessee. He held memberships in the Belle Meade Country Club, the Cedar Creek Yacht Club, the Beaver Creek Country Club, and the Hillwood Country Club. But rumors about the murder followed him for the rest of his life. He divorced his wife Helen Suddoth Powell and married businesswoman Debra Richardson, some 26 years his junior. William E. Powell died at the age of eighty-two.

There is no **Capitol Chevrolet** in Nashville anymore. Haynie Gourley's dreams of a future with his son Billy in the new Capitol Chevrolet headquarters at 600 Murfreesboro Road died with him on May 24, 1968. The grand building Haynie enjoyed for only a few short weeks no longer exists; it was torn down and, ironically, in its place sits the ultra-modern new headquarters of the Metropolitan Nashville Police Department.

With no more leads to pursue after the acquittal of Bill Powell, the **Metropolitan Police** and the District Attorney's office declared an end to the hunt for the mysterious assailant who vanished into thin air on May 24, 1968. There was no more investigation into the Gourley case, which, to this day, remains officially unsolved.

State of Tennessee vs. William E. Powell:

Nashville's Most Notorious

Unsolved Murder

Nashville Banner

2 Auto Firm Officials Shot

W. Haynie Gourley, Owner Of Capitol Chevrolet, Slain

$113 Million City Budget Presented

His Firm 1 Of Most Successful

State Opens $9,847,838 In Road Bids

EXTRA!

Negro Gunman Injures Powell In Robbery Try

Framed front-page copy of the May 24, 1968, *Nashville Banner* in a display case at the Nashville Archives, Nashville Public Library.

ACKNOWLEDGEMENTS

Much of the credit for *The Last Ride* goes to my daughters Anne Tate Pearce and Laura Tate Yellig, who, having heard Haynie Gourley's story since they were in elementary school, kept begging me to write a book. Their persistence finally gave me the courage to contact Billy Gourley, my college classmate and treasured friend, to ask if he would help me. It was scary because for fifty years he had turned down requests from the press and from numerous authors fascinated by the story. I am so thankful he said yes.

My four-year odyssey started out with numerous trips to Nashville. I owe a debt of gratitude to my Vanderbilt University classmate and brilliant, beloved sorority sister Martha Steinman Ballard and her husband Bill who welcomed me into their lovely home in Green Hills and provided me with meals and a safe place to stay while doing research and conducting interviews.

I will be eternally grateful to Hal Hardin, assistant district attorney at the 1969 trial, *State vs. William E. Powell*, who shared his recollections and insights and put me in touch with valuable sources. He has been a patient cheerleader for this project. I appreciate his sharing photographs and taking me back to the very courtroom I sat in for two weeks in the summer of 1969. Hal introduced me to William C. Koch Jr., president and dean of the Nashville School of Law, who graciously provided me with an invaluable 2016 video reenactment of news coverage of the murder and trial. This video, which featured a recording of the voice of defense lawyer Jack Norman Sr. reminiscing about the trial, also introduced me to journalist Ken Whitehouse, whose childhood experience is responsible for the shocking ending to this book.

I don't know what I would have done without entertainment lawyer and Billy Gourley's friend John Lentz, who grew up in Belle Meade not far from the Gourleys' home. John spent countless hours editing my original, much-too-long manuscript, checking legal terms, and providing the story of his own involvement in the case. To say that John made a profound impact on the final product would be a colossal understatement. John had a lot of experience when he voluntarily took on this project. He edited his wife Susan Lentz's engaging book *Kenneth,* a poignant true love story which had its beginnings in WWII. He also edited books for several of his clients, including *The Storyteller's Nashville* by Tom T. Hall, Doubleday, 1979; *The Songwriter's Handbook* by Tom T. Hall, Thomas Nelson, 2001; and *Stand By Your Man* by Tammy Wynette, Simon & Schuster, 1979.

I received the most amazing support and help from Nashville native Jane Hindman Kyburz, my little sister in the Kappa Alpha Theta sorority at Vanderbilt and sleuth extraordinaire. She had the idea to track down Sherman Nickens and Larry Brinton who were major players in this story. After doing her own detective work involving countless phone calls and emails, she located and contacted the two men, arranged a time and place for interviews, and even drove me to Nashville to meet with them. Jane's mother, Dot Hindman, owned several music publishing companies on Music Row. Jane bought me books I needed to reconstruct the history of the Grand Ole Opry and find information on Owen Bradley, bandleader, producer, and one of the founders of Music Row. Jane had danced to his orchestra countless times as a popular teenager in Nashville. Jane also lent me a vintage cookbook that included menus from Belle Meade's elite hostesses of the era. Joanne Fleming Hayes, another Kappa Alpha Theta sorority sister at Vanderbilt and a lifelong friend of Billy Gourley's, filled me in on life in Belle Meade in the late 1950s and 1960s and her parents' friendship with the Gourleys. Joanne's father, Sam Fleming, who was president of Third National Bank for decades, played an essential role in this story.

Dixie Johnson and the team at the Nashville Public Library, Special Collections, *Banner* Newspaper Collection, and Grace Hulme and colleagues at the Metropolitan Government Archives of Nashville and Davidson County at the Nashville Public Library were invaluable in helping me obtain period photographs, newsprint, and printed summaries of the witnesses in the trial. Without their assistance, I would have had few photographs or illustrations for the book.

I can never sufficiently thank Billy's wife Sherry Gourley for all she has done for this project. She located a letter from Haynie's nephew, Everett Gourley Jr., which contained important information about Haynie's parents and grandparents. From that letter I learned about Annece Haynie's elopement and details of the trip to St. Louis and the subsequent abandonment of the children. Sherry has been unwavering in her support of the book. Her contributions are too numerous to mention, but I want to thank her for not giving up on me when weeks turned into months and months into years. Most of the time I felt I was swimming in molasses, slogging through the trial transcript for months on end, yet she never lost her optimism or her faith that the book would see the light of day.

There is no way to thank Sherry enough for introducing me to Pam Grau who volunteered to take on the immense and tedious job of copyediting this book. I was slap-dash in my use of numbers and dashes and how to express time, among other stylistic sins. She rescued me by finding all the inconsistences and fixing them. Pam was the absolute right person for this monumental task, so knowledgeable and dedicated and patient and just a great editor. Pam enjoyed a career in the music industry as an independent journalist, publicist, copyright administrator, and as an editorial manager for Warner Bros. Records. She also served as program manager for the Vanderbilt Kennedy Center. Her confidence and competence were truly astounding and set my chaotic mind at ease. I can never thank her enough for her hard work which she carried out so cheerfully.

To all who read this manuscript on a computer or iPad and gave me their valuable feedback, I am so grateful. It helped to know that this book was, though disturbing, a decent read.

And to the immensely talented Mia Broder, who did the photography and laid out my previous book, *Margaret Moseley's A Garden to*

Remember, I am so deeply thankful. Her willingness to take on the design and formatting of this project gave me great peace of mind. It's so nice to have complete confidence in someone who has experience and a vision and who "loves to do books."

Finally, I will forever be grateful to Billy Gourley, who agreed to break fifty years of silence to share his painful story. Every one of my questions to him opened old wounds that took him back to an unspeakable time of trauma and heartbreak. With his wife Sherry supporting him at every turn, he bravely soldiered on and introduced me to Hal Hardin and John Lentz and the late Jimbo Cook, whose perspectives on the trial were invaluable. Billy ferried me up and down Elm Hill Pike, past 600 Murfreesboro Road where his father's new building once stood, and through Belle Meade where he grew up. He took me to the downtown Nashville Library where we were able to hold in our hands the 2,400-page typed transcript of the trial that changed his life. I am so grateful for his willingness to reach into the past and provide me with a portrait of his family, the Nashville he knew as a child, teenager, and young adult, and most of all the story of the father he loved so deeply.

SOURCES

All newspaper information for this book came from subscriptions to The Tennessean and Newspapers.com (Nashville Banner on-line through 1960); study of microfilm, Nashville Public Library, Special Collections, Nashville Banner Collection; clippings from both newspapers in the Metropolitan Government Archives of Nashville and Davidson County, Nashville Public Library

PROLOGUE
Interview with Billy Gourley
Information in morning paper read by Haynie: *The Tennessean*, p. 1, May 24, 1968
Trial testimony of Josephine Gourley
Headlines: *Nashville Banner*, p.1, Extra, Second Extra, May 24, 1968
CHAPTER 1:
History of founding of Cross Plains, Tennessee: *Across the Plains: A History of Cross Plains, Tennessee 1778-1986* by Rita A. Read, 1998, The Cross Plains Heritage Association pp. 2-6, 34, 59
Elopement, trip to St. Louis World's Fair, description of Annece Gourley, abandonment on train, Annece's talent and looks, trip to St. Louis World's Fair, train met in Springfield, Tennessee: Letter from Everett Gourley Jr. to Sherry and Billy Gourley, February 17, 2005
Abandonment of children: Interview with Billy Gourley; letter from Everett Gourley Jr.
Birth dates of children of Peter and Annece Gourley: Ancestry.com
Louisiana Purchase Exposition, 1904: Various web sites
1910 Census showing whereabouts of Haynie and brother: Ancestry.com
History of Nashville, Tennessee: Various web sites
Haynie Gourley's WWI service: Fold 3, Ancestry.com, and article on reunion of U.S. Army's 114th Field Artillery, Battery E, *Nashville Banner* on Newspapers.com
1920 Census, indicating Haynie's boarding house: Ancestry.com
Haynie Gourley in 1920s automobile industry: *Nashville Banner, The Tennessean*

articles and advertisements
The Fugitives: www.tennesseeencyclopedia.net and other web sites
1930 Census showing whereabouts of Haynie: Ancestry.com
CHAPTER 2
Hull-Dobbs-Maclin Automotive Company, Haynie's employment there, buying dealership: articles, ads in *The Tennessean; Nashville Banner*
History of Nashville dance clubs: Interview with Risley Lawrence
Courtship of Haynie Gourley and Josephine Saunders: Interview with Billy Gourley
Marriage announcement of Haynie Gourley and Josephine Saunders: *Nashville Banner*
Early years of Capitol Chevrolet: Articles, ads in *Nashville Banner, The Tennessean*
Society coverage of Haynie and Josephine Gourley: Articles in *Nashville Banner, The Tennessean*
CHAPTER 3
History of Ryman Auditorium: Ryman.com and other web sites
History of Grand Ole Opry: Various web sites; *America's Music: The Roots of Country* by Robert K. Oermann, Turner Publishing, Inc., 1996
History of Belle Meade Country Club: Interviews with John Lentz, Billy Gourley, Joanne Fleming Hayes, various web sites
Iroquois Steeplechase, Hillsboro Hounds: Iroquoissteeplechase.org; interviews with Billy Gourley
History of high school fraternities and sororities: Interviews with Jane Hindman Kyburz and Billy Gourley; articles in *The Tennessean, Nashville Banner*
Expansion of Capitol Chevrolet downtown: Articles in *The Tennessean*
CHAPTER 4
History of Owen Bradley and Music Row: *America's Music: The Roots of Country,* by Robert K. Oermann, Turner Publishing, Inc., 1996; various web sites; articles in *The Tennessean, Nashville Banner*
Saturday night dinners in Nashville: Interview with Joanne Fleming; menus of prominent Belle Meade hostesses in *Nashville Seasons Cook Book,* published by The Junior League of Nashville, Inc., first printing 1964, provided by Jane Hindman Kyburz
Haynie and Josephine's travels, interviews with Billy Gourley; articles in *The Tennessean, Nashville Banner*
James Lawson biography, history of Nashville's Civil Rights Movement: Wikipedia, www.tennessean.com; articles in *The Tennessean*
CHAPTER 5
JoAnn Gourley, courtship and marriage to William Bainbridge III: Articles in *Nashville Banner, The Tennessean*
History of Swan Ball: Articles in *The Tennessean;* Interview with Joanne Fleming Hayes
Fortnightly: Interviews with John Lentz, Billy Gourley, and Jane Hindman Kyburz; articles in *The Tennessean, Nashville Banner*

Billy Gourley's preparatory school, social life as teenager, Vanderbilt University: Articles in *The Tennessean;* interviews with Billy Gourley
Haynie Gourley's application for birth certificate: Ancestry.com
CHAPTER 6
Expansion of Capitol Chevrolet: Articles in the *Nashville Banner, The Tennessean*
Haynie hires Bill Powell: *The Tennessean*
Bill and Helen Powell: Articles in *Nashville Banner, The Tennessean*
Atmosphere at Capitol Chevrolet, 1966: Interview with Dr. Andy Rittenberry
CHAPTER 7
65th Anniversary Belle Meade Country Club: Article in *The Tennessean*
Capitol Chevrolet plans for new building: Interview with Billy Gourley; articles in *The Tennessean*
Perry Wallace integrates Vanderbilt basketball team: Author's recollections; articles in *The Tennessean*
Vanderbilt Symposium: Author's recollections; articles in *The Tennessean*
Billy Gourley in Tennessee Air National Guard: Interviews with Billy Gourley and John Lentz
Billy Gourley joins Capitol Chevrolet: Interview with Billy Gourley
CHAPTER 8
Grand Opening of Capitol Chevrolet's new location: Articles in *The Tennessean;* interview with Billy Gourley
Assassination of Dr. Martin Luther King: *Hellhound on His Trail* by Hampton Sides, Anchor Books, 2010
Nashville in aftermath of assassination: Articles in *The Tennessean*
Social life of Haynie and Josephine Gourley, 1968: Articles in *The Tennessean*
CHAPTER 9
Incident with borrowed demonstrator: Interview with Billy Gourley
Trip to Memphis: Testimony of Josephine Gourley, trial transcript, *The Tennessean*
Events of Wednesday, May 22, 1968: Testimony of Josephine and Billy Gourley, trial transcript, *The Tennessean,* Interview with Billy Gourley
Events of Thursday, May 23, 1968, day before slaying: Testimony of Sam Fleming, Josephine Gourley, Thomas Jackson, trial transcript, *The Tennessean*
PART II
Quote used by permission of Associated Press; Copyrighted 1936
CHAPTER 10
Haynie leaves for work: Testimony of Josephine Gourley, trial transcript, *The Tennessean*
Haynie's route to work: Interview with Billy Gourley
Events of May 24, 1968: Interviews with Billy Gourley, Hal Hardin, and Sherman Nickens; Capitol Chevrolet employees' testimonies from trial transcript, articles in *The Tennessean, Nashville Banner* microfilm
CHAPTER 11
Rivalry of *Nashville Banner* and *The Tennessean*: Various web sites; interview with

Larry Brinton, crime reporter for the *Nashville Banner*: *Nashville Banner* clippings, Metropolitan Government Archives of Nashville and Davidson County
Police response to slaying: Interviews with Bill Powell in hospital in *The Tennessean* articles
CHAPTER 12
Dr. T. E. Simpkins's examination and autopsy of Haynie Gourley: *The Tennessean*, articles, trial transcript.
Billy Dee Boyer: Trial transcript, *The Tennessean*
TBI agents and police response: *The Tennessean:* articles and trial transcript; interview with Sherman Nickens
Aftermath of shooting at General Hospital and Gourley home: Interview with Billy Gourley; recollections of author; *The Tennessean,* trial transcript and articles
Haynie Gourley's funeral: Recollections of author; list of pall bearers, *The Tennessean*
CHAPTER 13
Hunt for killer: *The Tennessean* articles and trial transcript; interview with Sherman Nickens
Reaction of Haynie's friend James Cook: Interview with son Jimbo Cook
Examination of car seat covers: *The Tennessean* articles and trial transcript
Retracing death route: *The Tennessean:* articles and trial transcript; interview with Sherman Nickens
CHAPTER 14
Chevrolet executives visit Josephine Gourley: *The Tennessean,* trial transcript
Description of murder of John Bolte, stabbing and rape of Barbara Bolte, murder scene: *The Tennessean* articles
Arrest of James Thomas Jefferson for Bolte murder: *The Tennessean* articles
Billy Gourley's return to work at Capitol Chevrolet: Interview with Billy Gourley
Haynie's reconditioned car is brought to showroom: Interview with Billy Gourley
CHAPTER 15
Discovery of pearl-handled pistol on Elm Hill Pike: *The Tennessean;* trial testimony of Henry Lewis
Police line-up, Bill Powell's identification of Gerald James Wingard: Interview with Sherman Nickens; articles in *The Tennessean*
Description of Gerald James Wingard in Job Corps, California: Articles in *The Tennessean;* interview with Sherman Nickens
CHAPTER 16
John Barros's claims of deception by Bill Powell and two other auto dealers; *The Tennessean* articles
CHAPTER 17
Grand Jury meets: *The Tennessean* articles
John Barros's claim of matching bullets: *The Tennessean* articles
Indictment and arrest of William E. Powell, March 1969: *The Tennessean* articles
Resignation of Billy Gourley from Capitol Chevrolet: Interview with Billy Gourley

John Barros files second lawsuit: *The Tennessean* articles
Bill Powell's attorney Cecil Branstetter files plea motion to dismiss case: *The Tennessean* articles
John Barros claims mysterious gun is left in mailbox: *The Tennessean* articles; interview with Hal Hardin
Gourley family hires their personal attorney John J. Hooker Sr. to act as special prosecutor in upcoming trial: *The Tennessean* articles; interviews with Billy Gourley and Hal Hardin
Bill Powell hires Jack Norman Sr. to assist in his defense: *The Tennessean* articles
Trial date set for July 14, 1968: *The Tennessean* article
CHAPTER 18
Requests from TV affiliates to broadcast trial from inside courtroom: *The Tennessean* article
Revelation that Metro patrolman Howard Kirkland working as investigator for defense: *The Tennessean* article
Weather at trial opening: *The Tennessean* front page
Atmosphere around opening of trial: Recollections of author; interview with Hal Hardin; *The Tennessean* articles
Description of Special Prosecutor John J. Hooker Sr.: Interview with Hal Hardin; *The Tennessean* articles about Hooker
Story of socialite Gene Beasley Wilson: *Nashville Scene* article by Larry Brinton
Hoffa trials: *The Tennessean* articles
Description of Jack Norman Sr.: Interview with Hal Hardin; *The Tennessean* articles
Description of District Attorney General Thomas Shriver: Interviews with Hal Hardin and John Lentz; articles in *The Tennessean*
Description of Assistant District Attorney Hal Hardin: Interviews with Hal Hardin; *The Tennessean* articles
Description of Cecil Branstetter: Interviews with Hal Hardin and John Lentz; *The Tennessean* articles
Description of Judge Allen R. Cornelius Jr.: *The Tennessean* articles; interviews with Hal Hardin and John Lentz
Account of *Nashville Banner* reporter Larry Brinton's persuading editor and owner James Stahlman to print trial transcript in full and *The Tennessean* editor to follow suit: Interview with Larry Brinton; articles in *The Tennessean*
CHAPTER 19
Description of Davidson County courthouse and Courtroom 611: Author's recollections; drawing of layout of courtroom, *The Tennessean*; author's visit with Hal Hardin to courtroom, 2019
Delay on first day of trial due to confession of James Joe Noe: *The Tennessean* article
Voir dire: *The Tennessean* articles
Description of families in courtroom: Author's recollection; *The Tennessean* articles
District Attorney Thomas Shriver insists on death penalty: *The Tennessean* articles; interview with Hal Hardin

Jurors allowed to watch moon landing: *The Tennessean* article; recollection of Hal Hardin
Witnesses' testimonies for the State: Transcript of trial in *The Tennessean*
Thoughts on testimony: Interviews with Billy Gourley and Hal Hardin
CHAPTER 20
Witnesses' testimonies for the State: Transcript of trial in *The Tennessean*
Thoughts on testimonies: Interviews with Billy Gourley and Hal Hardin
Atmosphere in courtroom, voices and gestures of attorneys: Recollections of author; articles in *The Tennessean*
Observations of two young lawyers: Recollections of author
CHAPTER 21
Witnesses for the defense: Trial transcript, *The Tennessean*: recollections of the author; interviews with Billy Gourley and Hal Hardin
Thoughts of George Crawford: Trial transcript, *The Tennessean*
CHAPTER 22
Story of discovery of how gun was found in 1968 on Elm Hill Pike: Trial transcript, *The Tennessean*
Witnesses for the defense: Trial transcript, *The Tennessean*
Thoughts on trial procedure: Interviews with Billy Gourley, Hal Hardin, and Jimbo Cook
CHAPTER 23
Meeting at Hooker's farm, contacts with FBI, Hal Hardin's private jet flight to Madison, Wisconsin, and back to Nashville: Interview with Hal Hardin
CHAPTER 24
Continuation of defense's case, witness testimonies: Trial transcript, *The Tennessean*
Defense rests: Trial transcript, *The Tennessean*
State's rebuttal: Trial transcript, *The Tennessean*
Thoughts on witness testimony, attorneys' actions: Interviews with Billy Gourley, Hal Hardin, and Jimbo Cook; recollections of author
CHAPTER 25
Revelation of ownership of gun found previous year on Elm Hill Pike: Interview with John Lentz
FBI and Charles Wilson testimonies: Trial transcript, *The Tennessean*
CHAPTER 26
Testimony of Bob Frensley: Interviews with John Lentz, Hal Hardin, Billy Gourley, author's recollections; trial transcript, *The Tennessean*
Witnesses for State regarding gun: Trial transcript, *The Tennessean*
Two young lawyers: Two recent graduates of Vanderbilt Law School in their first year of practice, seated with author in last week of trial; shared reactions, comments on proceedings. Classmates of acquaintances of author
CHAPTER 27
Surrebuttal by defense: Trial transcript, *The Tennessean*; interviews with Jimbo Cook and Hal Hardin

CHAPTER 28
Summation by District Attorney Thomas Shriver: Trial transcript, *The Tennessean*; Thoughts on performance by Thomas Shriver: Interviews with Billy Gourley, Hal Hardin, Sherman Nickens, and Jimbo Cook
CHAPTER 29
Jack Norman Sr. pulls stunt by refusing closing arguments: Trial transcript, *The Tennessean*; interview with Jimbo Cook; recollections of author
Judge charges jury: Trial transcript, *The Tennessean*
CHAPTER 30
Bill Powell, family, and friends wait for verdict: Article in *The Tennessean*
Gourley family and friends gather in hall and district attorney's office: Author's recollections; interview with Billy Gourley; article in *The Tennessean*
Jury enters courtroom, verdict is read, reaction of crowd: Recollections of author; Interviews with Billy Gourley, Hal Hardin, Jimbo Cook, and Sherman Nickens; articles in *The Tennessean*
Jurors interviewed: Articles in *The Tennessean*
Chevrolet executives demand Josephine Gourley sell her stock to Bill Powell: Interview with Billy Gourley; article in *The Tennessean*
CHAPTER 31
Scene in 1982 in Helen Suddoth's home: Panel discussion appearance by Ken Whitehouse in 2016 in video re-enactment of murder and trial by Nashville School of Law, DVD provided to author by William C. Koch, Jr., president, Nashville School of Law; subsequent interviews with Ken Whitehouse
EPILOGUE
Annece Bucher, location of grave: Ancestry.com; photograph of cemetery plaque, Ancestry.com
Thomas Shriver: Articles, obituary in *The Tennessean*
John J. Hooker Sr.: Articles, obituary in *The Tennessean*; interview with Hal Hardin
Jack Norman Sr.: DVD recording provided by William C. Koch Jr., president of Nashville School of Law; recording of voice of Jack Norman discussing case, originally provided in taped interviews made available to Nashville School of Law by his grandson; articles and obituary in *The Tennessean*
Cecil Branstetter: Obituary in *The Tennessean*; interview with Hal Hardin
Hal Hardin: Interviews with Hal Hardin; biographical information in *The Tennessean* articles
Sherman Nickens: Interview with Sherman Nickens; articles in *The Tennessean*; interview with Larry Brinton; *Nashville Scene* article on murder of Stringbean and his wife by Larry Brinton
Larry Brinton: Interview with Larry Brinton; interview with Sherman Nickens
Robert O. Frensley: Notes by John Lentz; obituary in *The Tennessean*
Josephine Gourley: Interview with Billy Gourley; statement by Joanne Fleming
Billy Gourley: Interview with Billy Gourley
Bill Powell: Obituary in *The Tennessean*; article in *Nashville Post* by Ken White-

house on the occasion of Powell's death, 2010

Sadly, Jimbo Cook, who attended the State vs. William E. Powell trial every single day, and Larry Brinton, crime reporter for the Nashville Banner in 1968-69, passed away after my interviews with them. I deeply appreciate their recollections which were invaluable in writing this story.

CPSIA information can be obtained
at www.ICGtesting.com
Printed in the USA
LVHW110739010223
738326LV00013B/366/J